Regional Differences in Women Entrepreneurship

Esra Sena Türko (ed.)

Regional Differences in Women Entrepreneurship

PETER LANG

Bibliographic Information published by the Deutsche Nationalbibliothek
The Deutsche Nationalbibliothek lists this publication in the Deutsche Nationalbibliografie; detailed bibliographic data is available online at http://dnb.d-nb.de.

Library of Congress Cataloging-in-Publication Data
A CIP catalog record for this book has been applied for at the Library of Congress.

ISBN 978-3-631-85344-3 (Print)
E-ISBN 978-3-631-85345-0 (E-PDF)
E-ISBN 978-3-631-86012-0 (EPUB)
DOI 10.3726/b18847

Peter Lang – Berlin · Bern · Bruxelles · New York · Oxford · Warszawa · Wien

This publication has been peer reviewed.

www.peterlang.com

Contents

Abbreviations

ACWF:	The All-China Women's Federation
AfDB:	African Development Bank
AU:	African Union
BRI:	The Belt and Road Initiative
GDP:	Gross Domestic Product
GEDI:	The Global Entrepreneurship and Development Institute
GEM:	Global Entrepreneurship Monitor
GFC:	Global Financial Crisis
GII:	Gender Inequality Index
ILO:	International Labour Organization
ITC:	International Trade Organization
MIWE:	MasterCard Index of Women Entrepreneurs
NTM:	Non-tariff measures
NUTS:	Nomenclature des Unités Territoriales Statistiques
OECD:	Organisation for Economic Co-operation and Development
PRC:	People's Republic of China
SMEs:	Small and medium-size enterprises
TEA:	Total early-stage Entrepreneurial Activity
UAE:	United Arab Emirates
UN:	United Nations
UNCTAD:	United Nations Conference on Trade and Development
UNDP:	United Nations Development Programme
UNECA:	United Nations Economic Commission for Africa
US:	United States
WB:	World Bank
WBL:	Women, Business and the Law
WTO:	World Trade Organization

Foreword

Women entrepreneurship can be seen as relatively a new research area and it may be assessed to be immature. Researches have focused on the differences between men and women entrepreneurs for a long time and this interest still continues. Researchers provided suggestions regarding examining this topic within various contexts in order to improve the discipline but, however, the research topics have not significantly diversified.

It can be seen that researchers having a regional perspective have not been interested in women entrepreneurship at a remarkable level. It is possible to investigate topic of women entrepreneurship based on entrepreneurship ecosystem, local economic development, and regional economy. Among these domains, especially the theoretical framework of the entrepreneurship ecosystem represents a very favorable basis for discussion on women entrepreneurship.

Among women entrepreneurship researches, number of studies reporting regional differences are very limited, except for those investigating the economies at the national level. However, comparative analyses always contribute to a better understanding of the subject. From this point of view, this book aims to represent the findings of women entrepreneurship studies from various theoretical frameworks, which address differences and similarities at regional level together, and reveal the big picture.

Regional differences in women entrepreneurship is a very comprehensive research topic. A relatively small portion of this comprehensive research topic could be presented in this book. Through their studies examining this topic within different contexts, the authors significantly contributed to this book. This book aims to contribute to better understanding the women entrepreneurship at any level.

Erzurum, 2021.

Esra Sena TÜRKO[1]

Introduction

Regional Differences in Women Entrepreneurship

In women entrepreneurship studies, the regional emphasis remained limited generally to the studies carried out within the scope of regional development. Regional differences were detected in many studies. However, unless the research was conducted within the theoretical framework of the regional economy, they were not discussed within this context. This book aims to represent the findings of studies on women entrepreneurship from various theoretical frameworks, which address differences and similarities at the regional level together and reveal the big picture.

Women entrepreneurship is relatively a new research topic. The first article on entrepreneurship dates back to 1930s, whereas the first manuscript on women entrepreneurship was published in 1976 by Schwartz (1976). The first conference paper on women entrepreneurship was presented by Hisrich & Brush (1983) in year 1983, whereas the first academic book was published by Goffee & Scase (1985) in 1985 and the first academic conference, Diana International Conference on Women's Entrepreneurship Research was held in 2003, and the first journal about women entrepreneurship, International Journal of Gender and Entrepreneurship, began to be published in 2009 (Yadav & Unni, 2016: 3).

It can be seen that the initial studies on women entrepreneurship focused on the differences between men and women entrepreneurs in the 1990s (Cromie, 1987; Birley, 1989; Brush, 1992; Fischer et al., 1993; Baker et al., 1997; Chell & Baines, 1998; Mirchandani, 1999). Nowadays, the differences between women and men entrepreneurs still draw researchers' attention. The studies using different theoretical frameworks continue investigating the differences by making use of gender variable (Baughn et al., 2006; Menzies, et al., 2006; DeTienne & Chandler, 2007; Eddleston & Powell, 2008; Uluköy & Demireli, 2014).

1 Assistant Professor Dr., Erzurum Technical University, Faculty of Economics and Administrative Sciences, Department of Economics, esturko@erzurum.edu.tr, ORCID ID: 0000-0002-9102-6120

Researchers have suggestions emphasizing different contexts regarding the need for expanding the theoretical framework. Gundry et al. (2002) stated that studies involving cross-sectoral comparisons are needed and they suggest that this subject should be examined within the context of developing countries. Ahl (2006) stated that the researches should be expanded in the way involving more factors and it is necessary to carry out contingency or comparative studies; the external factors affecting the women entrepreneurship could be examined by contingency studies. de Bruin et al. (2007) suggested expanding the theoretical frameworks used in the studies and that analyses conducted at multiple levels could improve the domain of women entrepreneurship. Brush et al. (2009) recommended the 5M approach by stating the need for a holistic approach, whereas Sullivan and Meek (2012) suggested that researches should be expanded in the way examining the relationships between psychology and entrepreneurship, and Hughes et al. (2012) recommended conducting the researches by using transnational networks beyond the national borders (Yadav & Unni, 2016).

Moreover, the studies are criticized from the aspect that the gender-based assumptions limit the epistemological scope of research and position the women entrepreneurs as unsuccessful or reluctant (Ahl & Marlow, 2012) and, while the large-scaled empirical studies focus on the differences between women and men, they provide less information about the industry or sampling method (Henry et al., 2016).

Involved as a variable in analyses, gender has transformed into a more specific research subject such as gender stereotypes, in the course of time (Gupta et al., 2008; Max & Ballereau, 2013). Especially the studies involving multiple countries significantly contributed to understanding the stereotypes against women entrepreneurship (Gupta et al., 2005; Gupta et al., 2009). Concurrently, the problems, which women entrepreneurs encounter, kept on being examined within the theoretical frameworks of different disciplines (Toksöz, 2007; Sarhan, 2019; Santos, 2009; Okafor & Amalu, 2010; Soysal, 2010; Upadhye, 2012; Chitsike, 2000; Tlaiss, 2015; Wahdiniwaty & Rustam, 2019).

It can be seen that a limited number of studies compared the women entrepreneurs operating in the same region or different regions. However, it can be thought that differences and similarities between the women entrepreneurs are suggestive about the factors affecting the women entrepreneurship. Comparing women and men entrepreneurs indicate the status of women relative to the men in the same region and it reveals gender-related problems. The studies comparing the women entrepreneurs allow investigating under which circumstances the gender-related issues affect women's entrepreneurial activities at high/low level.

Within this context, the research findings reported in studies on women entrepreneurs, which do not corroborate each other, should highly arouse curiosity. The determinants of women entrepreneurship might underlie the factors leading these differences. For this reason, examining the regional differences in women entrepreneurship may help us with understanding what kind of factors women entrepreneurship is influenced by, under which similar or different conditions. For such a point of view to turn into an efficient process, it is very important to well understand the limitations or general frameworks of the previous studies, because the research results reported do not apply to all conditions but are valid only for that sample. Achieving different results within different samples may be suggestive about the determinants of the mentioned variable.

In women entrepreneurship researches, the most important limitation of the studies, especially those investigating the problems that women encounter, is that the field survey results are confined to the region, where the survey was conducted. If the study does not include a comparative analysis or was not carried out in multiple regions or countries, it provides results confined to the local area or region, where the survey has been conducted. However, as a general tendency, these limitations of the research results are ignored by the other researchers.

Then, it can be thought that investigating the regional differences in women entrepreneurship brought a perspective that will contribute to the development of this field. It might also be evaluated that the regional perspective might correspond to new framework quest, needed in the women entrepreneurship studies.

The aim of this research is to investigate the regional differences in women entrepreneurship. The factors causing differences in women entrepreneurship at regional level and the topics, in which differences were observed, were examined within the regional borders defined at various levels. The research involves conceptual and applied studies.

In the introduction section, firstly, the causes of regional differences in women entrepreneurship, at which regional level they can be examined, and the differing topics are discussed. Then, the research results, involving regional emphasis in women entrepreneurship studies are presented and it is suggested that women entrepreneurship can be discussed within entrepreneurship ecosystem through a regional perspective. Finally, the chapters of this book are specified.

1. Regional Differences in Women Entrepreneurship

Examining the previous studies, it can be seen that they haven't presented the factors causing differences at regional level in women entrepreneurship, at which level these factors can be examined, and the topics, in which differences were observed, within a theoretical framework. However, when the studies on women entrepreneurship are examined as a whole, regardless of the context, such a framework can be drawn with a regional perspective.

The regional differences in women entrepreneurship may arise due to the following *reasons* (factors affecting the presence of difference at regional level):

1. Level of development
2. Economic resources
3. Human capital
4. Social structure and culture (gender, values, etc.)
5. Adopted political and economic system
6. Advantages and disadvantages brought by the region's geographical location in terms of transportation and logistical infrastructure (isolated region, harbor region, etc.)
7. Region's geographical location in stable or unstable regions, or proximity to these regions (being located in or near regions of instability, like the war zones etc., proximity to integration forms like EU, being located in or near a region with colonial past)

The regional differences in women entrepreneurship may arise or be examined at the following *levels*:

1. Between the local areas/sub-regions in regions constituting a country (e.g. NUTS[2] 3 level regions)
2. Between the regions constituting a country (e.g. NUTS 1 and 2 level regions, Eastern Anatolia, Bavaria, etc.)
3. Between the countries (Turkey, USA, Japan, etc.)
4. Between the regional groups constituted by countries (EU countries, ASEAN)

---

2 Nomenclature of territorial units for statistics, abbreviated NUTS (from French, Nomenclature des Unités Territoriales Statistiques) is used to subdivide the economic territory of the European Union (EU) into regions at three levels. NUTS 1, 2 and 3 respectively, move from larger to smaller territorial units (Eurostat, 2016).

5. Between geographical regions as big as to include multiple countries (Sub-Saharan Africa, Europe, Middle East, etc.)

Due to the aforementioned reasons, many topics in women entrepreneurship exhibit differences at regional level. The *domains of differences* can be listed as follows:

1. Profile of women entrepreneurs (why and how they became entrepreneurs, educational level, etc.)
2. Industry/branch of industry they are operating in, goods/services they produce
3. Work life, domestic life, and balance between them
4. Characteristics of the business, business ownership/management forms
5. Problems, pressures, and prejudices they encounter
6. Policies implemented and instruments used by governments in order to support the women entrepreneurs. Forms of fostering/restraining women, problems in participation and representation, and discrimination.
7. Supports provided by international organizations for women entrepreneurs, and support instruments.

2. Region Emphasis and Regional Differences in Women Entrepreneurship Studies

Women entrepreneurship can be considered as a new research area when compared to entrepreneurship. Consequently, the immaturity of the field and the problems related with the theoretical framework may seem reasonable. Regional perspective in women entrepreneurship researches is limited, similarly to entrepreneurship researches.

The results of the studies involving regional emphasis on women entrepreneurship are presented under this title, in four stages: Studies on entrepreneurship involving no gender emphasis but using regional context, studies on entrepreneurship involving gender emphasis and using regional context, studies on women entrepreneurship using regional context but not investigating the existence of regional differences, studies on women entrepreneurship using regional context and investigating the regional differences.

Regional context was used in several studies carried out on entrepreneurship, but the studies involved no gender emphasis. In a study carried out in 3 regions in Romania, regional differences were detected in entrepreneurial intentions, motivations, and obstacles against entrepreneurship. It was reported in this study that the differences detected, corroborated the theoretical aspect that the individual's motivation to become an entrepreneur is influenced by the environmental conditions (Nicolae & Nicolae, 2016).

In a study investigating the entrepreneurial processes in rural regions of Catalonia, regional differences were determined between the effects of role models (Lafuente et al., 2007). Individual differences in entrepreneurial processes were investigated in 3 regions of Netherlands and no gender gap or significant gender effect could be found for East-Groningen (Bosma et al., 2008). In a research, on a regional development project implemented in a region where entrepreneurial activities are comparatively lower than the other regions in Sweden, the experimental activities involving discourse pedagogy were explained (Berglund & Johansson, 2007).

Global Entrepreneurship Monitor (GEM) data were used in another study investigating the entrepreneurial activities in Germany within personal traits and regional contexts. This study indicated that both individual variables and regional variables have influence on the decision to become an entrepreneur (Bergmann & Sternberg, 2007).

In a study examining the causes of ongoing regional differences in entrepreneurial activities, the differences between the effects of cultural, personal, and institutional factors on the entrepreneurial activities in the USA and Europe were investigated. According to the survey results, fundamental differences were found between the USA and Europe in terms of start-up environment. In regions, where the start-ups are strong, the entrepreneur-friendly institutions and the networking activities between regional actors support the entrepreneurial spirit (Röhl, 2019).

According to a study comparing two cities from the northern and southern regions of Vietnam, entrepreneurs were reported to differ in terms of motivation, success factors, and perceived success (Benzing et al., 2005).

In several studies, carried out on entrepreneurship, both regional context was used and gender emphasis was placed. In these studies, the differences between women and men entrepreneurs were investigated at regional level.

In a study carried out in the USA and reporting the distinguishing effect of immigration gateways on ethnic entrepreneurship, it was determined that interaction effects shaped the women entrepreneurship in ethnic groups (Wang, 2010).

In a study examining the women and men entrepreneurship at the country level by using GEM data, the effects of various factors on women and men entrepreneurs in 29 countries were investigated. According to the results, the rates of entrepreneurial activities of women and men entrepreneurs are mainly affected by the same factors in the same direction. Differences were detected between the effects of variables such as unemployment and life satisfaction, on women and men entrepreneurship. At the same time, the study indicated that the factors influencing the number of women entrepreneurs might be different from the factors affecting the ratio of women entrepreneurs in the total entrepreneurs (Verheul et al., 2006).

The engagement of entrepreneurs in the entrepreneurship process occurs in five levels and these phases are named as "entrepreneurial ladder." It can be seen that these phases are ignored in women entrepreneurship studies. In a research using the data from a field survey conducted by the European Commission, the individual differences between women and men entrepreneurs in terms of entrepreneurial ladder were investigated in 36 countries. The research focused on the entrepreneurial environment. The research findings indicated that there were gender differences between the countries on the first and last phases of the entrepreneurial process (Van der Zwan et al., 2010; Van der Zwan et al., 2012).

Another study focusing on the differences between women and men entrepreneurs was carried out on Eastern Europe and Central Asia (ECA), Latin America (LA), and Sub-Saharan Africa (SSA) regions. The research indicated differences between entrepreneurs in 3 regions defined as developing ones. In all three regions, the scale of women entrepreneurs' businesses was smaller than that of men entrepreneurs' businesses. Gender-based difference was found to be at a lower level in terms of enterprise efficiency and growth but it maintained its validity in LA region. Women entrepreneurs in ECA region tended to request less use of formal financial resources than men. However, an opposite situation was observed in LA and SSA regions, compared to men, women entrepreneurs tended to request formal finance at higher levels. As an important result, the study reported no gender-based discrimination on access to formal finance (Bardasi et al., 2011).

Regional context was used in some studies carried out on women entrepreneurship but it was not investigated if there was any difference between the regions. In Southern Italy, in a study investigating the relationship between the challenges experienced by the women who had decided to become an entrepreneur and their motivations, the correspondence, canonical analysis, and cluster analysis were employed by taking the socioeconomic conditions of the region into account. It was determined that two-thirds of the women entrepreneurs were positively motivated and made their decision to become an entrepreneur with this motivation (Bianchi et al., 2016). In Romania, a sociological survey was conducted in three regions in order to evaluate the women entrepreneurship at regional level (Pocol & Moldovan-Teselios, 2014).

A literature review was conducted on women entrepreneurship in the Middle East and North Africa (MENA) region by grouping 271 studies published in the last decade under 9 main categories. In that study, 30 themes seemed to draw attention of the researchers. It was determined that women entrepreneurship and gender, youth entrepreneurship, entrepreneurship behavior and orientation categories were three categories affecting the entrepreneurial perspectives of the studies examining MENA region (Aljuwaiber, 2020).

It can be seen that countries, country groups and larger geographical regions consisting of countries were investigated in the studies examining women entrepreneurship within a regional context and exploring the regional differences. Remarkably, the MENA region has been studied much more extensively and a significant portion of studies use GEM data. Number of studies comparatively examining the regions within the borders of a single country is limited. It can be seen that the researches similarly focused on the motivations of women entrepreneurs and the problems they encountered.

The women entrepreneurs in transitional economies in Nigeria and China (Kitching & Woldie, 2004), similarities and differences between the problems women entrepreneurs encounter in six countries (McClelland et al., 2005), women entrepreneurs' ICT usage, and entrepreneurship barriers in 2 Gulf countries in the Middle East region (Mathew, 2010) were investigated. The motivations and entrepreneurial experiences of international small business owner women entrepreneurs in two Central European countries, Poland and the Czech Republic, were compared to those of women entrepreneurs in the Northern America (Lituchy & Reavley, 2004).

GEM is an important project providing a great contribution to investigating and understanding entrepreneurship at the global level for more than 20 years. The results obtained by using large datasets covering many countries are regularly published as reports. There are numerous researches carried out using the data of GEM. Women entrepreneurship, entrepreneurship ecosystem, and the reciprocal interaction between them were mentioned in the report published in 2019. It was reported that entrepreneurship ecosystems have changing effects on TEA rates depending on various factors (cultural factors, human capital, markets, presence of financial resources and infrastructural resources) and gender differences were detected on TEA ratios in 9 of 59 countries examined. Remarkably, women entrepreneurship was discussed within the entrepreneurship ecosystem, in the conclusion section of the report (GEM, 2019: 68–69).

In a research examining the women entrepreneurship in the MENA region, the studies involving macro, meso, and micro-level analyses were reviewed. In that research, it was determined that, in the studies carried out, the theoretical bases were insufficient, the macro-level data, such as culture and religion, were emphasized too much, and the organizational-level data were emphasized less. Besides, it was stated that the studies investigating women entrepreneurship within specific ethnic groups were insufficient and there were few studies on the region's complex social, cultural, and religious diversity; it was emphasized that the new regional incidents, such as immigrant crisis in the region, were not pointed out (Bastian et al., 2018).

In another research investigating the women entrepreneurship in MENA countries, an evaluation was performed using GEM research reports and the related literature together. The lack of reliable statistical data and the absence of literature discussing the women entrepreneurship within a regional framework were defined as limitations in this research (Hattab, 2012).

A detailed field survey on women entrepreneurs operating in Gulf Cooperative Council (GCC) countries was carried out in Saudi Arabia. The study incorporated comparisons between countries and between regions of Saudi Arabia. In that study, women entrepreneurs in Saudi Arabia, Bahrain, Jordan, Tunisia, Lebanon, and United Arab Emirates among MENA countries were asked about the subjects "they had more difficulties in only because they were women." Saudi women seemed to report higher level of problems in 5 out of 6 items when compared to the women from other countries. The level of problems encountered in joining formal networks and bureaucracy was significantly different from the other countries. Having higher-level problems compared to all countries in achieving the work-life balance, access to capital and managing male workers, Saudi women had the second-highest level of problem in being taken seriously as business owners, following Lebanon (Alturki & Braswell, 2010: 22). When all these problems are considered together, there are discriminative legal regulations affecting women.

In a study exploring the women entrepreneurship in GCC countries and using a regional context, the motivations of women entrepreneurs and the challenges they face in their entrepreneurial activities were examined. In GCC countries, women's entrepreneurial activities, challenges they face, and the support programs differ between countries. The most challenging issue faced by women entrepreneurs in Saudi Arabia was the access to capital, whereas a small portion of women expressed difficulty about this issue in Bahrein. Besides that, among the GCC countries, women entrepreneurship activities in Saudi Arabia, Bahrain, and United Arab Emirates were at a higher level when compared to Kuwait, Oman, and Qatar (Zeidan & Bahrami, 2011). It was observed that women entrepreneurs in Saudi Arabia had an optimistic attitude about the future of their enterprises and they wanted to grow their businesses and aimed to penetrate new markets. The problems women entrepreneurs encountered in Saudi Arabia were gender-related legal regulations, limited access to formal finance mechanisms, and need for sophisticated business tools (Alturki & Braswell, 2010: 8).

In a study investigating the motivations of women entrepreneurs for establishing a business in advanced and emerging economies, it was aimed to reveal the differences between women entrepreneurs in Norway, Russia, and Ukraine. Research findings indicated differences between advanced and emerging economies on women entrepreneurs' motivation for establishing a business. When compared to Russia and Ukraine, the women entrepreneurs in Norway had a higher level of desire to contribute to meeting the needs of the society. The study reported that women entrepreneurs in socially and culturally developed countries such as Norway are provided with more opportunities for self-realization. Besides, in this study, the profiles, problems, motivations, and entrepreneurial activities of women entrepreneurs constituting the sample were explained through country emphasis (Solesvik et al., 2019).

3. Need for a Regional Perspective to Women Entrepreneurship Studies

Interestingly, women entrepreneurship topic did not attract sufficient attention from researchers studying with regional economy perspective. Due to the multi-dimensional and gender-related nature of the subject, studying could be considered as difficult. Gender and discrimination theme of the research subject attracted attention of sociologists, whereas the economic activity aspect did attract attention of business administration researchers. Concentrating on the entrepreneur, behavioral scientists and management scientists focused on the individual and managerial characteristics of women entrepreneurs. Economists mostly examine the topic in terms of growth and employment at the national level. The distant stance of other disciplines delays the development of a holistic perspective, which will contribute to better understanding the women entrepreneurship.

It can be seen that a limited number of studies employing a regional perspective did not pass beyond the regional development and local economic development framework. Generally focusing on a single region, the researches do not involve interregional comparisons with a dynamic perspective. They are similar to the studies investigating the effects or contributions of entrepreneurship to local and regional development; and do not involve gender-based assessments. A limited number of studies focusing on women entrepreneurs' entrepreneurial activities and having a regional perspective emphasizes the gender-based problems and contributes to new research topics to come to the forefront in the agenda. Studies on the networking activities of women entrepreneurs can be given as examples within this context (McGowan & Hampton, 2006; Neumeyer et al., 2019; Mozumdar et al., 2019).

Yadav and Unni (2016) stated that the scope of women entrepreneurship researches needs to be expanded in terms of content and context and there is debate in the literature over whether or not a new theory for women entrepreneurship is needed. Many researchers suggest that the current concepts of entrepreneurship can be used by referring to feminist theories and, thus, the theoretical basis will expand (Yadav & Unni, 2016: 15–16). May the theories employing regional context be the frameworks, in which women entrepreneurship will be examined?

It is possible to examine more specifically how women entrepreneur manages her enterprise, the problems she encounters while managing, how she overcomes the problems in issues such as production, marketing and customer relations, and to ground these subjects within entrepreneurship ecosystem, local economic development, or regional economy. This type of research results allows developing programs and designing the instruments to support the entrepreneurial success of women, more specifically.

4. Discussing Women Entrepreneurship within the Entrepreneurship Ecosystem

Examining the factors discussed under previous titles and stated to cause differences in women entrepreneurship, it can be evaluated that these are the factors shaping the entrepreneurship ecosystem. Then, it is possible to think that the differences in women entrepreneurship arise from the entrepreneurship ecosystem. Each entrepreneurship ecosystem is unique (Isenberg, 2011). However, it should be noted at this point that the gender-related components in the entrepreneurship ecosystem are in interaction with all other components constituting the entrepreneurship ecosystem. For instance; social norms are in interaction with human capital. The conditions arising from the interaction of these components would not yield the same effect on women and men. When compared to men, these gender-related components impact women more and create a special area. Especially in an entrepreneurship ecosystem incorporating gender inequality, the deficiencies might create more severe adverse effects on the entrepreneurial activities of women. For instance; if there is a deficiency regarding the networks in the entrepreneurship ecosystem, women would remain outside these networks more than men. If there is a deficiency regarding the access to financial resources in the entrepreneurship ecosystem, the level of problems that women entrepreneurs encounter might be higher than those of men entrepreneurs.

An important problem in women entrepreneurship researches is the evaluation of the research results by combining and making generalizations, as if they represent a country and even all women entrepreneurs. It is possible to exemplify this case over Turkey. In Turkey, the conceptual researches investigating the women entrepreneurs' profiles paint a more pessimistic picture, compared to the applied researches. These researches examining the topic at national level evaluate the problems, which women entrepreneurs encounter within patriarchal social structure, social roles, low-level access to education, and family pressure. In fact, Turkey is a country with high regional disparities. Besides the differences, the problems encountered by women entrepreneurs also show similarities between regions. Discussing the topic at local or regional level will allow reaching more efficient results (Türko, 2016: 61). Especially examining the geographically large countries, where regional disparities and a rich cultural and ethnical structure exist, at national level would not yield information at desired specificity, particularly in researches conducted in order to improve the entrepreneurship ecosystem (Türko, 2020).

As many social, psychological, and sociopsychological factors, like culture, cooperation, personality traits of the entrepreneur, and gender roles affect entrepreneurship ecosystems, only the entrepreneurship ecosystems in geographically small countries may possibly give the same results with the national-level entrepreneurship ecosystem. Otherwise, in case of large geographical borders, cultural diversity, and regional disparities, the entrepreneurship ecosystem of each region will inevitably yield different results and the national entrepreneurship ecosystem will represent the average of these regions. Except for the assumption of small country, the author evaluates that the entrepreneurship ecosystem researches conducted at national level, would not provide much information about the entrepreneurship ecosystems beyond the adopted economic system's realization level (Türko, 2020).

The differences between women and men entrepreneurs are suggestive about the hindering aspects of the entrepreneurship ecosystem, whereas the differences between women entrepreneurs operating in different regions/the same region are suggestive about the factors influencing women entrepreneurship. Within the entrepreneurship ecosystem, it can be assumed that, without a gender discrimination, the entrepreneur is nurtured under equal conditions in the same entrepreneurial environment and has the ability to access facilities and opportunities presented by the entrepreneurship ecosystem at equal ratios. When classifying the main actor of the entrepreneurship ecosystem, the entrepreneur, using gender, sector, characteristic of the entrepreneurial activity or another variable, if one of the sub-groups is seen to have more limited access or lower level of realized benefit compared to other groups, then it can be thought that there is a faulting effect on the operation of the entrepreneurship ecosystem. The studies investigating the differences between women and men entrepreneurs, based on the gender variable, in fact, indicates the obstacles and deficiencies within entrepreneurship ecosystem, processing to the detriment of women entrepreneurs. For instance, one of the differences emphasized in the literature is that the women entrepreneurs tend to establish smaller scaled enterprises when compared to men. Examining the studies in further detail, it is seen that the women have low educational level and establish small enterprises operating in the service industry, and the determinant of enterprise scale is education level. Then, the fact that women entrepreneurs establish smaller scale enterprises compared to men should be attributed to the human capital component specific to the entrepreneurship ecosystem examined. Women have lower access to education when compared to men and it leads them to establish and manage small enterprises. The decision makers aiming to improve and develop the entrepreneurship ecosystem may try to contribute to alleviate this difference by designing policies and instruments to increase women's access to education. This example shows that, evaluating the findings within the theoretical framework of entrepreneurship ecosystem, non-complex route maps to diminish obstacles against women entrepreneurship could be determined. Several other examples can also be given. If it is determined that women entrepreneurs are engaged in entrepreneurial activities at lower levels since they cannot access to the same resources and opportunities with men due to reasons such as discriminative legal regulations and gender inequality, then the intervention area would be the improvement of the legal regulations and the practices aiming to eliminate the gender inequality.

Entrepreneurship ecosystem provides a favorable theoretical framework for women entrepreneurship researches, because all the factors (gender, values, etc.) causing women's entrepreneurial activities emerging as a special field are involved in the components and impact areas of the entrepreneurship ecosystem.

5. Book Plan

The aim of this research is to investigate the regional differences in women entrepreneurship. The factors causing differences in women entrepreneurship at regional level and the topics, in which differences were observed, were examined within the regional borders defined at various levels. The research involves conceptual and applied studies.

In the first chapter, Dr. Tuba Şahinoğlu investigates the differences in women entrepreneurship by the development level of countries. Motivations and current statuses of women entrepreneurs in least developed, developing, and developed countries are evaluated and the obstacles against women entrepreneurship were examined. Dr. Şahinoğlu concluded that making evaluations over the development level of countries might not always yield accurate results.

In the second chapter, Dr. E. Demet Ekinci Hamamcı examines the reflections of gender inequality to women entrepreneurship in her study, and aims to determine the relationship between gender equality and women participation in the labor force and entrepreneurial activities.

In the third chapter, Dr. M. Kürşat Timuroğlu carries out a literature review examining the entrepreneurial intentions and values and presents a theoretical basis for the entrepreneurial activities.

In the fourth chapter, Ahmet Kadiroğlu investigates the differences between activities of women entrepreneurs in rural areas, with a field survey carried out in two provinces in Turkey, with different climatic, geographic, social, cultural and economic characteristics. The research examines in detail and comparatively analyzes the entrepreneurial activities of women entrepreneurs, operating in the beekeeping industry.

The problems that women entrepreneurs encounter constitute the most frequently investigated topic in women entrepreneurship researches. Do the experiences of women entrepreneurs, in making the decision to become an entrepreneur, at start-up, and managing the business, differ by the countries? In the fifth chapter, Berrak Yellice assesses the problems of women entrepreneurs at country level through a comprehensive literature review.

In the sixth chapter of the book, Hasan Güneş examines the exporting women entrepreneurs. The obstacles against women entrepreneurs' participation in export activities, the profile and characteristics of women exporters, and women exporters in different countries and regions are evaluated in the study.

In the seventh chapter of the book, Dr. Burak Başkan approaches the issue of women entrepreneurship through the lenses of politics. By discussing the structural hegemonic dimension of popular culture, he endeavors to detect underlying conditions that limit women's actions in economic life. In this respect, he emphasizes processes as well as the content of popular culture on the terrain of gender politics.

In the eighth chapter of the book, Dr. Müge Yüce analyzes the effects of social and political factors on women entrepreneurship over the case of People's Republic of China.

References

Ahl, H. (2006). Why research on women entrepreneurs needs new directions. *Entrepreneurship Theory and Practice, 30*(5), 595–621. https://doi.org/10.1111/j.1540-6520.2006.00138.x

Ahl, H., & Marlow, S. (2012). Exploring the dynamics of gender, feminism and entrepreneurship: Advancing debate to escape a dead end? *Organization, 19*(5), 543–562. https://doi.org/10.1177/1350508412448695

Aljuwaiber, A. (2020). Entrepreneurship research in the Middle East and North Africa: Trends, challenges, and sustainability issues. *Journal of Entrepreneurship in Emerging Economies.* https://doi.org/10.1108/JEEE-08-2019-0123

Alturki, N., & Braswell, R. (2010). *Businesswomen in Saudi Arabia: Characteristics, challenges, and aspirations in a regional context.* Monitor Group. [Retrieved from https://www.academia.edu/35892321/Businesswomen_in_Saudi_Arabia_Characteristics_Challenges_and_Aspirations_in_a_Regional_Context]

Baker, T., Aldrich, H.E., & Liou, N. (1997). Invisible entrepreneurs: The neglect of women business owners by mass media and scholarly journals in the USA. *Entrepreneurship and Regional Development, 9*(3), 221–238. https://doi.org/10.1080/08985629700000013

Bardasi, E., Sabarwal, S., & Terrell, K. (2011). How do female entrepreneurs perform? Evidence from three developing regions. *Small Business Economics, 37*(4), 417–441. https://doi.org/10.1007/s11187-011-9374-z

Bastian, B.L., Sidani, Y.M., & El Amine, Y. (2018). Women entrepreneurship in the Middle East and North Africa: A review of knowledge areas and research gaps. *Gender in Management, 33*(1), 14–29. https://doi.org/10.1108/GM-07-2016-0141

Baughn, C.C., Chua, B.L., & Neupert, K.E. (2006). The normative context for women's participation in entrepreneurship: A multicountry study. *Entrepreneurship Theory and Practice, 30*(5), 687–708. https://doi.org/10.1111/j.1540-6520.2006.00142.x

Benzing, C., Chu, H.M., & Callanan, G. (2005). A regional comparison of the motivation and problems of Viatnamese entrepreneurs. *Journal of Developmental Entrepreneurship, 10*(1), 3–27. https://doi.org/10.1142/S1084946705000033

Bergmann, H., & Sternberg, R. (2007). The changing face of entrepreneurship in Germany. *Small Business Economics*, *28*, 205–221. https://doi.org/10.1007/s11187-006-9016-z

Berglund, K., & Johansson, A.W. (2007). Entrepreneurship, discourses and conscientization in processes of regional development. *Entrepreneurship & Regional Development*, *19*(6), 499–525. https://doi.org/10.1080/08985620701671833

Bianchi, M., Parisi, V., & Salvatore, R. (2016). Female entrepreneurs: Motivations and constraints. An Italian regional study. *International Journal of Gender and Entrepreneurship*, *8*(3), 198–220. https://doi.org/10.1108/IJGE-08-2015-0029

Birley, S. (1989). Female entrepreneurs: Are they really different? *Journal of Small Business Management*, *27*(1), 32–37.

Bosma, N., Schutjens, V., & Suddle, K. (2008). Whither a flat landscape? Regional differences in entrepreneurship in the Netherlands. *EIM Research Report*. https://core.ac.uk/download/pdf/7074439.pdf

Brush, C.G. (1992). Research on women business owners: Past trends, a new perspective and future directions. *Entrepreneurship Theory and Practice*, *16*(4), 5–30. https://doi.org/10.1177/104225879201600401

Brush, C.G., de Bruin, A., & Welter, F. (2009). A gender-aware framework for women's entrepreneurship. *International Journal of Gender and Entrepreneurship*, *1*(1), 8–24. https://doi.org/10.1108/17566260910942318

Chell, E., & Baines, S. (1998). Does gender affect business 'performance'? A study of microbusinesses in business services in the UK. *Entrepreneurship & Regional Development*, *10*(2), 117–135. https://doi.org/10.1080/08985629800000007

Chitsike, C. (2000). Culture as a barrier to rural women's entrepreneurship: Experience from Zimbabwe. *Gender & Development*, 8(1), 71–77. http://dx.doi.org/10.1080/741923408

Cromie, S. (1987). Motivations of aspiring male and female entrepreneurs. *Journal of Organizational Behavior*, *8*(3), 251–261. https://doi.org/10.1002/job.4030080306

de Bruin, A., Brush, C.G., & Welter, F. (2007). Advancing a framework for coherent research on women's entrepreneurship. *Entrepreneurship Theory and Practice*, *31*(3), 323–339. https://doi.org/10.1111/j.1540-6520.2007.00176.x

DeTienne, D.R., & Chandler, G.N. (2007). The role of gender in opportunity identification. *Entrepreneurship Theory and Practice*, *31*(3), 365–386. https://doi.org/10.1111/j.1540-6520.2007.00178.x

Eddleston, K.A., & Powell, G.N. (2008). The role of identity in explaining sex differences in business owners' career satisfier preferences. *Journal of Business Venturing*, *23*(2), 244–256. https://doi.org/10.1016/j.jbusvent.2006.11.002

Eurostat (2016, August 11). *Glossary: Nomenclature of territorial units for statistics (NUTS).* https://ec.europa.eu/eurostat/statistics-explained/index.php/Glossary:Nomenclature_of_territorial_units_for_statistics_(NUTS)#:~:text=The%20Nomenclature%20of%20territorial%20units,2%20and%203%20respectively%2C%20moving

Fischer, E.M., Reuber, A.R., & Dyke, L.S. (1993). A theoretical overview and extension of research on sex, gender, and entrepreneurship. *Journal of Business Venturing, 8*(2), 151–168. https://doi.org/10.1016/0883-9026(93)90017-Y

Global Entrepreneurship Monitor (2019). *2018/2019 Women's entrepreneurship report.* https://www.gemconsortium.org/report/gem-20182019-womens-entrepreneurship-report

Goffee, R., & Scase, R. (1985). *Women in Charge: The Experiences of Female Entrepreneurs.* London: George Allen & Unwin.

Gundry, L.K., Ben-Yoseph, M., & Posig, M. (2002). Contemporary perspectives on women's entrepreneurship: A review and strategic recommendations. *Journal of Enterprising Culture, 10*(1), 67–86. https://doi.org/10.1142/S0218495802000141

Gupta, V.K., Turban, D.B., Wasti, S.A., & Sikdar, A. (2005). Entrepreneurship and stereotypes: Are entrepreneurs from Mars or from Venus? *Academy of Management Proceedings,* C1. http://dx.doi.org/10.5465/AMBPP.2005.18778633

Gupta, V.K., Turban, D.B., & Bhawe, N.M. (2008). The effect of gender stereotype activation on entrepreneurial intentions. *Journal of Applied Psychology,* 93(5), 1053–1061. http://dx.doi.org/10.1037/0021-9010.93.5.1053

Gupta, V.K., Turban, D.B., Wasti, S.A., & Sikdar, A. (2009). The role of gender stereotypes in perceptions of entrepreneurs and intentions to become an entrepreneur. *Entrepreneurship Theory and Practice,* 33(2), 397–417. http://dx.doi.org/10.1111/j.1540-6520.2009.00296.x

Hattab, H. (2012). Towards understanding female entrepreneurship in Middle Eastern and North African countries: A cross-country comparison of female entrepreneurship. *Education, Business and Society: Contemporary Middle Eastern Issues, 5*(3), 171–186. https://doi.org/10.1108/17537981211265561

Henry, C., Foss, L., & Ahl, H. (2016). Gender and entrepreneurship research: A review of methodological approaches. *International Small Business Journal, 34*(3), 217–241. https://doi.org/10.1177/0266242614549779

Hisrich, R.D., & Brush, C.G. (1983). The women entrepreneur: Implications of family, education, and occupational characteristics. *Proceedings of the Babson Research Conference,* 255–270.

Hughes, K.D., Jennings, J.E., Brush, C.G., Carter, S., & Welter, F. (2012). Extending women's entrepreneurship research in new directions. *Entrepreneurship Theory and Practice*, *36*(3), 429–442. https://doi.org/10.1111/j.1540-6520.2012.00504.x

Isenberg, D. (2011). The entrepreneurship ecosystem strategy as a new paradigm for economic policy: Principles for cultivating entrepreneurship. *Presentation at Institute of International and European Affairs, May 12, 2011, Dublin, Ireland.* http://www.innovationamerica.us/images/stories/2011/The-entrepreneurship-ecosystem-strategy-for-economic-growth-policy-20110620183915.pdf

Kitching, B., & Woldie, A. (2004). Female entrepreneurs in transitional economies: A comparative study of businesswomen in Nigeria and China. In Gregson, T. (Ed.), *4th Annual Hawaii International Conference on Business. 2004 Conference Proceedings* (pp. 1–19). https://core.ac.uk/download/pdf/10873453.pdf

Lafuente, E., Vaillant, Y., & Josep Rialp, J. (2007). Regional differences in the influence of role models: Comparing the entrepreneurial process of rural Catalonia. *Regional Studies*, *41*(6), 779–796. https://doi.org/10.1080/00343400601120247

Lituchy, T.R., & Reavley, M.A. (2004). Women entrepreneurs: A comparison of international small business owners in Poland and the Czech Republic. *Journal of International Entrepreneurship*, *2*, 61–87. https://doi.org/10.1023/B:JIEN.0000026906.28190.df

Mathew, V. (2010). Women entrepreneurship in Middle East: Understanding barriers and use of ICT for entrepreneurship development. *International Entrepreneurship and Management Journal*, *6*, 163–181. https://doi.org/10.1007/s11365-010-0144-1

Max, S., & Ballereau, V. (2013). Theorizing about gender and entrepreneurship: Bridging the gap with social psychology. *International Journal of Gender and Entrepreneurship*, *5*(1), 97–110. http://dx.doi.org/10.1108/17566261311305238

McClelland, E., Swail, J., Bell, J., & Ibbotson, P. (2005). Following the pathway of female entrepreneurs A six-country investigation. *International Journal of Entrepreneurial Behaviour & Research*, *11*(2), 84–107. https://doi.org/10.1108/13552550510590527

McGowan, P., & Hampton, A. (2006). An exploration of networking practices of female entrepreneurs. In N. M. Carter, C. Henry, B. O. Cinneide & K. Johnston (Eds.), *Female Entrepreneurship: Implications for Education, Training and Policy* (pp. 110–133). New York: Routledge.

Menzies, T.V., Diohcon, M., Gasse, Y., & Elgie, S. (2006). A longitudinal study of female vs. male nascent entrepreneurs in Canada: Characteristics, process and out-come differences. *International Entrepreneurship and Management Journal*, *2*(4), 441–453. https://doi.org/10.1007/s11365-006-0013-0

Mirchandani, K. (1999). Feminist insight on gendered work: New directions in research on women and entrepreneurship. *Gender, Work and Organization*, *6*(4), 224–235. https://doi.org/10.1111/1468-0432.00085

Mozumdar, L., Hagelaar, G., Materia, V.C. et al. (2019). Embeddedness or over-embeddedness? Women entrepreneurs' networks and their influence on business performance. *The European Journal of Development Research*, *31*, 1449–1469. https://doi.org/10.1057/s41287-019-00217-3

Neumeyer, X., Santos, S.C., Caetano, A., & Kalbfleisch, P. (2019). Entrepreneurship ecosystems and women entrepreneurs: A social capital and network approach. *Small Business Economics*, *53*, 475–489. https://doi.org/10.1007/s11187-018-9996-5

Nicolae, M., Ion, I., & Nicolae, E. (2016). Regional differences in entrepreneurial perceptions and implications for the Romanian competitiveness policy. *Management & Marketing. Challenges for the Knowledge Society*, *11*(1), 394–409. https://doi.org/10.1515/mmcks-2016-0005

Okafor, C., & Amalu, R. (2010). Entrepreneurial motivations as determinants of women entrepreneurship challenges. *Petroleum-Gas University of Ploiesti Bulletin*, 62(2), 67–77.

Pocol C.B., & Moldovan-Teselios, C. (2014). Women entrepreneurship in Romania: A regional evaluation. *Bulletin UASVM Horticulture*, *71*(2), 408–416. https://doi.org/10.15835/buasvmcn-hort:10607

Röhl, K.H. (2019). Entrepreneurship: A comparative study of the interplay of culture and personality from a regional perspective. *Journal of Small Business & Entrepreneurship*, 31(2), 119–139. https://doi.org/10.1080/08276331.2018.1462621

Santos, F.J. (2009). Women entrepreneurs across racial lines: Issues of human capital, financial capital and network structures. *International Entrepreneurship and Management Journal*, 5, 341–344. https://doi.org/10.1007/s11365-007-0067-7

Sarhan, N. (2019). *Women entrepreneurs' access to justice in Egypt* [Unpublished master's thesis]. University of Sussex. [Retrieved from https://www.academia.edu/41672656/Women_entrepreneurs_access_to_justice_in_Egypt]

Schwartz, E.B. (1976). Entrepreneurship: A new female frontier. *Journal of Contemporary Business*, *5*(1), 47–76.

Solesvik, M., Iakovleva, T., & Trifilova, A. (2019). Motivation of female entrepreneurs: A cross-national study. *Journal of Small Business and Enterprise Development*, *26*(5), 684–705. https://doi.org/10.1108/JSBED-10-2018-0306

Soysal, A. (2010). Türkiye'de kadın girişimciler: Engeller ve fırsatlar bağlamında bir değerlendirme. *Ankara Üniversitesi SBF Dergisi*, 65(1), 83–114. https://dergipark.org.tr/tr/download/article-file/35924

Sullivan, D.M., & Meek, W.R. (2012). Gender and entrepreneurship: A review and process model. *Journal of Managerial Psychology*, *27*(5), 428–458. https://doi.org/10.1108/02683941211235373

Tlaiss, H. A. (2015). How Islamic business ethics impact women entrepreneurs: Insights from four Arab Middle Eastern countries. *Journal of Business Ethics*, *129*, 859–877. https://doi.org/10.1007/s10551-014-2138-3

Toksöz, G. (2007). İşgücü piyasasının toplumsal cinsiyet perspektifinden analizi ve bölgeler arası dengesizlikler. *Çalışma ve Toplum*, *4*, 57–79. [Retrieved from https://www.calismatoplum.org/makale/isgucu-piyasasinin-toplumsal-cinsiyet-perspektifinden-analizi-ve-bolgeler-arasi-dengesizlikler]

Türko, E.S. (2016). Can entrepreneurship education reduce stereotypes against women entrepreneurship? *International Education Studies*, *9*(11), 53–65. http://dx.doi.org/10.5539/ies.v9n11p53

Türko, E.S. (2020). *Girişimcilik Ekosisteminin Teorik Temelleri – Eleştirel Bir Yaklaşım*. İstanbul: Kriter Yayınevi.

Uluköy, M., & Demireli, C. (2014). Cinsiyetin girişimcilik profili üzerine etkisi: erkek girişimcilik ve kadın girişimciliğin karşılaştırmalı analizi. *Yönetim ve Ekonomi Araştırmaları Dergisi*, 22, 47–55. https://dergipark.org.tr/tr/pub/yead/issue/21809/234435

Upadhye, J. (2012). Entrepreneurship Among Poverty-ridden Women: The Confidence Building Index. *International Journal of Trade, Economics and Finance*, 3(2), 132–135. http://dx.doi.org/10.7763/IJTEF.2012.V3.186

Van der Zwan, P., Thurik, A. R., & Grilo, I. (2010). The entrepreneurial ladder and its determinants. *Applied Economics*, *42*(17), 2183–2191. https://doi.org/10.1080/00036840701765437

Van der Zwan, P., Verheul, I., & Thurik, A.R. (2012). The entrepreneurial ladder, gender, and regional development. *Small Business Economics*, *39*, 627–643. https://doi.org/10.1007/s11187-011-9334-7

Verheul, I., Van Stel, A., & Thurik, R. (2006). Explaining female and male entrepreneurship at the country level. *Entrepreneurship & Regional Development*, *18*(2), 151–183, https://doi.org/10.1080/08985620500532053

Wahdiniwaty, R., & Rustam D.A. (2019). Patriarchy as a barrier to women entrepreneurs in Indonesia. *IOP Conference Series: Materials Science and*

Engineering. 662(3), 1–4. http://dx.doi.org/10.1088/1757-899X/662/3/032042 [Retrieved from https://iopscience.iop.org/article/10.1088/1757-899X/662/3/032042]

Wang, Q. (2010). Immigration and ethnic entrepreneurship: A comparative study in the United States. *Growth and Change*, *41*, 430–458. https://doi.org/10.1111/j.1468-2257.2010.00532.x

Yadav, V., & Unni, J. (2016). Women entrepreneurship: Research review and future directions. *Journal of Global Entrepreneurship Research*, *6*(12). https://doi.org/10.1186/s40497-016-0055-x

Zeidan, S., & Bahrami, S. (2011). Women entrepreneurship in GCC: A framework to address challenges and promote participation in a regional context. *International Journal of Business and Social Science*, *2*(14). 100–107.

Tuba ŞAHİNOĞLU[1]

Differences in Women Entrepreneurship by the Development Level of Countries

Being one of the factors having a key role in development, entrepreneurship is generally considered as a male-dominated activity. On the other hand, the contribution of women employment and women entrepreneurship to economic development draws significant attention as a research subject. Thus, in the last 30 years, significant changes have been seen in the status and political place of women entrepreneurs and policies aiming to popularize the women entrepreneurship gained speed especially in developing countries (Minniti & Naude, 2010: 278; Vita et al., 2014: 451).

Women entrepreneurs are considered as a very important resource, which is not currently utilized, for the future (Beqo & Gehrels, 2014: 97). Besides its contribution to economic growth and development, this potential source has also potential to yield significant achievements such as human capital accumulation, wealth formation (Minniti & Naude, 2010: 277), social development, creating productive work, ensuring gender equality, and reducing poverty. For this reason, women entrepreneurship is of a significant place in future-oriented development policies and it is also an important driving force of economic growth. Hence, analyzing the fundamentals of women entrepreneurship and developing entrepreneurship-related policies are important to understand the competitive power and growth potential of a country (Vita et al., 2014: 451).

According to GEM (Global Entrepreneurship Monitor) 2020 report, high potential for establishment of new businesses and increasing policies addressing the empowerment of women from social and economic aspects gradually increase women entrepreneurship (GEM, 2020). In the USA, women-owned companies grow two times more than other firms and contribute approx. 3 billion USD to the economy. Moreover, in developing countries, there are approx. 8–10 million small and medium-size enterprises (SMEs) having a minimum of 1 female entrepreneur (WB, 2021a). However, as reported in World Bank's Business Statistics, only 30 % of registered businesses worldwide have women

1 Assistant Professor Dr., Atatürk University, Faculty of Economics and Administrative Sciences, Department of Economics, tsahinoglu@atauni.edu.tr, ORCID ID: 000-0002-5742-247X

entrepreneur. In other words, although women entrepreneurship constantly grows throughout the world and contributes to the growth of national economies and household incomes, women entrepreneurship is still at an insufficient level.

Ongoing difficulties in women entrepreneurship are actually not only seen in least developed and developing countries; they constitute a global problem. Because, the current data show that SMEs owned by women (even in developed countries) focus on sectors with low growth potential and profitability such as retail, beauty, and catering services. Focusing on these industries limits the financial opportunities and banks offer fewer investment opportunities. Especially in Africa and Asia, 75 % of women are working in such consumer-oriented sectors (Cornish, 2017).

On the other hand, by examining the women entrepreneurship rates by considering the development levels of countries, it can be seen that developed and developing countries have a homogeneous women entrepreneurship structure. Because, the time, human, physical, and social limitations hindering the women's skills of initiating an enterprise and growing current businesses vary depending on not only the development level of countries but also the specific dynamics of countries. Characteristics of country-specific sociocultural and institutional environments have a primary role in determining the women's access to entrepreneurship pathways, as well as their entrepreneurial success. Thus, belonging to specific cultures affects women entrepreneurs' experiences and attitudes (Vita et al., 2014: 451).

The lack of studies on women entrepreneurship in least developed and developed countries arises from the fact that heterogeneous structure of women entrepreneurship by the development level of countries is ignored. On the other hand, besides the recent studies in the literature discussing the differences between men and women entrepreneurs, there also are studies aiming to examine the differences in women entrepreneurship by the development level of countries. Understanding the difference and common points by the development levels is an important step in understanding the causes and effects of women entrepreneurship, as well as the potential suggestions for policies. Moreover, the objectives addressing the promotion of entrepreneurship in developing countries and empowering women in this process shall consider such differences and common points (Minniti & Naude, 2010: 278).

This chapter investigates the differences in women entrepreneurship by the development levels of countries. First, the differences between motives in women entrepreneurship by the development levels of countries are discussed. Then, the course of women entrepreneurship in least developed, developing, and developed countries is discussed using the current data and the prominent countries are emphasized. Finally, the barriers to women entrepreneurship were discussed from the aspect of countries' development level and the measures that should be taken are specified.

1. Motivational Factors in Women Entrepreneurship

In a long and difficult process such as entrepreneurship, motivational factors play a significant role in activation of potential entrepreneurs. Besides that, since entrepreneurship considered as the process of making use of opportunities is individual-oriented, motivation level and motivational factors differ from each other. Thus, motivational factors play determinant role in shaping and conducting the entrepreneurial activities (Özdemir, 2010: 118). For this reason, it should be determined if entrepreneurship motives differ between men and women.

In economies[2] involved in its 2019 Report, GEM comparatively examined the entrepreneurship motivations of men and women. Total Early-stage Entrepreneurial Activity (TEA) research results are presented in Tab. 1. Accordingly, in 36 of 50 countries, the number of women engaging entrepreneurship with the motive of "making a difference in the world" is higher than men with the same motive, whereas the situation in remaining 14 countries[3] is the opposite. Moreover, in 36 countries constituting three-quarters of total, the number of women engaging in entrepreneurial activities with the motive of "earning a living because jobs are scarce" is higher than that of men with the same motive. For this reason, in most of the economies analyzed, women have engaged in entrepreneurial activities with the motives of "making a difference in the world" and "earning a living because jobs are scarce." On the other hand, the motives of "building great wealth or very high income" and "continuing a family tradition" were more important for men than for women.

---

2 Armenia, Australia, China, India, Japan, Pakistan, Taiwan, Canada, Belarus, Croatia, Cyprus, Korean Republic, Germany, Greece, Ireland, Italy, Latvia, Luxemburg, Holland, Northern Macedonia, Norway, Poland, Portugal, Russia, Slovak Republic, Slovenia, Spain, Sweden, Switzerland, USA, United Kingdom, Brazil, Chile, Columbia, Equator, Guatemala, Mexico, Panama, Porto Rico, Egypt, Iran, Israel, Madagascar, Morocco, Jordan, Qatar, Saudi Arabia, South Africa, Oman, United Arab Emirates.

3 Korean Republic, Ireland, Latvia, Luxemburg, Poland, Slovenia, Spain, Sweden, United Kingdom, Columbia, Equator, Guatemala, Madagascar, Saudi Arabia.

Tab. 1: Importance of Motives for Entrepreneurship by Sex

Motive	Men > Women	Men < Women
Making a difference in the world	14	36
Building great wealth or very high income	30	20
Continuing a family tradition;	31	19
Earning a living because jobs are scarce	14	36

Source: Global Entrepreneurship Monitor, 2020.

Another interesting finding was that women were more target-oriented than women (GEM, 2020).

As can be understood from Tab. 1, the policies and practices considering the motives of women entrepreneurs are very important for popularizing the women entrepreneurship and achieving success in this objective. Different motives may create different desires for success and it would affect the entrepreneurship experience, entrepreneurial performance, and policy outcomes (Kobeissi, 2010: 30).

As in entrepreneurship in general, the motives in women entrepreneurship are classified as "push" and "pull" factors (Buttner & Moore, 1997). Push factors refer to the factors enforcing women to entrepreneurship in case of no other option, whereas pull factors are the factors making entrepreneurship attractive for women. It is important for countries to determine whether pull or push motives should be dominant in their policies aiming to support the women entrepreneurship. Because, in economies where the pull motives are dominant, women can make a sacrifice in the long-term in order to receive the fruits of their entrepreneurial activities. On the other hand, in economics where the push factors are dominant, women entrepreneurs need to achieve a good source of income in a period as short as possible (Kobeissi, 2010: 30).

Motivation sources vary depending on various factors such as ethnic origin, religious belief, and family structure, as well as economic and social structures of countries. They may even vary between various regions of a single country. In high-income advanced economies, women entrepreneurs are motivated by push factors such as wage discrimination and work dissatisfaction and pull factors such as sense of achievement and making use of an opportunity (Kobeissi, 2010: 30). In advancing societies, however, it can be seen that motives such as insufficient household income and need for flexible work schedule are more effective on women entrepreneurship. Women's motivation for being economically independent from their spouses and minimizing or recovering from men's effect and pressure or have a life in harmony life is very important in developing societies (Beqo & Gehrels, 2014: 97–100). Moreover, it can also be seen in these countries that the factors such as social status, power, and self-determination are also motivation sources, because, thanks to the entrepreneurship, women find an opportunity to expand their skills and experiences and to determine their destiny (Buttner & Moore, 1997: 41).

2. Women Entrepreneurship Profile by the Development Level

An important portion of studies on women entrepreneurship is carried out in developed countries and it is assumed that results obtained from these studies are valid for the entire world (Minniti et al., 2005). However, examining together with countries' development level and their own dynamics is very important for the studies on women entrepreneurship.

2.1. Women Entrepreneurship in Least Developed Countries

Development of women-owned firms in low-income societies is an option for eliminating the extreme poverty. Moreover, it would have a significant contribution in terms of reducing gender inequality and improving the economic and social rights of women. For this reason, while funding or supporting the development of women entrepreneurs, women in low-income countries should also be included.

However, in relevant countries, it is an important problem to access the data on women entrepreneurship for determining the current case. Especially because developing and least developed countries have no homogeneous data for specific statistics and the data are not consistently classified by sex, it becomes impossible to achieve accurate results in country comparisons.

World Bank Enterprise Surveys (2021d), one of the data sources for women entrepreneurship, aims to collect firm-level data from business owners and top managers.[4] The percentages of enterprises with women entrepreneur participation presented in Tab. 2 were calculated using Enterprise Survey data for low-income countries.[5]

4 Enterprise Surveys include various subjects such as corruption, crime, access to financial services, gender, shadow economy, enterprise characteristics, innovation and technology, performance, infrastructure, regulations, labor, taxes, and trade.

5 Especially for the least developed countries, the review was made with the data availability limitation.

Tab. 2: Percentage of Enterprises with Women Entrepreneur in the Total Enterprises in Low-Income Countries

	2009	2010	2013	2016	2017
Liberia	53				37.4
Madagascar	50		41.6		
Mali		58.3		15.3	
Niger	17.6				14.5
Nepal	27.3		21.8		
Yemen		6.4	6.6		
Togo	31.8			25.3	

Source: Prepared by author using data from World Bank Enterprise Surveys.

According to the data presented in Tab. 2, the highest percentages of enterprises with women entrepreneur participation were found in Liberia and Madagascar. In fact, Madagascan women have always been disposed to earn money to support their families. Moreover, Madagascar started implementing a gender-based policy aiming to support women entrepreneurs (GEM, 2020). On the other hand, the country with the lowest percentage as of year 2013 was Yemen with 6.6 %. Another interesting point here is the constant decrease in percentage of enterprises with women entrepreneur participation in low-income countries. The rate in Mali decreased from 58.3 % in year 2010 to 15.3 % in year 2016.

Another criterion used in quantitatively expressing the women entrepreneurship by the country is the Women, Business and the Law (WBL) index[6] established by World Bank. This index is used as a criterion to determine how women employment and entrepreneurship is affected by legal gender discrimination, as well as its economic outcomes. WBL index is the average of each economy's scores in 8 subjects. It consists of 35 items in 8 topics. Scored over 100 points, WBL index scores increase with increasing gender equality. In

6 In the last decade, WBL index measures the legal differences in access to economic opportunities between men and women in 190 economies. It incorporates scores of business place, mobility, wage, entrepreneurship, ownership, parenthood, marriage, and retirement.

Tab. 3: WBL Index and Women Entrepreneurship Scores of Low-Income Countries

Region	Countries	WBL Index	Women Entrepreneurship Score
Sub-Saharan Africa	*Burundi*	73.1	75
	Chad	66.3	50
	Congo Republic	78.8	100
	Ethiopia	71.9	75
	Guinea	65.0	100
	Madagascar	71.9	75
	Tanzania	84.4	75
	Mali	60.6	75
	Liberia	83.8	75
	Somali	46.9	75
	Uganda	73.1	75
	Niger	59.4	50
South Asia	*Afghanistan*	38.1	75
	Nepal	73.8	75
Middle East -North Africa	*Yemen*	26.9	75
Europe – Central Asia	*Tajikistan*	78.8	100

Source: World Bank, Women, Business, and the Law Data.

Tab. 3, WBL index and Women Entrepreneurship[7] scores of low-income countries are presented.

As seen in Tab. 3, except for Congo Republic, Guinea, and Tajikistan, the women entrepreneurship score of low-income countries is generally 75. On the other hand, the women entrepreneurship score of Chad and Niger was found to be 50. Considering the score of WBL index, Liberia (83.8 %) and Tanzania (84.4 %) had the highest scores, whereas Yemen (26.9 %) and Afghanistan (38.1 %) were found to have the lowest WBL index scores. From the aspect of the percentage

7 Questions asked in determining the women entrepreneurship scores are as follows.

- Can a woman sign a contract as a man does?
- Can a woman register a business as a man does?
- Can a woman open a bank account as a man does?
- Do the laws ban gender-based discrimination in access to loans?

Tab. 4: TEA, Women/Men TEA,[a] GDP per capita data of Low-Income Countries[b]

	2019			2018		
	Total TEA	**Women/ Men TEA**	**GDP per capita**[c]	**Total TEA**	**Women/ Men TEA**	**GDP per capita**
Madagascar	19.48	1.02	500.4	20.74	1.04	490.1
India	14.97	0.75	2151.72	11.42	0.62	2086.45
Morocco	11.40	0.51	3396.05	6.65	0.46	3361.22
Pakistan	3.65	0.30	1185.45			1197.91
Angola			3111.15	40.84	0.99	3233.9
Indonesia			4450.72	14.09	1.01	4284.68
Sudan			1724.08	22.17	0.62	1812.12
Armenia	20.97	0.64	4732.07			4406.7

a This ratio is calculated as the percentage of 18- to 64-year-old female population, who are either a nascent entrepreneur or owner-manager of a "new business," divided by the equivalent percentage for their male counterparts.
b Considering the income group classification made of World Economic Forum (WEF), GEM incorporates lower-mid-income group countries into lower-income group countries.
c Prices fixed to year 2010, in USD.
Source: GEM.

of enterprises with women entrepreneur participation in the total, Yemen had the lowest score. For this reason, they applied to ILO (International Labour Organization) in order to benefit from its experience in business development and to expand Yemen's technical specialty in women entrepreneurship.

Conducting entrepreneurship researches using country-level surveys, GEM is the only global research source directly collecting entrepreneurship-related data from individual entrepreneurs. GEM expanded its scope of data to 115 countries. The level of Total Early-stage Entrepreneurial Activity (TEA)[8] is an important parameter for GEM research. Tab. 4 represents the low-income countries.

From the aspect of women/men ratio in total early-stage entrepreneurial activity, Madagascar ranked 1st in both 2019 (1.02 %) and 2018 (1.04 %).

8 TEA is calculated by summing the entrepreneurs establishing a new business (new entrepreneur) and those operating an existing business (new business owner) and subtracting those in both categories. In other words, this parameter indicates the percentage of 18- to 64-year-old population who are owner-manager or founder of a new enterprise. The ones managing a company, which had paid wage for 42 months or more, are in the category "Established Business Owners."

This ratio indicates that women are as active in establishing their businesses as men. Madagascar implements a new gender-based policy in supporting women entrepreneurs. The lowest score was found to be 0.3 % in Pakistan in 2019. Since Pakistan has no data for year 2018, Morocco has the lowest score of women entrepreneurship with 6.65 %. One of the interesting points here is that Madagascar having the highest women entrepreneurship score has the lowest GDP (Gross Domestic Product) per capita (500 USD). Although India has approx. half of Armenia's income level, the ratio of women entrepreneurs in India is high. Moreover, whereas the total entrepreneurship score of Armenia is high, the women entrepreneurship score in this country is at low levels.

2.2. Women Entrepreneurship in Developing Countries

World Bank (2021c) emphasizes that elimination of poverty and increase in welfare could be achieved only through the full participation of men and women in economy. In the world, there are approx. 1 billion women having the potential of contributing to the economy and 812 million of these women live in developing countries having the highest need for an additional contribution. Empowering women entrepreneurs especially in rapidly growing industries and creating employment opportunities in these sectors would increase those countries' national income and contribute to saving thousands of families from poverty and creating greater economic and social transformation. For this reason, women and entrepreneurship attracted significant interest in recent years in developing countries and focusing on this "unused source" of growth became one of the inevitable goals of policymakers (Minniti & Naudé, 2010).

On the other hand, besides having fewer opportunities of establishing businesses when compared to men, women (especially those in developing countries) have businesses that tend to be smaller. Thus, it is estimated that, when switched to male-dominated industries, women might earn three times more than in traditionally women-dominated industries (Cornish, 2017). Moreover, when compared to men, women achieve lower revenues from entrepreneurial activities. Finally, rather than establishing a business, sustaining and growing it is a significant difficulty for all women, especially in developing countries.

Presented in Tab. 5, percentage of enterprises with women entrepreneur participation was calculated using World Bank's Enterprise Surveys for several countries in lower-mid- and upper-mid-income groups.

According to data in Tab. 5, although the percentage of enterprises with women entrepreneur participation is relatively higher in least developed countries, it has a heterogeneous structure. When compared to lower-mid-countries, the countries in the upper-mid-income group did not show better performance.

Tab. 5: Percentage of Enterprises with Women Entrepreneur Partnership in Total in Lower-Mid- and Upper-Mid-Level Income Countries

Lower-Mid-Income Group					Upper-Mid-Income Group			
Countries	**2009**	**2013**	**2019**	**2020**	**Countries**	**2009**	**2013**	**2019**
Egypt		16.1		5.2	*Albania*		13.1	20.7
Kirghiz Republic	60.4	51.2	45		*Turkey*		25.1	11.3
Moldavia	53.1	54.1	39.9		*Azerbaijan*	10.8	4	15.3
Mongolia	52	36.1	47.3		*Bosnia-Herzegovina*	32.8	22.8	24.6
Morocco		31.3	16.1		*Bulgaria*	33.9	41.5	41.7
Zambia		43.7	41.5		*Jordan*		15.7	22.6
Uzbekistan		29	25.9		*Kazakhstan*	34.4	29.6	30.5
Ukraine		32.2	38.6		*Kosovo*	10.9	13.2	7.3
Tunisia		49.5		40.1	*Lebanon*		43.5	9.9
					Romania	47.9	47.2	32.4
					Russia	33.1		34

Source: Prepared by author using data from World Bank Enterprise Surveys.

Among the countries in the lower-mid-income group, Egypt decreased from 16.1 % in 2013 to 5.2 % in 2020. An increase was observed in the percentage of enterprises with women entrepreneur participation in the total of Ukraine in lower-mid-income group and Albania, Azerbaijan, and Bulgaria in upper-mid-income group. Furthermore, the decrease in Lebanon in the upper-mid-income group draws attention.

Tab. 6 includes mid-level income group countries' scores of women entrepreneurship and WBL index, which is another criterion used by the World Bank for women employment and entrepreneurship.

Examining Tab. 6 in terms of income group, both WBL index and women entrepreneurship score have heterogeneous structures. Among the lower-mid-income group countries, the score of Equator Guinea was 0. Moreover, the women entrepreneurship score of Cameroon, Kenya, and Pakistan was found to be 50. Pakistan and Cameroon have low score in WBL index but the score of Kenya was found to be 80. On the other hand, in the countries in Latin America-Caribbean in the lower-mid-income group, WBL index and women entrepreneurship scores were higher than in other regions.

Considering the countries in the upper-mid-income group, although WBL index scores of countries in the lower-mid-income group were lower in general, the low scores in the Middle East – North Africa were attention-grabbing

Tab. 6: WBL Index and Women Entrepreneurship Scores of Countries in Lower-Mid- and Upper-Mid-Income Groups

Lower-Mid-Income Group				Upper-Mid-Income Group			
Region	**Countries**	**WBL Index**	**Women Entrepreneurship Score**	**Region**	**Countries**	**WBL Index**	**Women Entrepreneurship Score**
Sub-Saharan Africa	*Sudan*	29.4	75	*Latin America-Caribbean*	*Argentina*	76.3	75
	Angola	73.1	100		*Brazil*	81.9	75
	Cameroon	56.9	50		*Equator*	89.4	75
	Congo Republic	46.3	75		*Peru*	95.0	100
	Kenya	80.6	50		*Mexico*	83.8	100
	Nigeria	63.1	75	*Eastern Asia-Pacific*	*Philippines*	81.3	100
	Zimbabwe	86.9	100		*China*	75.6	75
	Equator Guinea	51.9	0		*Malaysia*	50.0	75
	South Africa	88.1	100		*Thailand*	78.1	75
South Asia	*Bangladesh*	49.4	75	*Middle East – North Africa*	*Egypt*	45.0	75
	India	74.4	75		*Iran*	31.3	75
	Pakistan	49.4	50		*Lebanon*	52.5	75
	Maldives	73.8	100	*Europe- Central Asia*	*Albania*	91.3	100
Latin America-Caribbean	*Bolivia*	82.5	100		*Armenia*	82.5	75
	El Salvador	88.8	100		*Azerbaijan*	78.8	100
	Nicaragua	86.3	100		*Bosnia-Herzegovina*	85.0	100
					Bulgaria	90.6	100
					Russia	73.1	75
					Turkey	82.5	75
					Romania	90.6	100

Source: World Bank, WBL Data.

(31.3 in Iran, 45 in Egypt, and 52.5 in Lebanon). On the other hand, women entrepreneurship scores ranged between 75 and 100. Moreover, regional effects played a significant role and women entrepreneurship scores were found to be 75 in Eastern Asia – Pacific and Middle East regions, while the scores were relatively better in Europe-Central Asia and Latin America countries. Given these results, it can be stated that the main characteristics of women entrepreneurship vary depending on the geographic region. Accordingly, besides the economic and legal conditions of country, entrepreneurship activity also depends on the sociocultural context (Vita et al., 2014: 454).

In their study, Vita et al. (2014) claimed that major factors determining the dynamics of women entrepreneurship differ between regions. While the effect of religion is more prominent in Eastern Asia and Pacific, role of networking comes to the forefront in Eastern Europe and Central Asia, social discrimination plays an important role in the Middle East, and social legitimacy of acting as an entrepreneur shapes the women entrepreneurship in South Asia and Sub-Saharan Africa (Vita et al., 2014: 452).

In conclusion, Tab. 7 lists the women entrepreneurship parameters and national income levels of countries in the mid-level income group within the scope of GEM report.

According to Tab. 7, the highest women/men TEA ratio was found to be 0.98 % in Brazil for the year 2019 and 0.96 % in Thailand for the year 2018. Among the countries with mid-level income, Brazil has the highest value with 11121.74 USD, whereas Thailand having 6501.55 USD of GDP per capita has not a high level of income. This ratio indicates that women are as active in establishing business as men. The country with the lowest score was Egypt with the scores of 0.44 % in 2019 and 0.38 % in 2018. This low score in women entrepreneurship draws the general score and TEA ratio was found to be 6.67 %. Moreover, Egypt also has the lowest GDP per capita among the other countries in the mid-level income group. On the other hand, another point to emphasize here is that Turkey has the higher GDP per capita among these countries but still has the second-lowest women/men TEA ratio (0.42 %) following Egypt.

2.3. Women Entrepreneurship in Developed Countries

Although the importance of women entrepreneurship for the development in developing countries has consistently been emphasized, it can be seen that different dimensions come to the forefront in developed countries. Especially for developed countries, one of the points to discuss about women entrepreneurship is the migrant women entrepreneurs, who have migrated from underdeveloped

Tab. 7: TEA, Women/Men TEA, and GDP per capita for Countries in Mid-Level Income Group[a]

	2019			2018		
Countries	**Total TEA**	**Women/ Men TEA**	**GDP per capita**[b]	**Total TEA**	**Women/ Men TEA**	**GDP per capita**
Belarus	5.78	0.82	6678.5			6586.29
Brazil	23.3	0.98	11121.74	17.88	0.93	11079.71
China	8.66	0.84	8254.53	10.39	0.82	7807.05
Columbia	22.28	0.88	7838.21	21.19	0.72	7694.42
Equator	36.2	0.86	5097.06			5180.59
Egypt	6.67	0.44	3010.15	9.84	0.38	2908.58
Guatemala	25.05	0.80	3413.23	27.52	0.8	3338.54
Iran	10.69	0.53	5922.52	9.71	0.50	6440.06
Jordan	9.11	0.59	3325.8			3309.75
Mexico	12.98	0.91	10267.05			10385.83
Russia	9.33	0.85	12011.53	5.55	0.53	11844.44
South Africa	10.77	0.89	7345.96			7433.61
Argentina			9742.45	9.11	0.81	10049.56
Bulgaria			9058.73	6.00	0.87	7807.05
Lebanon			5792.25	24.08	0.56	6214.35
Peru			6486.63	22.39	0.88	6453.56
Thailand			6501.55	19.68	0.96	6370.01
Turkey			15125.39	14.24	0.42	15190.1

a According to GEM classification, the countries in upper-mid level income group were included in mid-level income group.
b Prices fixed at year 2010, in USD
Source: GEM.

regions and are operating businesses in advanced economies. Besides their contribution to the economies of developed countries, these women want to support their countries and societies through global trade and employment creation. Due to the discrimination these women frequently face in their countries, entrepreneurship means a "self-survival strategy" for them (GEM, 2012; Vita et al., 2014: 452).

In Tab. 8, the percentages of enterprises with women entrepreneur participation calculated using World Bank's Enterprise Surveys for countries in the high-income group are presented. Accordingly, when comparing these data with those of least developed and developing countries, these data have

Tab. 8: Percentage of Enterprises with Women Entrepreneur Participation in Total in High-Income Group Countries

Countries	2009	2013	2019
Croatia		36.3	31.7
Czech Republic		30.4	29.9
Estonia		38.3	35.5
Hungary	42.4	48.7	51.9
Israel		27.3	
Italy			24
Latvia	46.3	41.6	46.6
Poland	47.9	40.9	37
Slovenia	42.2	38.5	34.1

Source: Prepared by author using data from WB Enterprise Surveys.

a more homogeneous structure and range between 24 % and 46 % for the year 2019. Among the countries analyzed here, Hungary has the highest score with 51.9 %, whereas Italy has the lowest score with 24 %. Considering the women's rate of participation in business ownership, Hungary draws attention with the increase in this parameter, whereas no significant change was observed in other countries.

On the other hand, the WBL index and women entrepreneurship scores presented in Tab. 9 belong to the countries in the high-income group. According to Tab. 9, the women entrepreneurship scores of countries in the high-income group, except for certain countries (Chile, Israel, Japan, Norway, Sweden, Singapore, Taiwan, UAE (United Arab Emirates), Qatar, and Kuwait), is 100 indicating a more homogeneous structure when compared to countries in low and mid-level income groups. Majority of countries with score of 100 are the OECD (Organization for Economic Co-operation and Development) member countries. WBL index score was, however, found to be 100 in Belgium, Canada, Denmark, France, Luxemburg, and Latvia. On the other hand, Qatar and Kuwait draw attention with WBL index score of 32.5 WBL. It can be seen that WBL index score was found to be low in Middle East – North Africa countries.

Finally, total TEA and women/men TEA ratios and GDP per capita values of countries in the high-income group are presented in Tab. 10. Accordingly, in Saudi Arabia with TEA ratio of 1.09, the number of women entrepreneurs is higher than men. Previous score of this country was 0.58 % in year 2018 and, thus, Saudi Arabia draws significant attention with such a rapid expansion

Tab. 9: WBL Index and Women Entrepreneurship Score of High-Income Group Countries

Region	Countries	WBL Index	Women Entrepreneurship Score
OECD	*Belgium*	100	100
	Canada	100	100
	Czech Republic	93.8	100
	Denmark	100	100
	Chile	77.5	75
	USA	91.3	100
	United Kingdom	97.5	100
	France	100	100
	Greece	97.5	100
	Germany	97.5	100
	Israel	77.5	75
	Italy	97.5	100
	Japan	81.9	75
	Australia	96.9	100
	Norway	96.9	75
	Spain	97.5	100
	Holland	97.5	100
	Luxemburg	100	100
	Switzerland	85.6	75
Eastern Asia-Pacific	*Singapore*	82.5	75
	Taiwan	91.3	75
Europe-Central Asia	*Latvia*	100	100
	Cyprus	91.3	100
Middle East- North Africa	*Kuwait*	32.5	75
	United Arab Emirates	56.3	75
	Saudi Arabia	70.6	100
	Qatar	32.5	75
	Malta	88.8	100

Source: World Bank, WBL Data.

in women entrepreneurship. On the other hand, its GDP per capita value of 20,542.17 USD falls behind the other countries in this group. Saudi Arabia is one of the countries making the highest level of reforms on women entrepreneurship. Moreover, Saudi Arabia equalized the age of retirement at 60 years for women and men and extended the working lives, contributions, and

Tab. 10: Total TEA, Women/Men TEA, and GDP per capita Values of High-Income Grup Countries

Countries	2019			2018		
	Total TEA	Women/ Men TEA	GDP per capita[1]	Total TEA	Women/ Men TEA	GDP per capita
Australia	10.52	0.72	57186.62			56832.05
Canada	18.16	0.71	51588.76	18.71	0.83	51476.20
Chile	36.71	0.79	15091.45	25.06	0.73	15111.7
Croatia	10.47	0.61	16509.91	9.61	0.59	15971.15
Cyprus	12.17	0.57	32093.03	3.86	0.60	31506.92
Germany	7.63	0.60	47446.73	4.97	0.50	47313.85
Greece	8.22	0.87	24024.23	6.35	0.45	23546.64
Ireland	12.41	0.57	79703.41	9.64	0.63	76662.67
Israel	12.69	0.69	35278.92	12.70	0.70	34749.68
Japan	5.35	0.37	49187.83	5.34	0.60	48766.13
Italy	2.79	0.60	35680.16	4.18	0.51	35485.11
Latvia	15.43	0.58	16722.10			16263.23
Luxemburg	10.20	0.69	111062.30	10.72	0.68	110701.9
Holland	10.38	0.80	55488.97	12.29	0.51	54894.13
Norway	8.36	0.44	92556.32			92119.52
Oman	6.94	0.72	15082.02			15796.73
Panama	22.68	0.74	11910.16	13.83	1.01	11755.11
Poland	5.39	0.90	17406.55	5.24	0.74	16648.77
Portugal	12.89	0.62	24658.50			24085.42
Puerto Rico	13.39	0.74	27684.46	11.61	0.55	27362.43
Qatar	14.69	1.00	63281.67	8.52	0.98	63932.66
Saudi Arabia	13.96	1.09	20542.17	12.09	0.58	20819.75
Sweden	8.25	0.55	58012.96	6.82	0.42	57911.23
Spain	6.15	0.94	33392.53	6.39	0.89	32949.08
UAE	16.41	0.70	41420.48	10.72	0.92	41327.38
Switzerland	9.77	0.59	79406.66	7.37	0.47	79234.96
Slovenia	7.80	0.56	27426.79	6.37	0.43	26760.48
United Kingdom	9.34	0.60	43711.71	8.24	0.49	43324.05
Austria			50552.91	10.90	0.57	50051.79
USA	17.42	0.91	55753.14	15.59	0.77	54832.98
France			44317.39	6.13	0.75	43720.03
Uruguay			14597.31	15.70	0.64	14617.46

1 Prices fixed at year 2010, in USD.
Source: GEM.

revenues of women in professional life. Furthermore, banning gender-based discrimination in access to financial services, Saudi Arabia supports women entrepreneurship (WB, 2021b). Besides, women have also recently been granted more personal freedoms in economic and social life.

With the score of 1 %, Qatar follows Saudi Arabia. Qatar has a high level of GDP per capita. One of the reasons for such a significant improvement in women entrepreneurship in Qatar is the educational opportunities provided for women. Women make use of programs provided by both governmental and private institutions. The lowest score for the year 2019 was found to be 0.37 % in Japan. This country, where the total entrepreneurship ratio was also found to be low, has a GDP per capita value of approx. 50,000 USD. Regarding total early-stage entrepreneurial activity, Chile draws attention with a high score of 36.71 %. However, women entrepreneurship ratio remained very low with the value of 0.79 %.

In conclusion, according to GEM 2019 Report, Saudi Arabia, Qatar, Madagascar, and Brazil were found to be economies with high women entrepreneurship in comparison to men, whereas the women entrepreneurship ratio was found to be low in Pakistan, Japan, Northern Macedonia, and Norway (GEM, 2020). In economies with a low level of women entrepreneurship, there are 2 early-stage men entrepreneurs per 1 early-stage women entrepreneur. Fig. 1 illustrates the expansion of women entrepreneurship in Saudi Arabia, Madagascar, and Qatar.

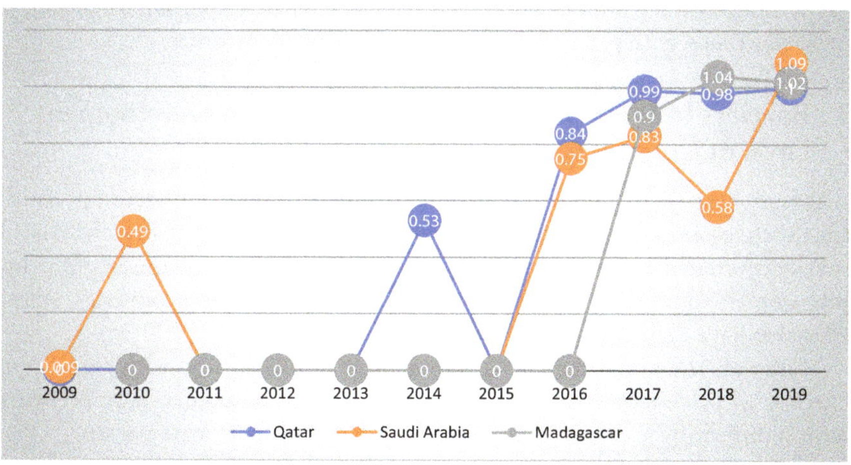

Fig. 1: Women/Men TEA ratios in Madagascar, Qatar, and Saudi Arabia

Source: Prepared by author using GEM data

Low level of women participation decreases the general entrepreneurial activities and it suggests that women entrepreneurs should be supported in these economies. Women have stronger and more significant roles in several economies, whereas significant advancements are necessary in some others. Gender inequalities in entrepreneurship continue draining new job stock and decreasing the economic potential (GEM, 2020).

When examining the women entrepreneurship in terms of the level of development, a heterogeneous structure draws attention especially in developing countries. On the other hand, even though Madagascar is a least developed country, it has a higher women entrepreneurship ratio. Although women entrepreneurship ratios seem to have a more homogeneous structure in developed countries, low ratios draw attention in countries such as Japan. Moreover, when examining the countries by development level in terms of women entrepreneurship, regional factors should not be ignored. The finding "women entrepreneurship is high in some regions and low in some others" cannot be generalized. However, it can be easily seen that the general level of entrepreneurship is high in countries including Latin America and Caribbean and Europe – Central Asian countries. In general, the countries in the Middle East and North Africa seem to have the lowest number of women entrepreneurs. However, Saudi Arabia and Qatar are the most remarkable exceptions. Thus, generalization over development status or on regional basis may not be always accurate. Countries' specific dynamics come to the forefront in women entrepreneurship. From this aspect, gender-empowering policies and success in this field are important for advancement of women entrepreneurship and permanence of outcomes.

3. Barriers to Women Entrepreneurship by the Development Level of Countries

Although barriers to women entrepreneurship are generally observed in countries with lower development status, women entrepreneurs face many different barriers even in developed countries. In general, besides the common problems that women entrepreneurs have in developed and developing countries, countries also have their specific problems.

While all the entrepreneurs in developing countries face with significant barriers in professional life, the findings indicate that women entrepreneurs have significantly greater barriers when compared to their male peers.

3.1. Gender Discrimination

Gender problems related with establishing and operating enterprises are among the factors negatively affecting women entrepreneurship. Intra- and transnational gender inequality is at higher levels in poorer and more isolated countries and the difference keeps expanding. Gender discrimination causes women to not efficiently use their entrepreneurial potential, besides bringing disadvantages for national economy. Thus, saving women from discriminative practices is required not only for the economic justice but also for the fact that excluding women from economic life would yield an unbearable cost for the economy (WB, 2021c).

Gender differences, which have been comprehensively examined by sociologists in studies on women entrepreneurship, play an important role in women's entrepreneurial preferences. For this reason, changing the policies and regulations resulting in discriminations against women such as inability of signing a contract on their own, barriers to access to bank accounts, or difficulties in women's business registrations is very important. On the other hand, gender differences in entrepreneurship do not always depend directly on the characteristics of women and they may be related with the industries, in which entrepreneurs are operating (Vita et al., 2014: 452–454).

Besides that, although economic growth is helpful in reducing gender inequality and improving the life standards of women especially in developing countries, it should be noted that economic growth is not the same as economic equality (Harrison & Bluestone, 1988).

3.2. Access to Financial Resources

Access to financial resources and achieving an initial capital constitute an important difficulty for any entrepreneur establishing a new enterprise. Since financial institutions consider women as "riskier clients with lower revenues," access to financial services is an important barrier to the development of women-owned businesses. Especially in developing countries, financial barriers combine with together with legal and political barriers and discrimination (Cornish, 2017).

Gallup's World Survey suggested that, in developing countries, there are significant differences between men-owned businesses' access to financial services and that of women-owned businesses. Accordingly, generally speaking, women have more limited access to basic banking services such as check and deposit accounts. In conclusion, many women entrepreneurs make use of their own savings, debts from family and friends, or micro-credits in funding their enterprises. On the other hand, since micro-credits provide a low amount of funds for a short term, they prevent women entrepreneurs from making long-term investments in their businesses (WB, 2021a).

On the other hand, besides the development level of country, the social structure may also play an important role in access to financial services. In a patriarchal social structure, all the properties that a family owns are generally registered in the name of the man of the house. It constitutes an important difficulty for the financial necessities of new women entrepreneurs (Beqo & Gehrels, 2014: 101).

3.3. Insufficient Education and Access to Information

Theory of Entrepreneurship asserts that skills and abilities of entrepreneurs constitute the primary human resource of a business. Thus, skills, abilities, and experiences of women provide positive or negative motivation, which possibly affects or starts women's business ownership (Kobeissi, 2010: 4).

One of the difficulties in women entrepreneurship in developing countries is the relative disadvantages of women in educations and skill trainings. Besides the lack of career, it also limits the access to various governmental or private support services regarding business development and business growth. But, learning and professional development are of critical importance for sustaining and growth of women entrepreneurship, besides being an important tool against gender discrimination (Davis, 2012: 20). Insufficient education that women have in underdeveloped societies increases the prejudice that women entrepreneurs face with.

On the other hand, women in developing countries do not have skills required for adapting to the effects of globalization, advancing technologies, and changing trade patterns (Vossenberg, 2013: 5). Lack of technologic knowledge and insufficient experience, as well as the lack of entrepreneurial and management skills, results in lower level of industrial entrepreneurial activities of women entrepreneurs (Drine & Grach, 2010: 453). For this reason, businesses established by women entrepreneurs tend to be informal, house-based, and small-scaled firms mainly focusing on retail and service sectors. Minimum 30 % of women working in non-agriculture sectors throughout the world are working in shadow sectors; this ratio reaches 63 % in Africa (WB, 2021a).

The fact that women entrepreneurs concentrate on education, tourism, and personal services industries becomes more apparent especially in developing countries (Bruni et al., 2005). Besides that, these sectors are deemed less necessary for development as high-technology or processing sectors and, thus, they are considered less valuable (Morched & Jarboui, 2018: 25).

Even if not directly, education has an important effect on women entrepreneurship. These findings highlight the importance of education for countries, especially for developing countries (Kobeissi, 2010: 23). The important point here is that women need a different education (Cornish, 2017). On the other hand, besides the fact that educational policies should vary between the countries, it may be necessary to adapt them to different regions of a country. For developing countries, education on women entrepreneurship should reach the rural areas because access to education is as important as the education itself. Sometimes policies might be more effective with increasing access to education (WB, 2001).

3.4. Legal Barriers and Procedures

Institutional and legal environment is of critical importance for the growth of women-owned businesses. For this reason, although varying depending on country, the lack of governmental support to required policies, laws, and services is defined as a barrier to women entrepreneurs (Vossenberg, 2013: 5). Discriminative regulations create a business environment threatening the women's economic security, career development, and work-life balance and not sufficiently supporting the working women.

Gender inequalities observed in several fields may be eliminated through economic development. For instance; the gender inequalities in education can be resolved with development but the same doesn't apply to gender inequalities in legal rights (WB, 2021a). The laws regulating the private area, especially those regulating the marriage, inheritance, and land ownership, may prevent the access of women to assets that can be pledged as security while getting a bank loan. According to the property score within the scope of World Bank's WBL index, countries in the low-income group such as Nepal (South Asia), Togo, and Mauritania have a score of 0 points. Women in the Middle East and North Africa have only half of men's legal rights but the average global ratio is 75 % (WB, 2021b).

3.5. Limited Network and Geographical Mobility

Considering the continuous information flow and the changes in global market, the importance of creating a network should be considered in women entrepreneurship. On the other hand, since women attach more importance to personal and emotional connections than men do, their networks are different from those of men (Beqo & Gehrels, 2014: 98). In developing countries, where they are given less authorization, women tend to have a significantly limited network and geographical mobility (Kobeissi, 2010: 10).

Especially in developing countries, women-created networks are recommended to women generally by their spouses or parents. Moreover, women entrepreneurs generally prefer women networks. Besides, they may need to participate in men-established networks because of the lack of alternatives and because men-established networks dominate the market (Beqo & Gehrels, 2014: 101).

3.6. Lack of Social Support

In several countries, normative limitations and social attitudes based on cultural and religious beliefs do not support the works of women entrepreneurs in general (Vossenberg, 2013: 5). Although social pressures on women may vary between countries, social norms generally limit women's participation in the economy by hindering their physical mobility or time available for running their business. For instance; social norms such as education are effective on many of women's economic activities and, thus, women cluster in service sectors with low productivity and growth potential (WB, 2021c).

4. Conclusion

Poverty and lack of opportunity can be considered among the most important reasons for inequality between men and women. For this reason, when poverty is reduced through economic advancements, women's status is improved in two ways because, in case of a decrease in poverty, an improvement is achieved in status of every individual and, because gender inequality reduces as the poverty decreases, women's status improves more than that of men. On the other hand, economic development may play an important role in decreasing the inequality between women and men but it might not be sufficient for ensuring the exact equality between women and men. Such that, discrimination against women might negatively affect the development process and, thus, additional policy actions may be needed in order to construct the gender equality (Duflo, 2012: 1053).

Although there is no significant difference between many developing and developed countries, there are differences between genders' entrepreneurship of countries. For this reason, in order to develop policies related with successful entrepreneurship, policymakers should consider the stages of country's economic development (Kobeissi, 2010: 29). But, the most important point here is that the development level of countries should not be the only criterion to be considered while developing policies for improving women entrepreneurship. The policies should also incorporate country-specific characteristics.

Thus, it is difficult to achieve homogeneous outcomes in assessing the entrepreneurship profiles of countries by considering the development levels of countries. According to GEM 2020 Report, there are 7 economies in which the women/men TEA ratio is 0.9 or higher. These countries are Madagascar, Saudi Arabia, Qatar (the Middle East and Africa), Mexico, Brazil (Latin America and Caribbean), Spain, and USA (Europe and North America). On the other hand, there also are 5 economies with more than 5 early-stage men entrepreneurs for every 1 early-stage women entrepreneur (Egypt, Norway, Japan, North Macedonia, and Pakistan). At this point, low participation of women also reduces the general entrepreneurial activities.

In most countries, entrepreneurial activities of men are higher than those of women, whereas there are 3 countries (Saudi Arabia, Qatar, and Madagascar), where women entrepreneurs outnumber the men entrepreneurs. Among them, Saudi Arabia and Qatar are developed countries, whereas Madagascar is categorized as a least developed country. Even this finding can show that an increase in development status is not a single way of empowering the women entrepreneurship. Thus, the interventions aiming to empower the women from economic aspect seem not sufficient for women to overcome the barriers. In order for those interventions to be transformative, they must pass beyond the basic access to financial and human capital and address the psychological, social, and skill limitations on women entrepreneurs (Siba, 2019: 1). Voosenberg (2013) argued that current policies promoting the women entrepreneurship absolutely provide benefits for women but, when the gender bias in which entrepreneurship is embedded is not addressed, all the efforts might fail.

At the same time, also the policies addressing the empowerment of gender may provide women with access to equal opportunities, they should never be considered as a single focus point. Besides empowering women from economic and gender aspects, policymakers should make effect to change the social perception of women entrepreneurs. This action would be more important especially in developing countries, in which the social acceptance of women entrepreneurs is lower than in developed countries. Actions such as promoting the entrepreneurship as a traditional career option in order to alter the perceptions, publicizing stories of successful women entrepreneurs (learning from a peer), and incorporating entrepreneurship as a part of curriculum in education might be used (Kobeissi, 2010: 28).

Especially the vocational training programs aiming to change the mentality and the skill training programs focusing on women are important. Women should be supported through effective business, management, and life skills in order for them to have significant contribution to family, society, and economy by developing their businesses. Successful interventions improving the women entrepreneurship generally combine basic work skills with soft skills such as leadership and mindset. Furthermore, the programs addressing the socially imposed gender roles improve women's understanding of preventing the normative assumptions (Siba, 2019: 4). In order for a support to be successful, providing women entrepreneurs with training suitable for their needs and cultural context and training the trainers within this context is important (WB, 2021c).

Besides the fundamental elements that they must have, the policies aiming to support women entrepreneurship should also incorporate characteristics that are specific to the developed and developing countries. Especially in developing countries, one of the methods aiming to change the social mentality is to encourage women for penetrating into male-dominated industries. Thus, women entrepreneurship would not be stuck in specific industries. Within this context, one of the supports is the programs supporting the women in switching to more productive industries or more valuable sectors in traditional industries.

Developing countries should also develop regulations to resolve the discriminative practices in laws and legal systems from the aspect of women entrepreneurship. Countries having easier bureaucratic procedures related with establishing a new business have significantly higher starts. For instance; the right of property, right to control, and right to participate in a contract (Davis, 2012: 24) can be given as examples. Besides the legal regulations, also the measures aiming to strengthen the institutions' capacity to implement and maintain the women entrepreneur supports in a non-discriminative way are very important (WB, 2021c).

References

Beqo, I., & Gehrels, S. A. (2014). Women entrepreneurship in developing countries: A European example. *Research in Hospitality Management*, *4*(1&2), 97–104. https://doi.org/10.1080/22243534.2014.11828320

Bruni, A., Gherardi, S., & Poggio, B. (2005). *Gender and Entrepreneurship: An Ethnographic Approach*. Taylor & Francis Group. https://doi.org/10.4324/9780203698891

Buttner, H. E., & Moore, D. P. (1997). Women's organizational exodus to entrepreneurship: Self reported motivations and correlates with success. *Journal of Small Business Management*, *35*(1), 34–46.

Cornish, L. (2017, December 20). *Are women entrepreneurs the key to global economic development?* Inside Development/Economic Development.

https://www.devex.com/news/are-women-entrepreneurs-the-key-to-global-economic-development-91010#:~:text=In%20developing%20countries%20in%20particular,gap%20remains%20a%20global%20phenomenon

Davis, P. J. (2012). The global training deficit: The scarcity of formal and informal professional development opportunities for women entrepreneurs. *Industrial and Commercial Training, 44*(1), 19–25. https://doi.org/10.1108/00197851211193381

Drine, I., & Grach, M. (2010). Supporting women entrepreneurs in Tunisia. *European Journal of Development Research, 24*(3), 450–464. https://doi.org/10.1057/ejdr.2011.13

Duflo, E. (2012). Women empowerment and economic development. *Journal of Economic Literature, 50*(4), 1051–1079. http://dx.doi.org/10.1257/jel.50.4.1051

GEM. (2012, December 09). *Global Entrepreneurship Monitor.* 2012 Global Report. https://www.gemconsortium.org/file/open?fileId=48545

GEM. (2020, December 11). *Global Entrepreneurship Monitor.* 2019/2020 Global Report. https://www.gemconsortium.org/report/gem-2019-2020-global-report

Harrison, B., & Bluestone, B. (1988) *The Great U-Turn: Corporate Restructuring and the Polarizing of America.* Basic Books.

Kobeissi, N. (2010). Gender factors and female entrepreneurship: International evidence and policy implications. *International Journal of Entrepreneurship, 8*, 1–35. https://doi.org/10.1007/s10843-010-0045-y

Minniti, M., Arenius, P., & Langowitz, N. (2005). *The 2004 global entrepreneurship monitor special topic report: Women in entrepreneurship.* Babson Park, MA: Center for Women Leadership, Babson College.

Minniti, M., & Naude, W. (2010). What do we know about the patterns and determinants of female entrepreneurship across countries? *European Journal of Development Research, 22*, 277–293. https://doi.org/10.1057/ejdr.2010.17

Morched, S., & Jarboui, A. (2018). Does female entrepreneurship add in economic growth? Evidence from twenty-five countries. *Journal of Academic Finance, 9*(2), 20–35.

Özdemir, A. A. (2010). Potansiyel girişimci olan kadınların motivasyon faktörleri ve Eskişehir'de bir araştırma. *Ege Akademik Bakış, 1* (1), 117–139.

Siba, E. (2019, February). *Empowering women entrepreneurs in developing countries: Why current programs fall short.* Africa Growth Initiative at Brookings. https://www.brookings.edu/wp-content/uploads/2019/02/Empowering-women-entreprenuers-in-developing-countries-190215.pdf

The World Bank (2001, January 01). Engendering development: Through gender equality in rights, resources, and voice. A World Bank Policy Research Report.

https://documents1.worldbank.org/curated/en/512911468327401785/pdf/multi-page.pdf

The World Bank (2021a, December 22). *Female entrepreneurship resource point – Introduction and module 1: Why gender matters.* https://www.worldbank.org/en/topic/gender/publication/female-entrepreneurship-resource-point-introduction-and-module-1-why-gender-matters

The World Bank (2021b, January 04). *Women, business and the law 2020.* https://datacatalog.worldbank.org/dataset/women-business-and-law

The World Bank (2021c, January 15). *Supporting high growth potential women entrepreneurs.* Innovation & Entrepreneurship. https://www.worldbank.org/content/dam/Worldbank/document/Trade/InnEntre_WomenEntrepreneurs.pdf

The World Bank (2021d, January 21). *Enterprise surveys.* https://www.enterprisesurveys.org/en/enterprisesurveys

Vita, L. D., Mari, M., & Poggesi, S. (2014). Women entrepreneurs in and from developing countries: Evidences from the literature. *European Management Journal, 32*, 451–560. https://doi.org/10.1016/j.emj.2013.07.009

Vossenberg, S. (2013). Women entrepreneurship promotion in developing countries: What explains the gender gap in entrepreneurship and how to close it? *Maastricht School of Management Working Paper*, No. 2013/08.

Emine Demet Ekinci HAMAMCI[1]

Gender Inequality and Reflections on the Women Entrepreneurship

Since the last quarter of 20th century, the lives of women started to change significantly and women had several achievements such as benefiting more from essential services like education and healthcare, participating more in labor force, having more political and legal rights, and participating more in social life when compared to the past. Besides that, these achievements couldn't be equally enjoyed by all the women in all the countries or couldn't equally reflect to all the dimensions of gender and women keep struggling with gender-based inequalities (WB, 2012).

Gender inequality refers to an individual's exposure to gender-based unequal behaviors, attitudes, and perceptions. The inequality arises from the differences between gender roles established by the society; in this process, gender norms and stereotyped attitudes limit the behaviors of women and men in the way causing inequality by intensifying the gendered identities (Ridgeway, 2011).

Gender inequality indicates not only the gender-based inequalities in access to and control of financial sources (Ridgeway, 2011), but also the gender-based differences distinguishing men from women in all the dimensions of social life such as family, law, education, politics, etc. The gender inequalities, women are generally exposed to, can be categorized as inequality in rights, in sources, in economic activities, in access to health and related services, in public life and politics as well as violence and abuse (Ecevit, 2003).

This study examined the gender inequality and its reflections on women's economic life and entrepreneurial activities. The gender inequalities, through the norms, behaviors, and roles attributed to women and the sociocultural roles and expectations, directly limits the participation of women in entrepreneurial activities, and prioritizes men. Moreover, gender inequality causes the emergence of an entrepreneur type distinguishing women from men and may cause women entrepreneurs to experience gender problems in professional life.

---

1 Assistant Professor Dr., Erzurum Technical University, Faculty of Economics and Administrative Sciences, Department of Economics, emine.hamamci@erzurum.edu.tr, ORCID ID: 0000-0003-2808-2186

The participation of women as an entrepreneur in economic life directly contributes to the economic growth and welfare of the country, similar to other entrepreneurial activities. However, the literature has pointed out the indirect effects of women entrepreneurs and reported that an increasing number of women entrepreneurs might provide more employment opportunities and contribute to gender equality, economic stability, and development (Lee Gosselin & Grise, 1990; Wells et al., 2003).

This study aimed to determine the relationships of women entrepreneurship with gender equality and women participation in the labor force. For this purpose, in this study, it was analyzed with Spearman correlation by using UNDP's gender inequality index, Global Entrepreneurship Monitor's female/male total early-stage entrepreneurial activity (TEA) ratio and female/male opportunity-driven TEA ratio, and World Bank's data on women's participation in labor force. The analysis has involved the data of 48 countries in high-income and mid-income groups for the year 2018.

The study consists of four parts. The first part discusses the concepts of gender and gender inequality, whereas the second examines the effects of gender inequality on women's economic life. The women entrepreneurship and the effects of gender inequality on women entrepreneurship are reviewed in the third part. The final part presents the relationship between gender inequality and women entrepreneurship.

1. Gender and Gender Inequality

Sex is defined as the biological, genetic, and physiological characteristics defining an individual as a woman or man. Gender, however, refers to the roles attributed to women and men in social life, and the behaviors and expectations arising from these roles (Cherry, 2005). In other words, sex is related with biological and anatomic differences between women and men, whereas gender refers to differences based on social and cultural factors (Sayer, 2011).

Rather than biological differences, gender is a concept related with how society considers, perceives, and thinks of us how we are supposed to behave as a man or woman (Dökmen, 2004). This concept refers to the roles, behaviors, and expectations that society constructs for women and men (Ecevit, 2003). However, gender now includes not only the socially created differences between women and men but also any discrimination distinguishing the female body from male body (Nicholson, 1994). In conclusion, the gender, regulating the social process in daily life, shapes the social organizations such as economy, ideology, family, politics, etc. by penetrating them (Onaran et al., 1998).

In 1950s, the term gender was first used in psychology in order to identify the self-perception of woman and man (cited by Sayer, 2011). Besides that, the use of gender concept with the meaning closest to current meaning was introduced in 1970s by American feminists claiming that gender-based discrimination was not biological but arising from the cultural and social structure (Scott, 2007).

Feminists used the term gender in order to criticize the biological determinism and the discrimination it created. According to biological determinism, the characteristics and behaviors of an individual have biological roots such as genetic structure and hormonal differences and, thus, women and men exhibit attitudes, behaviors, preferences, and selections differing by sex. However, this differentiation is accepted as natural and unchangeable, and triggers inequalities by affecting all the dimensions of social life between women and men. At this point, feminists ignore the biological determinism that is the basis of terms such as sex and sexual differences, and they advocate that biological characteristics shall not be the cause of social inequalities. Feminists emphasize that the differences between preferences and attitudes are largely "learned" ones, and are not innate. In other words, these differences are a result of culture and environment causing women and men to internalize the social norms and expectations (Scott, 2007). Gender differences arising from the social construction became gender inequalities in the society (Marshall, 2000).

Introduced by feminists, the concepts of gender and gender-based inequality increasingly were adapted by different social groups with time. In 1995, this concept was officially accepted in "4th World Women Conference" held in Beijing by United Nations (UN).

To emphasize the equal rights and their innate human dignity of men and women, in the declaration of Beijing conference, it was "reaffirmed to ensure the full implementation of the human rights of women and of the girl child as an inalienable, integral and indivisible part of all human rights and fundamental freedoms" (UN, 1995). Making effort to keep this subject on the agenda in the next years, the UN accepted the year 2013 as one of "Eight Millennial Development Objectives" and emphasized that gender equality is very important to achieve other seven objectives (UN, 2013).

Gender arises from and develops within an order. This order is gender order, which is defined as the general system where the gender relationships develop in a society. Lives of women and men are shaped by the gender order and, besides the gender-oriented division of labor in this order, reinforced by various means such as different sociocultural rules and expectations regarding women and men (Sayer, 2011). The operation of order begins with the birth of an individual;

girls and boys are loaded with the cultural meanings of their sexes, which can also be referred as gender roles.

Gender roles are the expectations and behaviors, which the society defines for women and men in a gender-oriented manner. Through the socialization process, girls and boys learn to classify the objects, activities, occupations, and even personality traits to be suitable or unsuitable for their sex (Dökmen, 2004). This learning process of children is affected by many institutions and persons such as family, school, social environment, and mass communication instruments; the stereotyped judgments are imposed on the basis of biological sex.

The meanings attributed to being a man or woman are stuck within the roles that are valid in social life and rooted in the public opinion and they become obligated to obey the roles imposed by the social paradigm (Caner, 2004). Thus, women are forced to fulfill the in-home responsibilities and be good mothers only, whereas men are supposed to earn money and protect his family (Moya et al., 2000). Moreover, according to these traditional roles, men are expected to have aggressive and dominant character, whereas women are expected to have a vulnerable, sensitive, and dependent character. But, when compared to women and women's roles and characteristics, the perspective based on the traditional roles attributes significantly higher value to men and their roles and characteristics (Lee, 2005). In other words, the gender-based division of labor creates inequality between sexes and puts men in an advantageous position (Butler & Scott, 1992). Thus, through the gender and gender roles, the equality between women and men is deteriorated and a gender inequality putting men into a superior position is created (Connell, 2003).

Gender inequality refers to any gender-based discrimination, deprivation, or limitation preventing or hindering or aiming to prevent or hinder the recognition, exercise, and enjoyment of women's fundamental freedoms and human rights in political, economic, social, cultural, and civil domains (Demirgöz Bal, 2014). According to World Bank (WB, 2012), gender inequalities refer to the power differences between two sexes arising from the social, behavioral, and cultural characteristics, expectations, and norms related to being a woman or man. In order words, gender inequality can be defined as qualitatively equal individuals' exposure to different treatments only because of their sex (Cesur, 2009).

In many developed or developing countries, there are practices and norms based on gender inequality and creating or increasing the conditions further impoverishing women and alienating and forcing them to submit (Vicente,

2005). Besides that, in patriarchal societies, the scope and context of inequality reach higher levels.

Gender inequalities are a cumulative outcome historically inherited between the generations (Sayer, 2011). Moreover, while gender differences trigger gender discrimination, gender discrimination creates gender differences and there is a bilateral interaction (Alptekin, 2014). As a result of this process, the sex factor becomes one of the most important axes of power relations in social life and it results in inequalities in various domains such as family, work, law, education, politics, etc.

Gender inequalities that women are exposed to vary among the countries, societies, and even families. For this reason, some women have a chance to live in a more equal world, whereas some others are exposed to more severe inequalities. Besides that, the gender inequalities women are generally exposed to are the inequalities in rights, resources, economic activities, and access to healthcare and related services, as well as violence, abuse, misuse, and inequalities in public life and political domain (Ecevit, 2003).

Some of the gender-based inequalities that women are exposed to can be listed as follows (Çağatay, 1998; Kümbetoğlu, 2002; Demirbilek, 2007; WB, 2013; Bal, 2014; İleri, 2016).

- Allocation of in-home responsibilities largely to women,
- Considering the responsibility of caring for children, patients, and disabled individuals as women's duty,
- Unequal distribution of household income and, thus, women's exposure to poverty and deprivation at a higher level,
- Higher level of exposure to domestic psychological, economic, and physical abuse,
- Women's lower schooling rates at any level of education,
- Higher death rates among women,
- Exposure to insufficient and unhealthy nutrition,
- Lower level of participation and activity in public domain,
- Lower labor force participation rates,
- Less employment opportunities in formal industry in comparison to men,
- Lower wages and violation of the rule of "equal pay for equal work,"
- Limitations in occupation preferences,
- Glass ceiling syndrome in promoting in business life,
- Lower chance to access to capital,
- Lower share from the national income,
- Absence of right to elect and be elected,

- Lower level of political representation,
- Having no chance to make a decision about political preferences,
- Lower level of participation in social life,
- Low level of no right of succession, divorce, possession, and travel, as well as many other legal rights.

Elimination of gender-based discriminations and ensuring the equality between women and men are very important for the societies. According to WB (2012), gender equality is important in itself because one of the fundamental rights is the right to live a self-determined life and be protected from essential deprivation and women and men should have equal rights. Second, gender equality is important as an instrument because the higher level of gender equality will contribute to economic productivity and other key developmental outcomes such as improving the opportunities of further generations and social policies/institutions.

2. Gender Inequality in Economic Activities

After the Industrialization Revolution, the labor of women has been incorporated into the public area and women have started to work in a paid job. In this process, the capitalists have intensely demanded the female labor considered as low-cost labor and women have had domestic conflicts with men, who have not accepted losing their power in home (Özer, 2017). Under the effects of these conflicts, women's labor force participation rate followed a fluctuating course. Besides that, the women's labor force participation rate increased with World War I and II. Especially in World War II, women have worked in war-related industries as factory workers and clerks and become an inseparable part of the formal economy (Neft & Levine, 1997).

Significant socioeconomic changes after World War II and the rapid growth trend increased the efforts to expand women's role in economic life. Thus, in year 1947, the "United Nations Commission on the Status of Women" has been established within the body of the United Nations and the statuses and problems of women in all the member countries have been investigated (Arıkan, 2002). In 1970s, with the positive effects of feminist movements, the UN declared the year 1975 as the "International Year of the Women." Hereby, the UN aimed to increase the equality between women and men, enable women to participate in all the efforts addressing economic development, and proclaim the contribution of women to world peace (Arıkan, 2002).

In 1970s, the efforts aiming to improve the status of women have brought positive results and it has been seen that, in comparison to the past, women have made more effort in order to participate in economic life. For instance, the women's labor force participation rate has been 43 % in 1970s but increased to 60 % at the end of 20th century. Similarly, the same rate has been 42.7 % in the United Kingdom and has increased to 54.5 % in 1999 (OECD, 2021). Women's labor force participation rate, which has peaked in 1990s, entered into a dramatic decreasing trend in 21st century. For instance, the women's global labor force participation rate was 57 % in 1990 but decreased to 55 % in 2012 (WB, 2013). However, this decreasing trend applies not only to women but also to men.

There have been many economic, social, and cultural transformations and advancements drawing women into the labor force more than past. Some of these factors can be listed as follows (Akoğlan, 1996; Barutçugil, 2002; Gökkaya, 2014):

- Women needed to contribute to the household income,
- Women's participation in working life granted them economic and social freedom,
- Participating in working life granted women with the sense of satisfaction and happiness,
- Increase in educational status of women,
- Elimination or decrease in prejudices objecting the women's participation in professional life,
- Advancements reducing the responsibility of women in services such as taking care of children, patients, and elders,
- Reduction in time allocated to domestic works thanks to the technological advancements,
- Decrease in rate of marriage, especially that of early marriages,
- Increase in divorce rates and in number of single-parent families, where the woman is the household head,
- Increase in demand for female employees due to structural transformation in national economies and rapid growth in service industry,
- Increase in the urbanization rate,
- Emergence of new occupations, which are suitable for women, as a result of knowledge era and advancements in management systems,
- Increase in the positive sexual discrimination towards women under the effects of feminist movements in Western countries,

- Increase in the laws and regulations protecting and supporting the working women,
- Emergence of, and increase in non-standard types of working.

As of the year 2019, the global number of labor force was approximately 3.5 billion and women constitute 389 % of this labor force (WB, 2020). Women's labor force participation rate is 47.2 % for year 2019. Besides that, men's labor force participation rate in year 2019 was 74.1 % but the global labor force participation rate was 60.7 % (ILO, 2020). This result indicates that the equality between labor force participation rates of women and men couldn't be achieved. However, the inequality between labor participation rates might reach very higher levels depending on the age and location of women.

Considering the national income level of countries, women's labor force participation rate is 63.2 % in low-income country group, 34.1 % in lower-mid-income group, 54.0 % in upper-mid-income group, and 53.2 % in high-income group, whereas the same rates for men are 78.4 %, 75.8 %, 74.5 %, and 68.4 %, respectively (ILO, 2020). Similarly, the difference between labor force participation rates of women and men varies depending on the age and, in many regions, the highest difference is at the age group of 25–34 as a result of the beginning of childcare responsibility (WB, 2013).

How and to what extent women would participate in labor force is closely related with economic development level and development strategy of countries (Dedeoğlu, 2000). Besides that, another important factor influencing the labor force participation rate is the gender roles and the gender inequality arising from these roles. Gender inequality originating from traditions, cultural characteristics, and biases of societies allocates roles and behavior patterns to women, creates social biases, and prevents the participation in labor force.

Traditional gender roles allocated duties such as taking care of children, patients, and elders to women, men are expected to earn money for household. Such a task distribution creates the most important obstacle for women's labor force participation (Önder, 2013) and even eliminates women's desire and thought of working. On the other hand, social biases such as considering the vocational education as a right of men and preventing girls from educational opportunities, society's negative thoughts about working women, and women's need for approval of family or husband in order to be able to work reinforce the gender roles and keep women away from the business life. Moreover, problems women have in their professional life, lack of policies to ensure the participation of women in economic life, and (if any) insufficient enforcement of regulations ensuring the women participation in professional life hinder the women's active participation in labor force (Çakır Hanbay, 2011).

Considering the world of work, the gender-based inequalities between women and men are not limited to the participation in labor force and they can be seen in any domain of economy such as employment, unemployment, wages, working conditions, business quality, etc. Some of the examples of problems that women from different countries have in their professional lives are as follows (WB, 2012; 2013):

- Women earn approximately 10–30 % less than men. Moreover, in many companies, women earn less money than men doing the same job.
- Women's opportunity to have a full-time job is 50 % less than men. In low-income countries, the ratio of women having a paid job decreases down to 9 %.
- Considering from the aspect of paid employment, men are generally employed in industries such as production, construction, transportation, and communication, whereas women are employed in industries such as healthcare, social services, and education. Besides the gender-oriented perspective, this difference is also based on education, training, occupational safety preferences, and need for flexible working hours.
- In all the regions other than Sub-Saharan Africa, the number of men working in informal sectors is exactly higher than that of women. Besides that, women in developing countries tend to be employed in non-agriculture informal industries.
- Women generally focus on "invisible duties" (domestic works and non-paid works). For instance, 27 % of all the paid female workers in Latin America and Caribbean and 14 % of paid female workers in Africa are employed in houses. Women constitute 83 % of all housemaids throughout the world. The majority of these maids enjoy none of the legal rights such as maximum weekly working hours, minimum wage, and maternity leave.
- Women achieved gender equality with men in positions such as parliamentarian, senior official, and manager in few countries (Columbia, Fiji, Jamaica, Lesotho, and Philippines).
- The share of women, who are subject to glass ceiling syndrome, has a share of 24 % in top management at a global scale.
- Women are not sufficiently represented in domains such as science, technology, engineering, and mathematics.
- Limited presence of women in several sectors and occupations (i.e., limited number of female employees in these sectors and occupations) reinforces the

discriminative opinions about the suitability of employment as worker and the productivity of women. If there is no mechanism to correct such beliefs, then the prejudices might become permanent.

- Women spend a minimum of two times more time for unpaid domestic works (child/elder care and house works) when compared to men. Moreover, even if women increase their working hours, they remain responsible for house works and etc.
- In majority of countries (128 countries), there is a minimum of 1 gender-based legal difference preventing the equal employment of women and men in professional life. These obstacles include women's access to institutions and services, property possession, access to credit, job search, etc. For instance, woman has to receive her husband's approval for employment.
- Many women have no access to land and financial capital. For instance; in Brazil, women own only 11 % of total agricultural lands and the lands owned by women are smaller than those owned by men. There are similar differences in use of fertilizers and improved seeds in agriculture.
- As a result of gender-specific limitations, women's harvest per land and rate of commercialization are lower when compared to men.
- Women are generally disadvantageous in domains such as access to financial services, technology, vocational education, information, and social networks. However, the support in access to information or in promotions or advancements comes in gender-oriented networks and women trying to enter a male-dominated area are harmed.
- In developing countries, there is a difference of approx. 9 % between the women and men having an account in an official financial institution.
- Throughout the world, 4 out of 10 people think that men have more right to work than women in cases of any employment limitation.
- Women entrepreneurs operate in industries with lower productivity and profitability levels and they have smaller-scale firms. For instance, in Latin America and Caribbean, there is no other employee in 50 % of firms owned by women. Thus, women have fewer opportunities for growing their businesses or for career development.
- Human and physical differences between women and men reinforce the differences in employment and wages. Despite the high educational status of women, there are still differences between the human capitals of women and men. These differences are years of schooling at older age groups and disciplines chosen by women and men at younger age groups.

Tab. 1 represents some of the statistical data of 2019 indicating the gender-based inequalities in working life.

Tab. 1: Selected Labor Force Statistics 2019 by Gender and National Income Groups

Country income group	Gender	Labor Force Par. Rate	Employment to pop. ratio	Informality level	Unemp. Rate (Urban)	Wage/ Salaried Worker	Employer	Extreme working poverty[a, b]
World	Total	60.7	57.4	61.2	6.5	52.8	2.6	7.1
	Female	47.2	44.6	58.1	6.9	53.2	1.4	7.5
	Male	74.2	70.3	63.0	6.3	52.5	3.4	6.9
Low income	Total	70.6	67.9	89.8	8.0	17.9	1.8	38.2
	Female	63,2	60.7	92.1	8.6	11.2	0.9	39.1
	Male	78.3	75.3	87.5	7.4	23.6	2.5	37.5
Lower middle income	Total	55.2	52.3	83.7	7.1	36.0	2.8	10.0
	Female	34.1	32.1	84.5	8.5	33.6	1.2	11.4
	Male	75.8	71.9	83.4	6.4	37.0	3.4	9.4
Upper Middle Income	Total	64.2	60.3	52.6	7.0	59.4	2.3	0.8
	Female	54.0	50.7	50.4	7.1	58.1	1.3	0.9
	Male	74.5	70.0	54.0	6.9	60.3	3.1	0.8
High income	Total	60.7	57.8	18.3	5.0	87.7	3.4	
	Female	53.2	50.4	17.6	5.3	90.2	2.1	
	Male	68.4	65.3	18.9	4.8	85.8	4.5	

a Extreme working poverty refers to earnings of less than US$1.90 PPP per day
b The ILO does not estimate extreme and moderate working poverty rates for most high-income countries, since the values would be very close to zero.
Source: ILO, 2020.

Woman is a value that generally remains in the background in professional life throughout the world regardless of time and space but plays an important role in the advancement of societies. Because this value is not appropriately appreciated by the society, women and society have significant economic and social losses.

Pushing women out of working life negatively affects their self-esteem and decreases their productivity. This problem creates a dilemma and further pushes women, who have lower productivity, out of professional life and limits the liberalization of women labor. Thus, it weakens the status of women in society. Moreover, the non-employed women have losses both from economic and familial aspects, as well as lower living standards. However, this problem doesn't remain at the individual level but it causes severe social and economic problems for the society.

Considering from the economic aspect, women constitute one of the important components of a country's limited sources and this source should be effectively used in order to achieve economic growth. Women play role in production as both employee and entrepreneur and diversify the production through the consumption. For this reason, allocation of this source to the production and utilization of revenues, which are obtained from its contribution to the production, through consumption or saving trigger economic growth.

From the social aspect, it can be seen that the problems arising from women's lack of employment opportunities cause many problems hindering the overall development of a country. For instance, when women are deprived of employment, many aspects such as reducing the poverty, participation of women in decisions regarding the social and family life, prevention of domestic violence, increasing the number of productive women who are open to innovation, better educational and medical opportunities provided for children, providing girls with educational and employment opportunities for future, preventing forced-marriages of girls at early ages, etc. are negatively affected. For this reason, supporting women in participating in social life would play a key role in the economic and social development of societies.

3. Gender Inequality and Women Entrepreneurship

Entrepreneurship means not only establishing or operating a company but the whole of activities positively affecting the economic growth and welfare of the region or the country, where the enterprise has been established. Having such significant effects, entrepreneurship has very modest beginnings, and emerges with entrepreneurial activities at the junction point of revenue opportunities and entrepreneur.

Entrepreneurial opportunity refers to revealing the new products, services, and organization methods and selling these economic values at a price higher than production cost (Hisrich et al., 2017). In short, entrepreneur is a person, who realizes the opportunity and consciously combines these production factors in order to produce services and goods. Entrepreneurs have certain characteristics such as innovativeness, risk-taking, and creativeness, as well as making the best use of opportunities. Thanks to the entrepreneurial personality traits, they provide economic development with dynamism and establish and improve businesses (Yetim, 2008).

Women entrepreneur is a woman taking risks estimated in the market economy, translating them into cash for the market, producing and selling goods and services, owning a business and registered in chambers of trade and commerce and in tax offices, working and employing individuals with social security institution registrations (Müftüoğlu & Durukan, 2004).

Being a part of entrepreneurship concept, women entrepreneurship is different and the definition should specify the limitations. Accordingly, the characters of women entrepreneurs are (Ecevit, 1993: 20):

- Having one or more businesses established by her outside the house,
- Working alone or together with employees in a firm or having the title of "firm owner,"
- Conducting the activities related with the production of any good or service,
- Conducting/organizing the distribution, marketing, and sales of produced good or service,
- Contacting various public and private institutions for professional purposes,
- Making plans for the future of firm,
- Having a word on the areas of investing and spending the revenues received from the firm, and
- Undertaking all the responsibilities in the name of her firm.

Despite the increasing opportunities in today's knowledge-oriented economies, when compared to men, women's chance to have or establish a firm is very lower and it even applies to industrialized countries (Allen et al., 2008). For instance; as of year 2019, the rate of female employers in labor market was 1.4 %, whereas that of men was 3.4 %. Considering the income group of countries, the rate of female employers is 0.9 % in low-income countries, 1.2 % in mid-income countries, and 2.1 % in high-income countries. Although there are relatively more female employers in high-income countries in comparison to the countries in other groups, the rate of male employers in high-income countries is 4.5 % and very higher than the global average (2.6 %) (ILO, 2020). However, the gender difference between women and men is not limited to the number of entrepreneurs and qualities of businesses also differ. Men entrepreneurs are founders, owners, and managers of larger-scale companies having higher revenues, offering more new goods and services, and employing more employees, whereas women establish and own smaller-scale companies with lower productivity (Allen et al., 2008).

The factors differing women and men entrepreneurs from qualitative and quantitative aspects are based on, as in other dimensions of economic life, the gender concept and the inequality it creates. With this concept, the roles and behavior patterns imposed on women and men might prevent women from entrepreneurship, cause the emergence of a different type of entrepreneur distinguishing women from men, and create gender inequality-based problems in professional life to the detriment of women.

Women generally remain fall behind in terms of utilizing the entrepreneurial opportunities when compared to men. It might arise from the personality traits of woman, while it may also be based on the social characteristics. First of all, women are imposed with merciful, sensitive, submissive, and dependent personality traits. However, in society, the entrepreneur is correlated with personality traits such as go-getter, dynamic, brave, self-esteem, risk-taking, etc. (Ertübey Özgen, 1993). For this reason, some women think that they do not have such important personality traits and are scared of entrepreneurship, while some societies have negative biases about women entrepreneurship. Especially the patriarchal societies are not accustomed to women in business life and, thus, women having entrepreneurial plans get reactions from their families and relatives. Women, who have established their businesses despite these reactions, have to struggle with social and environmental reactions while operating their businesses (Özyılmaz, 2016). The in-home responsibilities allocated to women and the responsibility of being a good mother and wife prevent them from entrepreneurship. Believing that they cannot fulfill the responsibilities given by the sexist division of duties and the responsibilities arising from operating an enterprise, many women prefer the in-home duties or being forced to prefer them.

The gender-based factors such as roles, behaviors, culture, lifestyle, etc. limiting the women entrepreneurship causing women entrepreneurs have different characteristics than men entrepreneurs. For instance; main motivations of women entrepreneurs arise from the personal expectations such as demand for independence, work satisfaction, and desire for achievement, whereas the

Tab. 2: Characteristics Distinguishing Women and Men Entrepreneurs

Characteristics	Women Entrepreneurs	Men Entrepreneurs
Source of motivation	Desires to achieve success since she has never been let progress.	Intention of controlling and guaranteeing the future.
İnitial financial sources	Personal assets and savings	Personal equity and bank credits and personal loans
Previous professional experiences	Mid-level manager in service industry	Production, finance, and technical fields
Personality traits	Lower self-esteem and more normative	Self-esteem, more flexible, more tolerant
Age of entrepreneurship	Between 35 and 40 years	Between 25 and 35 years
Educational status	Liberal art education (in general)	Technical and business administration education (in general)
Main supporters	Spouses, close friends, and professional unions	Advisors (Lawyer, Financial Advisor) and spouses
Industry of enterprise	Service industries such as public relations, retail sale, and education	Production, foreign trade, and advanced technology

Source: cited by İpçioğlu, 2011.

main motivations of men are based on rational factors such as controlling and guaranteeing the future. Moreover, women are shier and have more self-esteem problems, whereas men have higher levels of self-esteem. However, these differences may cause women to own or manage smaller-scale firms with lower productivity. Some of the characteristics distinguishing women and men entrepreneurs are presented in Tab. 2.

In its nature, entrepreneurship is a concept incorporating many economic, social, and psychological risks. For this reason, entrepreneurs undertake the problems arising from risks and uncertainties throughout their lives and make effect to tolerate them. However, besides these problems, women entrepreneurs also face different gender-based problems.

The gender-based problems that women entrepreneurs face are based on factors such as social relationships, resource procurement, obligation of fulfilling the professional responsibilities with domestic ones, cultural and traditional resistance, etc. (Ertürk, 1993). The problems of women entrepreneurs can be categorized as follows (İlter, 2008):

- Micro problems: Inexperience, lack of knowledge, being alone, inability to participate in the social information network, lack of communication with customers, familial reactions, intense workload, negative attitudes from peers and customers, etc.
- Macro problems: Lack of education, procurement of capital and material, finding a place for business, procurement of equipment, hardware, etc., communication with government institutions, lack of qualified personnel, fluctuations in market, payments, and lack of organization with other women entrepreneurs.
- Problems related with introduction to market

As with other entrepreneurial activities, women entrepreneurship contributes to the economic growth and welfare of regions and countries by translating savings into investments, producing more goods and services, and expanding the employment opportunities. Moreover, by creating innovations in production, production process, and organization structure, they positively contribute to the other industries. However, the increase in number of women entrepreneurs contributes not only to the economic growth but also to the economic development of countries.

As role models, women entrepreneurs allow increase in the number of women entrepreneurs, as well as creating more employment opportunities for women, decreasing women unemployment, increasing the women's labor force participation through flexible working hours, reducing the poverty through contributions to household income, sustainability of local economies, and social interaction (Lee-Gosselin & Grise, 1990; Wells et al., 2003; Bertaux & Crable 2007; Sarfaraz et al., 2013). Thus, women entrepreneurship changes and reinforces the role and status of women in society and may act as an instrument in ensuring gender equality.

4. The Relationship between Gender Inequality and Women Entrepreneurship: Spearman's Correlation Analysis

4.1. Methodology

The empirical studies generally pointed out that gender equality increases the women's labor force participation rates and the number of women entrepreneurs by enabling women to participate more in economic activities. On the other hand, it was also indicated that an increasing number of women entrepreneurs positively contributes to women's participation in labor force as employer or employee and to gender equality. From this aspect, in this study it has aimed to determine the relationships of women's participation in entrepreneurial activities with women labor force participation and gender inequality.

In the study, it has been analyzed with Spearman's correlation by using Perez's gender inequality index (GII) for gender inequality, Global Entrepreneurship Monitor (GEM)'s female/male total early-stage entrepreneurial activity (TEA) ratio and female/male opportunity-driven TEA ratio and World Bank's female labor force participation rate for women entrepreneurship.

Gender inequality index (GII) is a human development index annually calculated by UNDP. While calculating the index, women health (maternal mortality ratio and adolescent birth rates), empowerment of women (proportion of parliamentary seats occupied by females and proportion of adult females and males aged 25 years and older with at least some secondary education), and economic status of women (female labor force participation rate) are considered (UNDP, 2020). Index score ranges between 0 and 1. The higher GII values indicate increasing inequality between women and men, whereas lower scores indicate that the gender equality is achieved.

Female/male TEA ratio and female/male opportunity-driven TEA ratio are important indicators annually calculated by GEM. Female/male TEA ratio refers to percentage of female 18–64 population, who are either a nascent entrepreneur or owner-manager of a "new business," divided by the equivalent percentage for their male counterparts, whereas female/male opportunity-driven TEA ratio is defined as percentage of those females involved in TEA who (i) claim to be driven by opportunity as opposed to finding no other option for work; and (ii) who indicate the main driver for being involved in this opportunity is being independent or increasing their income, rather than just maintaining their income, divided by the equivalent percentage for their male counterparts (GEM, 2020).

With these two entrepreneurship indicators, GEM reports the difference between considering entrepreneurship as an obligation and considering it as an opportunity (Perez & Hernandez, 2016). Accordingly, female/male TEA ratio defines the sum of entrepreneurs considering entrepreneurship as both the best available option and an opportunity, whereas female/male opportunity-driven TEA ratio incorporates the ones considering entrepreneurship as an opportunity.

The analysis included data of totally 46 countries in high-income group (Austria, Canada, Chile, Croatia, Cyprus, France, Germany, Greece, Ireland, Israel, Italy, Japan, Luxemburg, Netherlands, Panama, Poland, Qatar, Saudi Arabia, Slovakia, Slovenia, South Korea, Spain, Sweden, Switzerland, United Arab Emirates, United Kingdom, USA, and Uruguay) and mid-income group

(Angola, Egypt, India, Indonesia, Morocco, Sudan, Argentina, Brazil, Bulgaria, China, Colombia, Guatemala, Iran, Lebanon, Peru, Russia, Thailand, and Turkey) for 2018. These countries have involved since they have both gender inequality index and female/male TEA ratio and female/male opportunity-driven TEA ratio data.

In order to determine the relationships of women's labor force participation and women entrepreneurship with gender inequality, Spearman's rank correlation analysis was used. Spearman's rank correlation is a method investigating the direction, level, and significance of a relationship between two variables. Spearman's correlation analysis is preferred if the variables were obtained with ratio or interval scale, but not have normal distribution.

Since the data has not normally been distributed (One-Sample Kolmogorov-Smirnov Test: $p<0.05$), Spearman's rank correlation analysis method has been used in the study.

The hypotheses are as follows;

- **H_1:** There is a negative and significant relationship between GII and female/male TEA ratio in high-income countries.
- **H_2:** There is a negative and significant relationship between GII and female/male TEA ratio in mid-income countries.
- **H_3:** There is a negative and significant relationship between GII and female/male TEA ratio in all countries.
- **H_4:** There is a negative and significant relationship between female/male opportunity-driven TEA ratio in high-income countries.
- **H_5:** There is a negative and significant relationship between female/male opportunity-driven TEA ratio in mid-income countries.
- **H_6:** There is a negative and significant relationship between female/male opportunity-driven TEA ratio in all countries.
- **H_7:** There is a positive and significant relationship between labor force participation rate and female/male TEA ratio in high-income countries.
- **H_8:** There is a positive and significant relationship between labor force participation rate and female/male TEA ratio in mid-income countries.
- **H_9:** There is a positive and significant relationship between labor force participation rate and female/male TEA ratio in all countries.
- **H_{10}:** There is a positive and significant relationship between labor force participation rate and female/male opportunity-driven TEA ratio in high-income countries.
- **H_{11}:** There is a positive and significant relationship between labor force participation rate and female/male opportunity-driven TEA ratio in mid-income countries.

- **H_{12}:** There is a positive and significant relationship between labor force participation rate and female/male opportunity-driven TEA ratio in all countries.

4.2. Findings

Tab. 3 represents Spearman's correlation coefficients between gender inequality index and female/male TEA ratio, female/male opportunity-driven TEA ratio.

Given the Spearman's correlation coefficients presented in Tab. 3, there is no significant relationship between gender inequality index and female/male TEA and female/male opportunity-driven in high-income and mid-income countries. Thus, hypotheses H_1, H_2, H_4, and H_5 were rejected. It was also determined that there is a negative and significant relationship between gender inequality and female/male opportunity-driven TEA in all countries ($p<0.027$, $r=-0.326$) and H_6 hypothesis has been supported. In other words, there is a positive relationship between gender equality and number of opportunity-driven women entrepreneurs.

Tab. 3: Correlation Coefficients between Gender Inequality Index (GII) and Female/Male TEA, Female/Male Opportunity-Driven TEA

Factors compared	**High-income countries (28)**		**Mid-income countries (18)**		**All countries (46)**	
	r	p	r	p	r	p
GII and female/male TEA	0.330	0.086	0.005	0.984	0.240	0.108
GII and female/male opp.-driven TEA	-0.342	0.075	-0.176	0.484	**-0.326**	**0.027***

p<0.05.

Tab. 4: Correlation Coefficients between Labor Force Participation Rate and Female/Male TEA, Female/Male Opportunity-Driven TEA

Factors compared	**High-income countries (28)**		**Mid-income countries (18)**		**All countries (46)**	
	r	p	r	p	r	p
Labor force participation rate and female/male TEA	-0.093	0.637	**0.720**	**0.001***	0.273	0.066
Labor force participation rate and female/male opp.-driven TEA	**0.603**	**0.001***	-0.267	0.284	0.264	0.077

p<0.01.

In Tab. 4, Spearman's correlation coefficients between women's labor force participation rate and female/male TEA ratio, female/male opportunity-driven TEA ratio are shown.

Given the correlation coefficients in Tab. 4, it can be seen that there is a positive and significant relationship between labor force participation rate and female/male opportunity-driven TEA in high-income countries ($p<0.001$, $r=0.603$) and between labor force participation rate and female/male TEA in mid-income countries ($p<0.001$, $r=0.720$). Thus, hypotheses H_8 and H_{10} have been supported.

5. Conclusion

On one hand, increasing the investment, production, innovation, and employment, women entrepreneurship positively contribute to economic growth of region or country. On the other hand, it also supports the women's participation in labor force, increase in the number of women entrepreneurs, decrease in women unemployment, and elimination of poverty, as well as supporting socioeconomic development by enabling gender equality. However, although they significantly contribute to country's economic growth and development, the number of women entrepreneurs is very low throughout the world and below the number of men entrepreneurs. Moreover, when compared to men entrepreneurs, women entrepreneurs generally establish and own lower-scaled firms with lower productivity and less revenue. The factors distinguishing women and men entrepreneurs from qualitative and quantitative aspects are based on, as in other dimensions of economic life, the gender concept and the inequality it creates.

Gender and the norms, attitudes, and judgments it creates impose a gender-based life to women and men and trigger the gender inequalities in such a life. These inequalities can be seen in household, business life, political life, art, and cultural activities, as well as religion and even language, and weaken the role and power of women in socioeconomic life. However, keeping women constituting approx. 40 % of the total labor force in the background would have important socioeconomic costs. For this reason, in order for societies to achieve economic growth and development, societies should allow women to explore their skills and capabilities. Besides that, rather than suppressing their skills, societies should support women and incorporate them in social and economic life.

References

Akoğlan, M. (1996). *Konaklama endüstrisinde kadın yöneticiler.* Anadolu Üniversitesi yayınları, No: 994.

Allen, I. E., Elam, A., Langowitz, N., & Dean, M. (2008). *Global entrepreneurship monitor: 2007 Report on women and entrepreneurship.* The Center for Women's Leadership at Babson College, Babson Park, MA.

Alptekin, D. (2014). Toplumsal cinsiyet eşitsizliği örüntüsünde kadının yoksulluğu ve yoksunlukları. In Topçuoğlu, A. (Ed.), *Yoksulluk ve kadın* (pp. 15–33). Ayrıntı Yayınevi.

Arıkan, S. (2002). *Girişimcilik temel kavramlar ve bazı güncel konular.* Siyasal Kitabevi.

Barutçugil, İ. (2002). *İş yaşamında kadın yönetici.* Kariyer Yayınevi.

Bertaux, N., & Crable, E. (2007). Learning about women, economic development, entrepreneurship and the environment in India: A case study. *Journal of Developmental Entrepreneurship, 12*(04), 467–478.

Butler, J., & Scott, J. (1992). *Feminists theorize the political.* Routledge.

Caner, E. (2004). *Kutsal fahişeden Bakire Meryem'e toprak ve kadın.* Su Yayınevi.

Cesur, E. (2009). İşgücünün kadınsılaşması ve çalışan yoksullar. Sakarya Üniversitesi: *Uluslararası Disiplinler arası Kadın Çalışmaları Kongresi,* 1. Cilt, 55–64.

Cherry, A. L. (2005). *Examining global social welfare issues.* Thomson Brooks.

Connell, R. W. (2003). The role of men and boys in achieving gender equality. http://www.un.org/womenwatch/daw/egm/menboys2003/Connell-bp.pdf.

Çağatay, N. (1998). *Gender and poverty.* UNDP: Social Development and Poverty Elimination Division, Working Paper Series, WP5.

Çakır Hanbay, E. (2011). Kadın istihdamında yerel yönetimlerin rolü, görevleri ve sorun alanları. *TEPAV: Kadın Emeği Konferans,* 75–86.

Dedeoğlu, S. (2000). Toplumsal cinsiyet rolleri açısından Türkiye'de aile ve kadın emeği. *Toplum ve Bilim, 86,* 139–170.

Demirbilek, S. (2007). Cinsiyet ayrımcılığının sosyolojik açıdan incelenmesi, *Finans Politik & Ekonomik Yorumlar, 44*(511), 12–27.

Demirgöz Bal, M. (2014). Toplumsal cinsiyet eşitsizliğine genel bakış. *Kadın Sağlığı Hemşireliği Dergisi, 1*(1), 15–28.

Dökmen, Z. Y. (2004). *Toplumsal cinsiyet.* Remzi Kitapevi.

Ecevit, Y. (1993). Kadın girişimciliğin yaygınlaşmasına yönelik bir model önerisi. In Altınel, A. (Ed.). *Kadını girişimciliğe özendirme ve destekleme paneli bildiriler ve tartışmalar,* Devlet Bakanlığı Kadın ve Sosyal Hizmetler

Müsteşarlığı Kadının Statüsü ve Sorunları Genel Müdürlüğü, Eğitim Serisi, Yayın No: 74, 15–34.

Ecevit, Y. (2003). Toplumsal cinsiyetle yoksulluk ilişkisi nasıl kurulabilir? Bu ilişki nasıl çalışılabilir? *Cumhuriyet Üniversitesi Tıp Fakültesi Dergisi, 25*(4), 83–88.

Ertübey Özgen, H. N. (1993). Türkiye'de kadın girişimciliği: mevcut durum, sorunlar ve öneriler. In Necla Arat (Ed.), *Türkiye'de Kadın Girişimcilik*, No: 7, TES-AR.

Ertürk, Y. (1993). Girişimcilikte örgütlü dayanışma yaklaşımı. In Altınel, A. (Ed.). *Kadını girişimciliğe özendirme ve destekleme paneli*, Devlet Bakanlığı Kadın ve Sosyal Hizmetler Müsteşarlığı Kadının Statüsü ve Sorunları Genel Müdürlüğü, Eğitim Serisi, Yayın No: 74, 43–48.

Global Entreprenuership Monitor. (2020). Entrepreneurial behaviour and attitudes. https://www.gemconsortium.org/data/key-aps

Gökkaya, V. B. (2014). Cam tavan, kadın ve ekonomik şiddet. *Journal of Academic Social Science Studies*, (26), 371–383. doi:10.9761/JASSS2385

Hisrich, R. D., Peters, M. P., & Shepherd, D. A. (2017). *Entrepreneurship.* (10th Edition), McGraw Hill.

International Labor Organization. (2020). *World employment and social outlook: Trends 2020.* ILO.

İleri, Ü. (2016). Sosyal politikalarda kadın ve cinsiyet ayrımcılığı ile ilgili başlıca uluslararası ve ulusal hukuki düzenlemeler. *Hak İş Uluslararası Emek ve Toplum Dergisi, 5*(12), 128–153.

İlter, B. (2008). *Girişimcilik sürecinde kadın girişimcilerin karşılaştıkları sorunların analizi: KAGİDER Örneği* (Unpublished doctoral thesis). Afyon Kocatepe Üniversitesi.

İpçioğlu, İ. (2011). Kadın girişimcilik. In Erdoğan, B. Z. (Ed.). *Girişimcilik ve KOBİ'ler: Teori ve uygulama* (pp. 97–110), Ekin Kitabevi.

Kümbetoğlu, B. (2002). Afetler sonrası kadınlar ve yoksulluk. In Özdek, Y. (Ed.). *Yoksulluk, şiddet ve insan Hakları* (pp.129–142), TODAİE.

Lee, J. W. (Ed). (2005). *Gender roles.* Nova Science.

Lee-Gosselin, H., & Grise, J. (1990). Are women owner-managers challenging our definitions of entrepreneurship? An in-depth survey. *Journal of Business Ethics, 9*(5), 423–433.

Marshall, B. L. (2000). *Configuring gender: Explorations in theory and politics.* CANCOPY.

Moya, M., Expósito, F., & Ruiz, J. (2000). Close relationships, gender and career salience. *Sex Roles, 42*, 825–846. https://doi.org/10.1023/A:1007094232453.

Müftüoğlu, T., & Durukan, T. (2004). *Girişimcilik ve KOBİ'ler.* Gazi Kitabevi.

Neft, N., & Levine, A. D. (1997). *Where women stand: An international report on the status of women in 140 countries 1997-1998.* Random House.

Nicholson, L. (1994). Interpreting gender. *SIGNS: Journal of Women in Culture and Society, 20*(1), 79–105.

OECD. (2021). Labour force participation rate (indicator). https://doi.org/10.1787/8a801325-en

Onaran, O., Büker, S., & Bir, A. (1998). *Eskişehir'de erkek rol ve tutumlarına ilişkin alan araştırması*, Anadolu Üniversitesi.

Önder, N. (2013). Türkiye'de kadın işgücünün görünümü. *ÇSGB Çalışma Dünyası Dergisi, 1*(1), 35–61.

Özer, M. M. (2017). Ataerkil kapitalist çalışma yaşamından kadın tanıklıkları. *Çalışma ve Toplum* 2017/3, 1397–1424.

Özyılmaz, A. M. (2016). *Türkiye'de kadın girişimciliği ve girişimci kadınların karşılaştıkları sorunlar üzerine bir araştırma* (Unpublished master's thesis). Hacı Bektaş Veli Üniversitesi.

Perez-Perez, C., & Aviles-Hernandez, M. (2016). Explanatory factors of female entrepreneurship and limiting elements, *Suma de Negocios, 7*, 25–31.

Ridgeway, C. (2011). *Framed by gender: How gender inequality persists in modern World.* Oxford University.

Sarfaraz, L., Mian, S., & Karadeniz, E. E. (2013). Female entrepreneurship, internationalization and trade liberalization: The case of Iran, Pakistan, and Turkey. *Proceedings of the 16th Annual McGill International Entrepreneurship Conference*, August 1–5. Montréal, Canada, McGill University.

Sayer H. (2011). *Toplumsal cinsiyet eşitliğine erkeklerin katılımı* (Uzmanlık Tezi), TC Başbakanlık Kadının Statüsü Genel Müdürlüğü, Ankara.

Scott, J. W. (2007). Toplumsal cinsiyet: Faydalı bir tarihsel analiz kategorisi. D. Demirler & F. Dinçer (Translators). *Kültür ve Siyasette Feminist Yaklaşımlar, 12*, 112–138.

United Nations. (1995). Fourth world conference on women: Beijing Declaration. https://www.un.org/womenwatch/daw/beijing/platform/declar.htm.

United Nations. (2013). *Millennium development goals and beyond 2015.* https://www.un.org/millenniumgoals/bkgd.shtml.

United Nations Development Programme. (2020). *Human development reports, gender inequality index.* http://hdr.undp.org/en/content/gender-inequality-index-gii.

Vicente, E. (2005). From the feminization of poverty to the feminization and democratization of power, *Sela Panel 1: The Obligation to Eradicate Poverty*, Puerto Rico.

Wells, B. L., Pfantz, T. J., & Bryne, J. L. (2003). Russian women business owners: Evidence of entrepreneurship in a transition economy. *Journal of Developmental Entrepreneurship*, *8*(1), 59–72.

World Bank. (2012). *Toplumsal cinsiyet eşitsizliği ve kalkınma: Genel bakış*. Dünya Kalkınma Raporu. World Bank.

World Bank. (2013). *Gender at work: A companion to the World development reports on jobs*. https://www.worldbank.org/content/dam/Worldbank/document/Gender/GenderAtWork_web.pdf.

World Bank. (2020). *Gender indicators*. https://data.worldbank.org/indicator

Yetim, N. (2008). Sosyal sermaye olarak kadın girişimciler: Mersin örneği. *Ege Academic Review*, *2*(2), 79–92.

Muhammed Kürşat TİMUROĞLU[1]

Entrepreneurial Intention and Values

Popularization and development of entrepreneurship positively affect many fields and are very important for development and advancement. One of the points to consider in discussing the entrepreneurship is the entrepreneurial intention because the entrepreneurial activities cannot be conducted without an entrepreneurial intention. Researchers investigating the entrepreneurial intention from the aspect of personal characteristics aimed to explain the entrepreneurship by examining the individual's psychological, demographical, and personality characteristics. From this perspective, entrepreneurs have unique specific values, attitudes, and necessities, and certain personal variables such as current psychological state, personal characteristics, and experiences affect the spirit of entrepreneurship (Naktiyok, 2005: 14). The idea of discussing the entrepreneurship from a scientific perspective drew significant interest among educators and researchers in recent years. Measuring the individuals' intention to establish a new enterprise has been one of the fundamental foci of researchers studying the area of entrepreneurship.

In this chapter, the concepts of entrepreneurship, women entrepreneurship, entrepreneurial intention, and values are discussed in detail and the studies examining the relationship between entrepreneurial intention and values and contributing to the literature are reviewed.

1. Entrepreneurship

Before describing the concept of entrepreneurship, the entrepreneur, who is responsible for all the entrepreneurial activities, should be explained. Used by Richard Cantillon, a French economist, in the early 18th century for the first time, the entrepreneur has been defined as the person buying and producing the production inputs and services in order to sell them at an undetermined price in the future (Çelik & Akgemci, 1998: 17).

---

1 Associate Professor Dr., Atatürk University, Faculty of Economic and Administrative Sciences, Department of Business Administration, timuroglu@atauni.edu.tr, ORCID ID: 0000-0003-2028-9764

The concept of entrepreneur is associated with the characteristics of benefiting from opportunities, organizing the production factors in order to create new opportunities, and taking risk. In lexical meaning, entrepreneur is defined as "a person starting an enterprise by investing capital in fields such as trade, industry, etc." Entrepreneur is a person, who can observe the opportunities in the market, introduce these opportunities to the market as commercial ideas, use his/her skills in this process, undertake risk, and create innovation.

Nowadays, in addition to the conventional production factors of labor, capital, and nature, also the entrepreneur is considered as a production factor. Thus, the entrepreneur can be defined as the person combining the other production factors in order to make production. Fidan defined the entrepreneur as a person noticing the products and services, which people need and demand, making effort to produce them, and taking risk with his/her labor and capital for business he/she deems feasible (Fidan & Yılmaz, 2001: 10). Mucuk described the entrepreneur as a person finding and appropriately combining the production factors of labor, capital, and nature in order to produce products and services, which will meet the needs of others. Entrepreneur is the fourth production factor seeking profit and undertaking risk (Mucuk, 2001: 6). According to Drucker, the entrepreneur is the person establishing the order in fuzzy and variable world. For this purpose, entrepreneur combines and organizes the resources that might yield wealth (Drucker, 1986: 2). Schumpeter defined the entrepreneur as a person creating new combinations for the business such as developing new processes, producing new products, finding new markets, finding new raw material sources, and establishing a new organizational structure (Güney, 2008: 10).

The concept of entrepreneurship has been derived from the French word "entreprendre," which means "to undertake." According to Hisrich and Peters, entrepreneurship is a process of creating a different value by undertaking economic, psychological, and social risks and spending time and making effort. Beyond creating revenue, they considered the entrepreneurship as constructing a change in business and social lives (Henry, 2003: 11). However, Brezeal described the entrepreneurship as benefiting from the opportunities that other people do not notice (Brezeal, 1999: 3). Entrepreneurship may appear as recognizing the opportunities in market or revealing the opportunities that have not been noticed before.

The concept of entrepreneurship can be defined as the process of combining the production factors or making innovations in the production processes in order to establish creative, active, and flexible organizations that are producing goods and services, which are needed by individuals, and rapidly responding to the environmental by observing the opportunities in market and considering the risks in order to achieve the objectives such as making profit, pioneering innovations, growth, and reputation.

Entrepreneurship is the key factor of economic structuring in underdeveloped economies, of economic development in developing economies, and of dynamism in developed economies. These objectives refer to creating wealth and welfare because contributing to the gross national product by establishing new companies, renewing the processes, and making social improvements is the driving force of creating economic values. The activities required for creating economic values are performed by individuals named "entrepreneur" (Naktiyok, 2004: 11).

Main activities of entrepreneurs are to create new products, differentiate the products, and increase the value of products. Such activities gained more importance under today's fluctuating environmental conditions, in which markets have hyper-level competitiveness and customers have much more options. This is because entrepreneurs direct the change by acting as an instrument of change.

2. Women Entrepreneurship

Women entrepreneurs can be defined as women having business outside the home, working alone or together with employees in that business, having the title as business owner, performing the activities related with the production of any good or service, and having a voice on the investment and use of revenue gained (Tikici & Aksoy, 2009: 22).

Women entrepreneurship is a specific field of general employment and women employment. The studies examining the participation of women in the labor force increased in Turkey since the 1980s. The interest in women's employment is closely related with the development strategies mainly adopted in developing countries (Yetim, 2002: 79).

The recent increase in the number of women entrepreneurs despite the difficulties the women entrepreneurs face during the process of making entrepreneurial decision can be explained with women's fear of losing their current jobs, their idea that they would not promote, and the sociocultural changes. It is seen that the women having care responsibilities make their entrepreneurial decision when they find chance to fulfill their care responsibilities and turn their hand skills into a commercial benefit (Çakır, 2013: 27).

3. Entrepreneurial Intention

Entrepreneurship is widely known as the main catalyzer of economic growth in a country. Entrepreneurship and entrepreneurs have significant importance in the era of globalization. Competitive strength of a country is determined by the innovation and the spirit of entrepreneurship. Entrepreneurship has been an interesting area not only for economists and sociologists but also for the psychologists. During the advancement of the theory of entrepreneurship, the definitions of entrepreneur and entrepreneurship have also changed (Mat et al., 2015: 1016–1017).

The idea of approaching the entrepreneurship from the cognitive perspective drew gradually increasing interest among the educators and researchers. The importance given to cognitive aspects of entrepreneurship and the unique characteristics of entrepreneurs can be considered as an answer to the conflicting results reported in previous studies. Thanks to entrepreneurs and their cognitive characteristics, recognizing the opportunities, performance, business growth, and decision of being an entrepreneur play a critical role in the entire process (Pihie et al., 2013: 174).

Entrepreneurs do not only establish new businesses but they also develop business opportunities pioneering the new technologies, findings, and inventions. The main findings in the 20th century were the entrepreneurship-related initiatives. Many countries have made significant multidimensional benefits of entrepreneurship. Moreover, society also made benefit of entrepreneurship's economic advantages in terms of gaining strength in industry, as well as the benefits related with life standard (Iskandarini, 2014: 166).

Before the entrepreneurial intention, it might be more appropriate to define the concept of intention. The intention is a state of mind directing the individual's attention to a path, an object drawing the attention of individual, or a purpose (Bird, 1988: 442). The entrepreneurial intention was defined as "the commitment to establishing a new business" (Sabuncu, 2017: 13). This concept has also been defined as an individual's commitment to the activities aiming to establish and manage individual's own business. This activity generally depends on the individual's entrepreneurship desire and enthusiasm. From this aspect, this concept was also defined as an individual's intentional and volitional behavior (Timuroğlu & Çakır, 2014: 121).

According to Bird (1988), intention also refers to an individual's emotional state canalizing individual's attention, experience, and behaviors to a specific objective or the achievement of success. From this aspect, the intention is like a prediction of a planned action. Then, the entrepreneurial intention can be defined as an "intended action" or, in other words, as an "indicator of planned entrepreneurial activity" (Marangoz et al., 2014: 79).

The entrepreneurial intention is defined as the level of commitment to making entrepreneurial effort to establish a business for individual's own employment. Entrepreneurial intention "aims to establish a new enterprise or create new values in existing enterprises and guides the business activities such as target setting, communication, commitment, organization, etc." (Çetin et al., 2015: 32). Entrepreneurial intention is "an individual's effort made in order to put the thought into action and to achieve success in the process of establishing his/her own business" (Şeşen et al., 2014: 94). Being the driving force of entrepreneurial activities, the entrepreneurial intention reflects "the idea of establishing a business and initiating an enterprise to benefit from potential opportunities rather than other career options" (Çelik et al., 2014: 114).

Examining the individuals' intention to establish a new enterprise has been one of the main areas of interest among the entrepreneurship researchers and educators. The gradually increasing interest in exploring the entrepreneurial intentions is of critical importance in estimating the individuals' professional entrepreneurial plans and their actual participation (Pihie et al., 2013: 175).

There are three models known and used in expressing the entrepreneurial intention. First of them is Shapero and Sokol's (1982) "Entrepreneurial Event Model, the second one is Bird's (1988) 'Entrepreneurial Intentionality Model'," and the third one is Ajzen's (1991) "Theory of Planned Behavior" (Fayolle & Klandt, 2006: 79).

The Entrepreneurial Event Model of Shapero and Sokol (1982) focused on the idea of establishing a new business. According to this model, the individual makes assessment about if he/she could initiate the business he/she aims to establish and if that business is suitable for him/her, and then takes action by undertaking the risk after analyzing the opportunities (Schlaegel & Koeing, 2014: 294).

Bird's (1988) entrepreneurial intentionality model includes different perspectives regarding the opinions of individuals on entrepreneurship (Fayolle & Linan, 2014: 665). According to this model, entrepreneurial intention comes into effect after analyzing the factors of rationalism, thinking of cause and effect, previous experiences, goals, and individual's vision (Schneider, 2009:10).

Ajzen's (1991) theory of planned behaviors emphasizes that the more positive the intention of an individual to a behavior is, the more likely the behavior will be acted. The point here is the behavior. The factors influencing the intention are attitude, control, and subjective values. Attitude refers to a demeanor exhibited before taking action by assessing (not only emotionally but also rationally) the person's opinions about an object together with his/her previous experiences. Control refers to considering the results before making a decision about a behavior. Subjective values refer to the social pressure experienced before the behavior (Ajzen, 1991: 181).

Entrepreneurship is a process that continues for a period. When considering the entrepreneurship as a process, then the intention is a natural indicator of entrepreneurial activity. Krueger stated that the entrepreneurship is a voluntary phenomenon in nature; it comes on purpose, not accidentally. Environment provides a selection for entrepreneurial activity proven in studies of Obschonk and Schmitt-Rodermund. The effort that a person makes in order to maintain his/her entrepreneurial behaviors determines the entrepreneurial intention. This intention depends on three major motivational factors influencing the final behavior. Attitude towards beginning is related with positive or negative personal thoughts on entrepreneurship. Subjective norm is a perception of approval by a relevant person (spouse, family) and the perceived behavioral control is related with ease or difficulty of transforming into an entrepreneur. The factors related with this perception allow understanding the complex aspect of entrepreneurship process (İsmail et al., 2015: 350). Entrepreneurial activity generally arises from a person's desire and will. From this aspect, the entrepreneurial activity is an intentionally planned behavior.

4. Entrepreneurial Intention and Values

The concept of value was defined by Rokeach as the fundamental component of cognitive system. It was emphasized that values precede beliefs and behaviors (Mayberry, 2006: 6). Bardi and Schwartz stated that value is a motivational structure and it refers to what is important for us, as well as the broad objectives (Bardi & Schwartz, 2003: 1208). The value can be defined as the whole of principles and standards of a society, organization, and individual (Kenny, 1994: 17). Playing an important role in selection and decision-making, values are also important in solving problems and conflicts (Russell, 2001: 77).

Analyzing the values dominating the person's character is the best way of understanding and knowing the person because the value reflects the valuable and important factors in assessing the organizational or personal behavior in personal or collective life (Schwartz et al., 1997: 6; McEwan, 2001: 45) since the sense of appreciation influences the selection of explicit or implicit behaviors or concepts determining the characteristic of an individual or organization (Hofstede, 1980: 19). Many researchers consider the value as the main belief underlying the opinion motivating an individual. For this reason, the value guides the actions and behaviors of an individual. In other words, what and how a person does is shaped by his/her values (Kenny, 1994: 17). From this point of view, it can be stated that the values would shape the decision, behavior, and objectives of an entrepreneur.

There are studies examining the effects of values on entrepreneurial intention (Davidsson & Wiklund, 1997: 188; Tan et al., 2003: 2; Douglas & Fitzsimmons, 2005: 5; Kellermanns & Eddleston, 2006: 811; Llano, 2006: 22). The most important common point of these studies is that values and beliefs influence the entrepreneurial intention. In a study carried out on MBA students in Singapore, it was emphasized that a settled value related with innovativeness affected the entrepreneurial intention. In the same study, it was also reported that the students being ashamed of failure had less entrepreneurial intention when compared to others (Tan et al., 2003: 4).

Examining the concept of entrepreneurship, the first point is the individuals and their behavior processes. Values function as standards guiding the assessment or selection of behaviors, persons, and events (Schwartz & Bilsky, 1987: 551). Allport explained the value as a belief that individuals act in accordance with their preferences. The author explained this statement as follows: if it is known what a person will cause in future, then it can be discussed if that the person is good or bad. Shaping of future by the relevant person depends primarily on his/her personal values (Herriot, 1976: 18).

Besides that, especially in the studies in discipline of social sciences, it was discussed that life values described as an important distinctive characteristic or an expressed characteristic of an organization are considered as the phenomena underlying the behavior and functioning as a criterion or standard in person's assessments and they were defined as the facts influencing the personal attitudes and cognitive processes and reflecting the cultural patterns (Kilby, 1993: 31; Schwartz et al., 1997: 6; McEwan, 2001: 45). Moreover, it was also reported that the entrepreneurship is a value-attributed lifestyle. Activities or lifestyles of entrepreneurs include their values, way of working and entertaining, leadership preferences, commitment, order, and esthetic. In a study carried out on advanced-technology entrepreneurs, it was found that these entrepreneurs attach more importance to esthetic and theoretical values when compared to religious and economic ones. Similarly, it was also emphasized that these entrepreneurs attach importance to values such as independence, loyalty, success, and target-orientation. It was also stated that several entrepreneurs make use of their positions in the organization in improving the activity, which they personally pay attention to. Some of these entrepreneurs aimed to build professional values, whereas some others made effort to improve the social values (Bird, 1989: 95). Considered as the principles directing the individual's life and instruments allowing the expression of human needs, the values shape the current and future behaviors and function as a standard guiding the individual activities, an instrument promoting the ideal behavior style, an acquired rule, a behavior sanction, and a plan in decision-making and solving the conflicts (Kenny, 1994: 17, Small & Dickie, 1999: 629; Russell, 2001: 76–77).

Analyzing the human behaviors started drawing more attention in recent years (Elizur, 1996: 25). Most of these scientific studies have been affected by Schwartz's Theory of Values (Bilsky & Koch, 2002: 2). Empirical studies generally focused on measurement and typology of values (Elizur et al., 1991: 22). The relationships between value and attitude, objective, and behavior are the other important research subjects. One of the most important studies on this subject is Milton Rokeach's (1973) Theory of Human Values (Zhao et al., 1998: 23). While some of the scientists focusing on researching this subject advocate that there were differences between attitude and values (Rokeach, 1973), researchers such as Levy and Guttman emphasize that values constitute a sub-group of behaviors (Elizur, 1996: 25). Many researchers define the values as the main belief underlying the thought motivating an individual. For this reason, value guides the actions and behaviors of individuals. In other words, what a person does and how he/she does it are shaped by his/her values (Kenny, 1994: 17).

After Rokeach (1973) and Allport (1961) arguing in their value definitions that values guide the behaviors and Kristiansen and Hotte (1996) and McClelland (1985) arguing that values rarely guide the behavior, many studies have been carried out on this subject. It is not clear if specific values are related with specific behaviors or if the values in general are related with behavior. However, it is assumed that the relationship between values and behaviors is managed by a simple motivational structure (Bardi & Schwartz, 2003: 1207).

The values are considered as motivational purposes or personal principles in person's life and, as standards, they guide which behavior the person would exhibit. In Schwartz's theory, it was asserted that fundamental human values are the cognitive reflections of biological needs, social needs, group welfare need (Glazer et al., 2004: 324). Individuals make effort in their daily lives in order to meet these needs. They are satisfied meeting these needs and they consider having such needs as a must-have purpose. Besides that, it is asserted that the values would vary depending on the motivational orientation. Bilsky and Schwartz (1994) emphasized that different value types represent ascending or descending needs (Hofer et al., 2006: 307). In conclusion, examining the values, Schwartz determined 10 motivational types of value (Devos et al., 2002: 482;

Bardi & Schwartz, 2003: 1208; Glazer et al., 2004: 324; Knafo & Schwartz, 2004: 440; Bilsky, 2006: 74). These types are:

- Power,
- Achievement,
- Hedonism,
- Stimulation,
- Self-direction,
- Universalism,
- Benevolence,
- Tradition,
- Conformity,
- Security.

Each of these motivational types of value represents a motivational purpose and also affects the behaviors (Gibson & Schwartz, 1998: 52). Examining the relationship between entrepreneurial intention and value types mentioned above, the relationship between power and entrepreneurial intention will be discussed first.

Power refers to the importance of social status, prestige, and control or authority on resources and persons. The values in this dimension are social status, wealth, public image, and social recognition (Bardi & Schwartz, 2003: 1208; Schwartz & Boehnke, 2004: 239). In their studies, Peay and Dyer examined the personality traits of entrepreneurs and aimed to explain the relationship between power and entrepreneurial intention. They reported that entrepreneurs are motivated by both social and personal power needs (Peay & Dyer, 1989: 52). In literature, Bhandari emphasizing that social status and prestige affect the entrepreneurial intention could not prove this relationship in his study carried out on students in India (Bhandari, 2006: 177). Previous studies reported that there is a positive and strong relationship between entrepreneurship and wealth, which is classified within the power (Hurst & Lusardi, 2004: 320).

Achievement refers to the personal success expressed over the skills in accordance with social standards. The values in this dimension are success, ambition, skill, intelligence, and effectiveness (Routamaa & Heinasuo, 2006: 2). Previous studies emphasized that the need for achievement motivated entrepreneurs about establishing a business (Franke & Lüthje, 2004: 272). There is an important relationship between entrepreneurship and need for achievement. Need for achievement is one of the motivational factors influencing the entrepreneurial intention (Douglas & Fitzsimmons, 2005: 2). In studies carried out on entrepreneurs, it was observed that entrepreneurs have high level of need for achievement (Sadler-Smith et al., 2003: 48).

Hedonism is related with passion and loving the life. The values in this dimension are the passion and the love of life (Sawyerr et al., 2005: 500). In his studies on entrepreneurship, Schumpeter examined the dynamic and static types of behavior in parallel with hedonistic impulses and stated that these impulses affect the behavior (Ebner, 2006: 504).

Stimulations are related with the search for excitement, novelty, and challenge in life (Devos et al., 2002: 482). The values in this dimension are interesting life, varied life, and exiting life. One of the important research subjects is the effects of today's life conditions and styles on the entrepreneurial intention. The studies on this subject reported that entrepreneurial intention is affected by the obstacles and support factors the persons perceive in their environment (Lüthje & Franke, 2003, 137).

Self-direction refers to thought and action independence. The values in this dimension are independence, creativeness, choosing own goals, self-respect, and curiosity (Knafo & Schwartz, 2004: 440). Examining the effect of political independence on entrepreneurial intention Wee-Liang Tan reported strong relationships between economic independence, sociocultural factors, and environmental factors and entrepreneurship (Tan et al., 2003, 2). It was also stated that it was not surprising that there was a relationship between creativity and entrepreneurship (Ward, 2004, 174).

Universalism refers to preserving, accepting, and understanding the humanity and nature. The values in this dimension are equality, peaceful world, unity with nature, social justice, thought independence, protecting the nature, and inner harmony (Schwartz & Boehnke, 2004: 239). Lee and Peterson claimed that universalism contributed to entrepreneurship (Elam, 2006: 6). Kumar stated that, as a result of universalism and standardization, entrepreneurship culture and postmodern culture played a role in development of individual thinking and behavior styles (Nicholson & Anderson, 2005: 156).

Benevolence refers to preserving and increasing the welfare of others, whom the person is in personal contact with. The values in this dimension are helpfulness, responsibility, forgiving, and social justice (Gibson & Schwartz, 1998: 53). Despite those arguing that entrepreneurship is motivated by economic or sociobiological factors, it is also claimed that it is motivated by helpfulness and altruism (Montanye, 2006: 552).

Tradition refers to the respect to the traditions and thoughts of culture and religion imposed to the individual. The values in this dimension are respect to tradition, humbleness, moderateness, devout, and detachment

(Bardi & Schwartz, 2003: 1208). It was emphasized that tradition plays an important role in the process of adaptation and socialization and it is effective on the cognitive styles (Licht & Siegel, 2006: 11). It can be stated that tradition might contribute to the effect of surrounding culture on entrepreneurial intention.

Conformity is related with limiting the desires, activities, and emotions violating the social expectations and norms or harming the others. The values in this dimension are politeness, honor, obedience, and honest family (Routamaa & Heinasuo, 2006: 2). In their study on entrepreneurs, Sexton et al. reported that conformity is at a lower level among entrepreneurs when compared to business administrators but entrepreneurs have a higher level of energy and they undertake more risk (Naffziger, 1995: 35).

Security refers to the stability, harmony, and security of individual's relationship and society. The values in this dimension are social order, family security, national security, health, and sense of belonging (Devos et al., 2002: 482). It was emphasized that the entrepreneurial efforts without cultural values creating and supporting the social being and trust would fail (Ceylan & Demircan, 2002: 3).

5. Conclusion

Examining the literature on entrepreneurial intention and values, it can be seen that entrepreneurial intention is in apparent relationship with the values power, achievement, hedonism, stimulation, self-direction, universalism, benevolence, conformity, tradition, and security.

Many researchers define the value as the main belief underlying the thought stimulating an individual. For this reason, the values guide the actions and behaviors of individuals. In other words, the values shape what and how a person does (Kenny, 1994: 17). When considered from this aspect, it can be stated that the values would shape the decisions, behaviors, and goals of an entrepreneur. That is to say, values influence the entrepreneurial intention of an individual.

References

Ajzen, I. (1991). The theory of planned behavior. *Organizational Behavior and Human Decision Processes*, *50*(2), 179–211. https://doi.org/10.1016/0749-5978(91)90020-T

Allport, G. W. (1961). *Pattern and growth in personality.* New York: Holt, Rinehart & Winston.

Bardi, A., & Schwartz, S. H. (2003). Values and behavior: Strength and structure of relations. *Personality and Social Psychology Bulletin, 29*(10), 1207–1220. https://doi.org/10.1177/0146167203254602.

Bhandari, N. C. (2006). Intention for entrepreneurship among students in India. *Journal of Entrepreneurship, 15*(2), 169–179. https://doi.org/10.1177/097135570601500204.

Bilsky, W., & Koch, M. (2002). On the content and structure of values: Universals or methodological artefacts? In Blasius, J., Hox, J., De Leeuw, E., & Schmidt, P. (Eds.), *Social science methodology in the New Millennium. Updated and extended proceedings of the Fifth International Conference on Logic and Methodology, held at Cologne, Germany, October 3–6, 2000* (pp. 1–12). Leske & Budrich.

Bilsky, W., & Schwartz, S. H. (1994). Values and personality. *European Journal of Personality, 8*, 163–181. https://doi.org/10.1002/per.2410080303

Bird, B. (1988). Implementing entrepreneurial ideas: The case for intention. *Academy of Management Review, 13*(3), 442–453. https://doi.org/10.2307/258091

Bird, B. J. (1989). *Entrepreneurial behavior.* Scott Foresman & Co.

Brezeal, D. V., & Herbert, T. (1999). The genesis of entrepreneurship. *Entrepreneurship Theory and Practise, 23*(3), 29–46. https://doi.org/10.1177/104225879902300303.

Çakır, S. (2013). *Girişimcilerin yeni bir girişim yapma niyetlerinin risk alma eğilimi ile ilişkisi* [Unpublished master's thesis]. Atatürk University.

Çelik, A., & Akgemci, T. (1998). *Girişimcilik kültürü ve KOBİ'ler.* Nobel Yayın Dağıtım.

Çelik, A., İnce, M., & Bozyiğit, S. (2014). Üniversite öğrencilerinin girişimcilik niyetlerini etkileyen ailesel faktörleri belirlemeye yönelik bir çalışma. *Niğde Üniversitesi İktisadi ve İdari Bilimler Fakültesi Dergisi, 7*(3), 113–124. https://dergipark.org.tr/tr/pub/niguiibfd/issue/19756/211501

Çetin, A., Şentürk, M., & Alacalar-Çakır, A. (2015). Mesleki ilgi alanı ve kişisel ahlak felsefesinin girişimciliğe yönelik tutum ve girişimcilik niyetine etkisi: Üniversite öğrencileri üzerine bir araştırma. *AİBÜ Sosyal Bilimler Enstitüsü Dergisi, 2*(15), 25–35. https://www.researchgate.net/publication/330346739_Mesleki_Ilgi_Alani_ve_Kisisel_Ahlak_Felsefesinin_Girisimcilige_Yonelik_Tutum_ve_Girisimcilik_Niyetine_Etkisi_Universite_Ogrencileri_Uzerine_Bir_Arastirma

Ceylan, A., & Demircan, N. (2002). Girişimcilerin başarı, güç ve yakın ilişki ihtiyaçlarının kişilik özellikleriyle ilişkisi üzerine Düzce Bölgesi'ndeki

KOBİ'lerde bir araştırma. *21. Yüzyılda Kobi'ler: Sorunlar, Fırsatlar ve Çözüm Önerileri*, Doğu Akdeniz Üniversitesi, İşletme Fakültesi, 1–19.

Davidsson, P., & Wiklund, J. (1997). Values, beliefs and regional variations in new firm formation rates. *Journal of Economic Psychology, 18*(2–3), 179–199. https://doi.org/10.1016/S0167-4870(97)00004-4

Devos, T., Spini D., & Schwartz, S. H. (2002). Conflicts among human values and trust in institutions. *The British Journal of Social Psychology, 41*(4), Health & Medical Complete, 481–494. https://doi.org/10.1348/014466602321149849

Douglas, E. J., & Fitzsimmons, J. R. (2005). Entrepreneurial intentions towards individual vs. corporate entrepreneurship. *Paper presented at the SEAANZ 2005 Conference, Armidale, N.S.W.* https://eprints.qut.edu.au/6488/1/6488.pdf

Drucker, P. F. (1986). *The frontiers of management: Where tomorrow's decisions are being shaped today*. Harvard Business Review Press, Harper & Row.

Ebner, A. (2006). Institutions, entrepreneurship, and the rationale of government: An outline of the Schumpeterian theory of the state. *Journal of Economic Behavior & Organization, 59*(4), 497–515. https://doi.org/10.1016/j.jebo.2005.06.003

Elam, A. B. (2006). *Gender and entrepreneurship across 28 countries: A multilevel analysis using GEM data*. (Unpublished Doctoral dissertation), The University of North Carolina.

Elizur, D. (1996). Work values and commitment. *International Journal of Manpower, 17*(3), 25–30. https://doi.org/10.1108/01437729610119496

Elizur, D., Borg, I., Hunt, R., & Beck, I. M. (1991). The structure of work values: A cross cultural comparison. *Journal of Organizational Behavior, 12*(1), 21–38. https://doi.org/10.1002/job.4030120103

Fayolle, A., & Klandt, H. (2006). *International entrepreneurship education: Issues and Newness*. Edward Elgar Publishing Limited. http://www.untag-smd.ac.id/files/Perpustakaan_Digital_1/ENTREPRENEURSHIP%20International%20Entrepreneurship%20Education.pdf

Fayolle, A., & Linan, F. (2014). The future of research on entrepreneurial intentions. *Journal of Business Research, 67*(5), 663–666. https://doi.org/10.1016/j.jbusres.2013.11.024

Fidan, M., & Yılmaz, Ş. (2001). *Müteşebbislik*. Tubitay.

Franke, N., & Lüthje, C. (2004). Entrepreneurial intentions of business students: A benchmarking study. *International Journal of Innovation and Technology Management, 1*(3), 269–288. https://doi.org/10.1142/S0219877004000209

Glazer, S., Daniel, S. C., & Short, K. M. (2004). A study of the relationship between organizational commitment and human values in four countries. *Human Relations, 57*(3), 323–344. https://doi.org/10.1177/0018726704043271

Güney, S. (2008). *Girişimcilik-temel kavramlar ve bazı güncel konular* (4th ed.). Siyasal Kitabevi.

Henry, C., Hill, F., & Leitch, C. (2003). *Entrepreneurship education and training.* Ashgate Publishing.

Herriot, P. (1976). *Values, attitudes and behavior change*, Mathuen & Co. Ltd.

Hofer, J., Chasiotis, A., & Campos, D. (2006). Congruence between social values and implicit motives: Effects on life satisfaction across three culture. *European Journal of Personality, 20*, 305–324. https://doi.org/10.1002/per.590

Hofstede, G. (1980). *Culture's consequences: International differences in work related values.* SAGE Publications Ltd.

Hurst, E., & Lusardi, A. (2004). Liquidity constraints and entrepreneurship. Household wealth, parental wealth, and the transition in and out of entrepreneurship. *Journal of Political Economy, 112*(2), 319–347. https://doi.org/10.1086/381478

Iskandarini. (2014). The impact of entrepreneurial barrier toward entrepreneurial intention for decreasing unemployment through community empowerment. *Social and Behavioral Sciences, 115*(2014), 166–174. https://doi.org/10.1016/j.sbspro.2014.02.425

İsmail, K., Anuar, M. A., Omar Wan, Z. W., Aziz, A. A., Seohod, K., & Akhtar, C. S. (2015). Entrepreneurial intention, entrepreneurial orientation of faculty and students towards commercialization. *Social and Behavioral Sciences, 181*, 349–355. https://doi.org/10.1016/j.sbspro.2015.04.897

Kellermanns, F. W., & Eddleston, K. A. (2006). Corporate entrepreneurship in family firms: A family perspective. *Entrepreneurship Theory and Practice, 30*(6), 809–830. https://doi.org/10.1111/j.1540-6520.2006.00153.x

Kenny, T. (1994). From vision to reality through values. *Management Development Review, 7*(3), 17–20. https://doi.org/10.1108/09622519410060375

Kilby, R. (1993). *The study of human values.* University Press of America.

Knafo, A., & Schwartz, S. H. (2004). Identity formation and parent-child value congruence in adolescence. *The British Journal of Developmental Psychology, 22*, 439–458. https://doi.org/10.1348/0261510041552765

Kristiansen, C. M., & Hotte, A. M. (1996). Morality and the self: Implications for when and how of value-attitude-behavior relations. In C. Seligman, J. M. Olson, & M. P. Zanna (Eds.), *The Ontario Symposium: Vol. 8. The psychology of values.* Hillsdale, NJ: Lawrence Erlbaum.

Licht, A. N., & Siegel, J. I. (2006). The social dimensions of entrepreneurship. In Casson, M. & Yeung, B. (Eds.), *Oxford handbook of entrepreneurship* (pp. 1–43). Oxford University Press.

Llano, J. A. (2006). *The university environment and academic entrepreneurship: A behavioral model for measuring environment success*. Work paper, 1–27.

Lüthje, C., & Franke, N. (2003). The making of an entrepreneur: Testing a model of entrepreneurial intent among engineering students at MIT. *R&D Management, 33*(2), 135–147. https://doi.org/10.1111/1467-9310.00288

Marangoz, M., Kaya, F., & Bakan, H. (2014). Eğitim alanı girişimcilik niyetini nasıl etkilemektedir? Üniversite öğrencilerine yönelik bir inceleme. *Journal of Economics and Management Research, 3*(1), 75–96. http://eyad.mu.edu.tr/index.php/eyad/article/view/90

Mat, S., Maat, S., & Mohd, N. (2015). Identifying factors that affecting the entrepreneurial intention among engineering technology students. *Social and Behavioral Sciences, 211*, 1016–1022. https://doi.org/10.1016/j.sbspro.2015.11.135

Mayberry, C. (2006). Social entrepreneurs: Is it a new breed of entrepreneur? *OIKOS Ph.D. Summer Academy 2006 Sustainability and Corporate Strategy*, pp. 1–14.

McClelland, D. C. (1985). *Human motivation*. Glenview, IL: Scott, Foresman.

Mcewan, T. (2001). *Managing values and beliefs in organizations*. Prentice Hall Inc.

Montanye, J. A. (2006). Entrepreneurship. *The Independent Review, 10*(4), 549–571. https://www.independent.org/pdf/tir/tir_10_4_03_montanye.pdf

Mucuk, İ. (2001). *Modern İşletmecilik*. Türkmen Kitabevi.

Naffziger, D. (1995). Entrepreneurship: A person-based theory approach. Advances in entrepreneurship, firm emergence, and growth. *JAI Press, 2*, 21–50. https://numerons.files.wordpress.com/2012/04/8entrepreneurship-a-person-based-theory-approach.pdf

Naktiyok, A. (2004). *İç girişimcilik*. Beta.

Nicholson, L., & Anderson, A. R. (2005). News and nuances of the entrepreneurial myth and metaphor: Linguistic games in entrepreneurial sense-making and sense-giving. *Entrepreneurship Theory & Practice Journal, 29*(2), 153–172. https://doi.org/10.1111/j.1540-6520.2005.00074.x

Peay, T. R., & Dyer, W. G. (1989). Power orientations of entrepreneurs and succession planning. *Journal of Small Business Management, 27*(1), 47–52.

Pihie, Z., Bagheri, A., & Sani, Z. (2013). Knowledge of cognition and entrepreneurial intentions: Implications for learning entrepreneurship in public and private universities. *Social and Behavioral Sciences, 97*, 174–181. https://doi.org/10.1016/j.sbspro.2013.10.219

Prince-Gibson, E., & Schwartz, S. H. (1998). Value priorities and gender. *Social Psychology Quarterly, Academic Research Library, 61*(1), 49–67. https://www.jstor.org/stable/2787057

Rokeach, M. (1973). *The nature of human values*. The Free Press.

Routamaa, V., & Heinasuo, K. (2006). Type and values over generations, psychological type and culture. *East & West: A Multicultural Research Conference held at Honolulu, Hawaii, January 6–8.*

Russell, R. F. (2001). The role of values in servant leadership. *Leadership & Organization Development Journal, 22*(2), 76–83. https://doi.org/10.1108/01437730110382631

Sabuncu, R. G. (2017). *Anadolu üniversitesi işletme fakültesi öğrencilerinin girişimcilik niyetleri ve çevresel tutumlarını ölçmeye yönelik bir araştırma* [Unpublished master's thesis]. Anadolu Üniversity.

Sadler-Smith, E., Hampson, Y., Chaston, I., & Badger, B. (2003). Managerial behavior, entrepreneurial style, and small firm performance. *Journal of Small Business Management, 41*(1), 47–67. https://doi.org/10.1111/1540-627X.00066

Sawyerr, O. O., Strauss, J., & Yan, J. (2005). Individual value structure and diversity attitudes: The moderating effects of age, gender, race, and religiosity. *Journal of Managerial Psychology, 20*(6), 498–521. https://doi.org/10.1108/02683940510615442

Scheiner, C. W. (2009). *Fundamental determinants of entrepreneurial behavior.* Gabler.

Schlaegel, C., & Koenig, M. (2014). Determinants of entrepreneurial intent: A meta-analytic test and integration of competing models. *Entrepreneurship Theory and Practice, 38*(2), 291–332. https://doi.org/10.1111/etap.12087

Schwartz, S. H., & Boehnke, K. (2004). Evaluating the structure of human values with confirmatory factor analysis. *Journal of Research in Personality, 38*(3), 230–255. https://doi.org/10.1016/S0092-6566(03)00069-2

Schwartz, S. H., & Bilsky, W. (1987). Toward a universal psychological structure of human values. *Journal of Personality and Social Psychology, 53*(3), 550–562. https://doi.org/10.1037/0022-3514.53.3.550

Schwartz, S. H., Verkasalo, M., Antonovsky, A., & Sagiv, L. (1997). Value priorities and social desirability: Much substance, some style. *British Journal of Social Psychology, 36*(1), 3–18. https://doi.org/10.1111/j.2044-8309.1997.tb01115.x

Şeşen, H., Soran, S., & Caymaz, E. (2014). Toplumsal kültürün üniversite öğrencilerinin girişimcilik niyetine etkisi: Sosyal ağ ve kullanımının aracılık rolü. *Dumlupınar Üniversitesi Sosyal Bilimler Dergisi, 41*, 93–106. https://dergipark.org.tr/tr/pub/dpusbe/issue/4783/65955

Shapero, A., & Sokol, L., (1982). The social dimensions of entrepreneurship. In *Encyclopedia of entrepreneurship*. Englwood Cliffs: Prentice Hall.

Small, M. W., & Dickie, L. (1999). A cinematograph of moral principles: Critical values for contemporary business and society. *Journal of Management Development, 18*(7), 628–638. https://doi.org/10.1108/02621719910284477

Tan, Wee-Liang; Denis H. Y., Leung & Thomas, B. (2003). *The influence of political factors on entrepreneurship intentions*. Working Paper, 12/2003, 1–10.

Tikici, M., & Aksoy, A. (2009). *Girişimcilik ve küçük işletmeler*, Nobel Yayın Dağıtım.

Timuroğlu, K., & Çakır, S. (2014). Girişimcilerin yeni bir girişim yapma niyetlerinin risk alma eğilimi ile ilişkisi. *Afyon Kocatepe Üniversitesi İktisadi ve İdari Bilimler Dergisi, 16*(2), 119–136. https://doi.org/10.5578/jeas.8189

Ward, T. B. (2004). Cognition, creativity, and entrepreneurship. *Journal of Business Venturing, 19*(2), 173–188. https://doi.org/10.1016/S0883-9026(03)00005-3

Yetim, N. (2002). Sosyal sermaye olarak kadın girişimciler: Mersin örneği. *Ege Akademik Bakış, 2*(2), 79–92. https://dergipark.org.tr/tr/pub/eab/issue/39833/472261

Zhao, J., He, N., & Lovrich, N. P. (1998). Individual value preferences among American police officers The Rokeach theory of human values revisited. *Policing: An International Journal of Police Strategies & Management, 21*(1), 22–37. https://doi.org/10.1108/13639519910271210

Ahmet KADİROĞLU[1]

Differences among Women Entrepreneurs in Rural Areas: A Survey in Beekeeping Industry

In general, development of women is a necessity for development of society and nation (Mishra & Kiran, 2014). Women entrepreneurship is important for the benefit of rural populations. Rural women entrepreneurship is considered as a potential instrument for alleviating the relative difficulties that the women in rural areas have and a method for utilizing the unused economic development potential of women in the rural areas. Furthermore, women entrepreneurship is expected to grant women economic independence. For this reason, women entrepreneurship is the key to both women's liberalization and national development (Kungwansupaphan & Leihaothabam, 2016).

In rural areas, entrepreneurship has two main goals, which are economic and social ones. Economic goals include increasing the income, transforming the capital, improving the use of credit, facilitating the investments, minimizing the entrepreneurial risks, increasing productivity, improving the sales opportunities, ensuring the functionality of the marketing chain, and rationalizing the company's management and organization structure. Social goals include improving the allocation of work hours and spare time, taking measures required for social security, eliminating the individuals' risk of disease or accident for any reason, improving the severe conditions of women, and facilitating the agricultural duties of women and children (Sosyal, 2013; Nguyen et al., 2014; Dutta, 2018).

In rural areas, women entrepreneurs generally operate in sectors such as herbal marketing, rural tourism, weaving, poultry raising, animal husbandry, dairy farming, and plant nursing (Hashemi et al., 1996; Sharma et al., 2012). Areas of activities of women living in rural areas may differ depending on various factors.

The objective of this chapter is to investigate the regional differences between women entrepreneurs operating in rural areas. For this purpose, the present

1 Lecturer, Bingöl University, Social and Economic Studies Application and Research Center, akadiroglu@bingol.edu.tr, ORCID ID: 0000-0002-0818-5324

research focused on the activities of women entrepreneurs operating in the same industry in different regions. In order to make a comparative analysis, a field survey was conducted with 137 rural women entrepreneurs operating in the beekeeping industry in Ordu and Bingöl provinces, which have different geographical, climatic, social, cultural, and economic characteristics, in Turkey. The data collected were first analyzed using descriptive statistics and frequency tables. The dataset was analyzed using One-Sample Kolmogorov-Smirnov test and non-parametric Mann-Whitney U test. In this study, the activities of rural women entrepreneurs operating in the beekeeping industry were comparatively examined.

1. Women Entrepreneurs in Rural Areas

In the global world, the importance of entrepreneurship for the national economy has increased and been investigated in many scientific studies. When compared by the level of importance, it can be seen that the subject of women entrepreneurship has not drawn such an importance in scientific researches. There are few studies carried out on the entrepreneurial activities of women entrepreneurs living in rural areas (Marangoz et al., 2016). Emphasizing that human, social, institutional, and financial capital revenues should be achieved in entrepreneurial activities, the subject of rural women entrepreneurship has been first studies by Wernerfelt (1984). Besides the studies examining the problems in rural women entrepreneurship (Goyal & Parkash, 2011; Patel & Chavda, 2013; Pharm & Sritharan, 2013; Nguyen et al., 2014; Limbu & Bordoboloi, 2015; Muhammad et al., 2016; Ghouse et al., 2017), there also are studies examining the capital factor in rural women entrepreneurship (Poon et al., 2012; Vosta & Jalilvand, 2014; Dastourian et al., 2016; Kungwansupaphan & Leihaothabam, 2016). Studies examined the efficiency of micro-credits in rural areas on women entrepreneurship (Afrin et al., 2008; Egyir, 2010; Maru & Chemjor, 2013; Nukpezah & Blankson, 2017; Khan et al., 2020).

1.1. Entrepreneurial Activities of Women in Rural Areas

Women entrepreneurship in a society depends largely on the economic, social, religious, cultural, and psychological factors in the society (Vosta & Jalilvand, 2014). There are many causes or encouraging factors for women living in rural areas to establish businesses or engage in economic activities. They include, earning money, having a desirable source of income, increasing the life standards, personal satisfaction, self-esteem, desire to utilize one's own skills and abilities, desire to own one's own business and employing others, access to credit, appropriate governmental policies, impressiveness of success stories, unsuitable working conditions, career guarantee, family security, fulfilling the liabilities to creditors, working at family business, inability of finding a suitable occupation or job, and economic needs (Jyoti et al., 2011).

In rural regions, women are related to agriculture-related activities such as farming, sericulture, aquaculture, etc. However, these are considered as their daily duties and they are kept away from financial sources. They have all the sources such as human power, raw material, knowledge, hardworking nature, etc. However, transforming the women in rural areas into entrepreneurs requires mindset, education, access to finance, credit, and market opportunities. Nowadays, entrepreneurship is the only solution for providing the rural youth with employment. In rural areas, women can prove themselves and increase their individual and social statuses by means of micro-credits and micro-entrepreneurship (Padmavathi, 2011).

1.2. Problems of Rural Women Entrepreneurs

Rural women entrepreneurs have more problems when compared to men living in rural areas and women living in urban areas. This is not only because of gender discrimination or literacy problem (Manjunatha, 2013). Behara and Niranjan (2012) discussed the problems of rural women entrepreneurs as follows. However, it should be noted that the following problems have been listed for women entrepreneurs operating in disadvantaged rural areas and they might not apply to the regions having different development levels.

a. *Financial insufficiency*: Women and micro-entrepreneurs always suffer from insufficient financial sources and circulating capital. They are deprived of external funds due to the lack of collaterals and credits. Women generally do not own properties in their names.
b. *Ineffective regulations for marketing and sales*: Women entrepreneurs are generally at the mercy of intermediaries, who generally receive the majority of profit, in marketing their products.
c. *Raw material insufficiency*: Women entrepreneurs have difficulties in the procurement of raw materials and other required inputs. Many raw materials have very high prices.
d. *Intense competition*: Most of the women entrepreneurs work with a non-perfect organizational structure. They face severe competition from the organized industries and men entrepreneurs.

e. *High production costs*: Another problem limiting the progression and decreasing the productivity of women entrepreneurship is the high production costs.
f. *Low mobility*: One of the most important limitations for women entrepreneurs is mobility or transportation. Women have difficulties in finding accommodation on their own in small counties.
g. *Family responsibilities*: Familial bonds significantly decrease the energy and time to be allocated to the business. Married women entrepreneurs should establish a good balance between business and home.
h. *Social attitudes*: The most important problem of a women entrepreneur is the social attitude and the limitations she has to cope with. Despite the constitutional equality, women are subjected to discrimination. In tradition-bound societies, women suffer from men's prejudicial attitudes regarding the roles and capacity of women. In rural areas, women have to cope with not only the men but also women accepting the inequality.
i. *Low level of risk-taking skills*: Since they maintain a protected life, women have relatively less skills regarding coping with economic and other risks.
j. *Educational deficiency*: Due to the educational insufficiencies, most women are not aware of technological advancements, marketing knowledge, etc. Insufficient knowledge and experience creates more problems in establishing and running businesses.
k. *Low need for success*: Need for success, independence, and autonomy are important prerequisites for succeeding in entrepreneurship. However, women are proud of achievements of their parents, husbands, sons, etc.

1.3. Why Is Rural Women Entrepreneurship Important?

Women participation in entrepreneurial activities contributes to the economic growth in many countries. In the last decade, it was documented that women entrepreneurship is a significant and unused source for economic growth. Although the ratio of women participation in entrepreneurship is lower than men, women generally prefer establishing and managing businesses in different industries when compared to men. Improving the entrepreneurship in women living in rural areas would be useful in improving the personal skills of women, as well as their status in decision-making in family and society (Padmavathi, 2011; Mennakanti, 2017). Because of the important role of entrepreneurship in economic development, the studies on entrepreneurship have expanded in the way including various aspects such as entrepreneurship in rural areas. Rural women entrepreneurship is one of these specific areas (Kungwansupaphan & Leihaothabam, 2016).

A characteristic of women entrepreneurs operating in rural areas is their struggle with poverty. The goals of contributing to the family economy and increasing the life standards increased the women participation in entrepreneurship in disadvantaged rural areas (Healey, 2012; Gautam & Mishra, 2016). Utilization of women's entrepreneurial potential may create employment opportunities for more individuals throughout the world. From the aspect of the dynamic effects on the rural economy, it is very important for women to develop skills and be successful under supportive policy conditions. Utilization of women's entrepreneurial skills is an effective strategy for struggling with unemployment and poverty in rural areas (Parveen, 2014). Rural women entrepreneurship contributes to increasing rural welfare by means of the use of local sources and better distribution of agricultural products. Moreover, it also contributes to the rural development thanks to its fundamental characteristics such as decreasing discrimination, offering alternative occupations against the rural-to-urban migration, and providing the rural population with human power, fund, material, machinery, management, and market opportunities (Lawatre, 2016).

1.3. Supporting Rural Women Entrepreneurship

Due to family responsibilities and social and cultural obstacles, most women are deprived of the opportunity of being employed as a paid worker. Within this context, self-employment or establishing their own businesses provides women with an opportunity to gain an income and achieve financial security. Advancement of entrepreneurship contributes to decreasing unemployment and, consequently, decreasing various unemployment-related social problems of the society. For this reason, advancing the entrepreneurship among women can be considered as an approach aiming to economically strengthen women (Choudhary, 2015).

One of the important instruments to be used to improve women entrepreneurship is the microcredits. Micro-credit program has an important effect on the socioeconomic lives, incomes, and economic security of women living in rural areas. It increases the incomes of women and allows them to spend more money for the development of themselves and their families. It also contributes to increasing the household income that improves the consumption patterns and lifestyles of rural families (Afrin et al., 2008).

Poon et al. (2012) examined the role of social capital on rural women entrepreneurship in two regions of Northern Vietnam via a field survey on micro-credit programs implemented between 1991 and 2007. In their study, it was observed that the distance to public markets significantly increased the possibility of women entrepreneurship. Moreover, they also reported that access to capital, i.e. the number of micro-financial loans and minimum amount of credits, has a positive effect on the women entrepreneurship. Khan et al. (2020) empirically analyzed the results of micro-finance on the rural women entrepreneurs in Punjab state of Pakistan. As a result of their study, the authors determined that micro-finance programs addressing women did not only make indebted women from financial aspect by increasing their incomes and consumptions but also they contributed to many local shareholders. In their study on 183 rural entrepreneurs in Malaysia, Zin and İbrahim (2020) empirically examined the relationship between the rural entrepreneurs' business performance and the entrepreneur supports such as entrepreneurship education, market support, business networking, and financial support. The results suggested that governmental supports increased the business performances.

2. Rural Women Entrepreneurs: Literature Review with a Regional Emphasis

Petridou and Glaveli (2008) carried out an experimental study on the rural women entrepreneurs managing cooperatives in Greece. Their study on 104 cooperative-member rural women entrepreneurs aimed to examine the effects of educational support on their skills and attitudes, livability of cooperatives, growth expectations, and work-life balance. According to the results they reported, it was determined that, after the trainings, participants showed more positive attitudes towards determining new business opportunities, flexibility in decision-making, effective cooperation, and entrepreneurship in terms of skills development. Moreover, their perceptions about the development and growth expectations of cooperative and the work-life balance were also positively affected. Iakovidou et al. (2009) carried out a research more closely examining the women entrepreneurs in rural regions of Greece. In their research, authors conducted a survey on 516 women entrepreneurs operating in 5 different rural areas in Northern Greece and closely examined the characteristics of rural entrepreneurship the causes of entrepreneurial activities. As a result of their research, it was observed that women entrepreneurship remarkably differed in relation with the rural reality. In rural regions of Greece, families play determining role in women's engagement in entrepreneurial activities. In general, the entrepreneurial activities of women in rural areas are not driven by the personal goals and entrepreneurial objectives. Gender issues and social recognition are still effective on the preservation of intra-family employment and women.

In their field survey on 63 women entrepreneurs in Tehran city of Iran, Lashgarara and Ghashghaei (2014) determined the factors influencing the development of rural women entrepreneurship. As reported by rural women entrepreneurs, education was determined to be the most important factor influencing the rural women entrepreneurship. The participation of women in rural development in rural areas can be achieved by organizing briefings and informative courses through mass media (radio, TV, etc.). Specialists might further direct the women, who live in rural areas, into entrepreneurship through educational visits in entrepreneurship plans. Considering the needs of women in rural areas might play an important role in drawing their attention to entrepreneurship.

Rezaei-Moghaddam et al. (2019) investigated the marketing activities of women entrepreneurs in rural regions. They conducted a survey on 307 women entrepreneurs, who were the entrepreneurs of enterprises that were members of a holding specialized in agricultural development, in Fars state of Iran. According to the findings, marketing methods such as face-to-face advertising, phone-calls, exhibitions, and SMS are widely used by the women entrepreneurs.

In a study empirically examining the effect of social capital on women entrepreneurship in rural regions of Iran, the results suggested that social capital has a positive and significant effect on rural women entrepreneurship. It was determined that three social capital factors (structural, relational, and cognitive) explained the differences in entrepreneurs' psychological characteristics such as achievement, innovation, self-control, self-esteem, opportunism, autonomy/independence, and risk/uncertainty (Vosta & Jalilvand, 2014).

Driga et al. (2009) examined the effects of selected institutional factors on the entrepreneurial activities of rural women and men entrepreneurs. Using the logistic regression model, they analyzed the data of the Spanish Global Entrepreneurship Monitor 2004. According to the results, it was determined that, in Spain, women in rural regions tend to engage in entrepreneurial activities less than men in rural regions, women are less optimistic about their entrepreneurial skills, and they do not consider the fear of failure as an important problem regarding the engagement in entrepreneurial activities.

In their study, Rathee and Yadav (2017) examined the status of women entrepreneurship in rural regions of India, rural regions' contributions to economic improvement, women entrepreneurs' expectations from the future, and government policies and provided strategies for empowering women in rural regions. In their study, the authors used secondary data obtained from books, journals, articles, websites, and government reports. As a result of assessments, it was observed that women entrepreneurs were not limited to small companies but they also started large and medium-scale enterprises. In their study, they reported that government should play a facilitating role and more banks and financial institutions should improve the access to funding that has an encouraging role in entrepreneurial activities.

In order to determine the strategy of women, who live in rural regions of Punjab-India, regarding the strengthening the farm and house-based entrepreneurship, Sidhu and Kaur (2006) conducted a field survey on 250 women living in rural regions. According to the findings, women in rural regions are engaged in various activities in farms and houses. It was determined that women entrepreneurs have basic knowledge, skills, and potential resources that might be useful in establishing and managing the enterprises.

Another study was carried out in rural regions of India by Gautam and Mishra (2016) in order to discuss the problems in women entrepreneurship, examine the supportive governmental policies, and determine the position of rural women entrepreneurs in India. In their study, it was determined that women's problems include imbalance between family and career responsibilities, low level of financial independence among women in rural areas, lack of entrepreneurial skills, fund, self-esteem, and education among rich and poor women, low level of risk-taking skills, and inability to work with male workers.

Pharm and Sritharan (2013) examined the relationship between motivational strengths, socioeconomic backgrounds, and entrepreneurial characteristics of women entrepreneurs living in Erode region of India. As a result of their research, the authors determined that women were ready to confront the difficulties related with establishing a business. Society and families were exactly open to the concept of women entrepreneur. Women were working to satisfy their inner creative impulses and prove their skills, not to survive. The education of women significantly contributes to her social transformation. Important problems of women entrepreneurs include the factors in social background, the type and function of enterprise, and the education programs. It is expected that more women will penetrate sectors that are currently dominated by men.

Limbu and Bordoloi (2015) investigated the reasons for the slow growth of women's entrepreneurial activities in Assam-India. Kumari et al. (2010) conducted a field survey on 60 women living in rural areas of Rajasthan-India (30 women engaging in entrepreneurial activities and 30 women not) and examined the problems of rural women entrepreneurs. It was determined that women entrepreneurship was negatively affected by several factors such as repayments, lack of education, weak skills, problems related with marketing deficiencies, mobility limitations, prejudices towards women, and low payment capacity due to the infrastructural support deficiencies.

In their field survey conducted on 342 women living in rural regions of Pakistan, Li et al. (2019) examined the effects of gender-related factors on women entrepreneurship. In their study, it was determined that gender discrimination, educational deficiencies, and lack of access to capital were positively related with each other and were the main problems in women entrepreneurship in rural regions of Pakistan. Moreover, the major factors preventing women from entrepreneurship were found to be illiteracy, limitations, low status, women's weak role in decision-making, early marriages, negligence of the government, lack of familial support, culture, tradition, and male competitors' attitudes in the market.

Yu and Cui (2019) investigated the relationship between e-commerce, entrepreneurship and gender in rural regions of China. In their study, authors advocated that socioeconomic opportunities of women do not necessarily translate into cultural and political empowerment. Activation of women's entrepreneurship potential has become complex due to traditional limitations on women and digital capitalist exploitation of women labor force's affordable, flexible, and passive nature.

In a field survey conducted on 45 rural women entrepreneurs in Rathnapura region of Sri Lanka, the new technologies adopted by young rural women entrepreneurs and their difficulties were determined. The study revealed that the government encouraged rural women for using the new technologies in their small-scale businesses. In this study, it was reported that gender roles in small-scale flower planting businesses changed and educational level had no relationship with women entrepreneurs' use of technology (Edirisinghe, 2013).

Gürbüz and Özkan (2020) carried out a study in order to determine to what extent the women entrepreneurs operating in rural areas of 7 different regions of Turkey are affected by environmental pollution and climate change and to what extent they will be affected in the next 5 years throughout Turkey. The problems of women entrepreneurs in rural regions became more complex due to environmental pollution and climate change. Important environmental problems result in loss of income, assets, and animal among women entrepreneurship, as well as the loss of potable water. It was projected that women entrepreneurs would be negatively affected by the environmental problems in the next 5 years in terms of customer demands, quality of raw material used, and quality of products. On the other hand, there was no consensus on if the environmental problems would affect their business places, as well as investment in technology and equipment. Moreover, it was also observed in their study that none of the participants have disaster insurance and none of them were member of any environmental organization.

2.1. Rural Women Entrepreneurs in Beekeeping Industry

The contributions of the activities of women, who are living in rural areas of developing countries, in the beekeeping industry to both family economy and national economy were investigated (Ejigu et al. 2008; Mburu et al., 2015; Pocol & McDonough, 2015; Mwakatobe et al., 2016). Pocol and McDonough (2015) reported that women living in Salaj and Cluj regions of Romania were engaged in beekeeping as subsistence activity and the beekeeping activities were at a small scale. Moreover, it was also observed that beekeeping yielded improvements in their household incomes and women participation in the beekeeping industry. It was determined that the bee products produced by women entrepreneurs were generally sold by these women. Besides, together with the positive thoughts of women about beekeeping, women continued their activities together with their husbands or other male family members rather than on their own.

According to the studies carried out in Africa, it was found that beekeeping is mainly dominated by men and women remained in the background (Mwakatobe, 2001; Mujuni et al., 2012; Austin et al., 2020). In Kajiado region of Kenya, the success possibility of studies aiming to increase women participation in beekeeping industry by using modern technologies in beekeeping industry was analyzed. According to the results obtained, it was determined that the variables such as sex of head of house, farmer's marital status, household size, land size, and educational level have a significant contribution to the adaptation to new technologies (Muya, 2014; Muya, 2018). In studies examining the women's role in beekeeping in Ethiopia and contribution to improving the household's source of income, it was determined that, although beekeeping is considered as a men's job, women may earn an income by selling honey in the market and producing other value-added products (Ejigu et al., 2008; Olana & Demrew, 2018).

3. A Comparative Survey

3.1. Objective and Method

The number of women beekeepers registered in Bingöl Beekeepers Union and operating in Bingöl province is 70, whereas the number of women beekeepers operating in Ordu province and registered in Ordu Beekeepers Union is 321. The universe of present research consists of 391 women beekeepers registered in Bingöl Beekeepers Union and Ordu Beekeepers Union. The sample was calculated to be 234 in total (175 for Ordu and 59 for Bingöl) at a 95 % confidence level and 0.05 confidence interval on www.surveysystem.com website (Survey System, 2020).

The questionnaire form was prepared by the researcher after a comprehensive literature review on rural women entrepreneurship, examining the previous field survey. As a result of the meetings with Bingöl Beekeepers Union, the question groups of beekeeping activities, problems in beekeeping and honey marketing, and support requests from the ministry were prepared with the guidance of the Union. In order to determine the items that are not well understood or controversial, a preliminary survey was conducted with 20 rural women entrepreneurs in Bingöl and Ordu. Thus, before giving the questionnaire its final shape, the questionnaire form was tested and the understandability of items, order of asking, and answering time were determined.

The questionnaire, which was developed for the data collection, was conducted between November and December 2020 on women entrepreneurs, who were operating in Bingöl and Ordu provinces, through phone calls due to the COVID-19 pandemic. Within the scope of the field survey, 391 entrepreneurs were called; 137 entrepreneurs accepted the participation and 25 entrepreneurs refused. Furthermore, it was found that phone numbers of 229 women beekeepers were not up-to-date and not in harmony with the records obtained from Union. For this reason, no questionnaire was conducted with these entrepreneurs. Within the scope of the field survey, 137 questionnaires were performed in total.

The questionnaire form consists of 50 questions (72 items). In the form, women entrepreneurs were asked about demographic information, beekeeping activities, industry-related problems, industrial supports, and difficulties of operating as a women entrepreneur.

In the present study, descriptive statistics were used for summarizing the raw data. Moreover, the differences between groups were measured using Mann-Whitney U analysis. The analyses were performed using IBM SPSS Statistics 25 package software.

3.2. Statistical Analysis

3.2.1. General Information

The ages of women participants are presented in Tab. 1. Of women entrepreneurs in Ordu province, 2 % were aged between 18 and 25 years, 16.8 % were aged

Tab. 1: Age

Province		18–25	26–35	36–45	46-55	56 and more	Total
Ordu	N	2	17	33	32	17	101
	Local	2.0 %	16.8 %	32.7 %	31.7 %	16.8 %	100.0 %
Bingöl	N	5	10	10	7	4	36
	Local	13.9 %	27.8 %	27.8 %	19.4 %	11.1 %	100.0 %

Tab. 2: Place of Residence

Province		Hamlet	Village	District	City	Total
Ordu	N	1	48	24	28	101
	Local	1.0 %	47.5 %	23.8 %	27.7 %	100.0 %
Bingöl	N	0	15	13	8	36
	Local	0.0 %	41.7 %	36.1 %	22.2 %	100.0 %

between 26 and 35 years, 32.7 % were aged between 36 and 45 years, 31.7 % were aged between 46 and 55 years, and 16.8 % were aged 56 years or higher. Of women entrepreneurs in Bingöl province, 13.9 % were aged between 18 and 25 years, 27.8 % were aged between 26 and 35 years, 27.8 % were aged between 36–45 years, 19.4 % were aged between 46 and 55 years, and 11.1 % were aged between 56 years and higher.

In Tab. 2, the information about the residential areas of women entrepreneurs is presented. In Ordu, there was only 1 women entrepreneur living in hamlet, whereas there was no women entrepreneur living in hamlet in Bingöl. The ratio of those living in village was 47.5 % in Ordu and 41.7 % in Bingöl. The ratio of those living in district was 23.8 % in Ordu and 36.1 % in Bingöl; whereas the ratio of those living in city center was 27.7 % in Ordu and 22.2 % in Bingöl.

The educational level of women entrepreneurs is presented in Tab. 3. There was 1 woman without any educational background in each province. Among the women living in Ordu, 45.5 % were elementary school graduates, whereas 25 % of women living in Bingöl were elementary school graduates. The ratio of those with middle-school/high-school graduation was 45.5 % in Ordu and 50 % in Bingöl. The portion of those with associate/Bachelor's degree was 7.9 % in Ordu and 16.7 % in Bingöl, whereas the ratio of postgraduates was 5.6 % in Bingöl and there was none in Ordu. It can be seen that the women entrepreneurs in Bingöl have a higher educational level when compared to Ordu.

Tab. 3: Educational Level

Province		None	Elementary School	Secondary-High school	Associate / Bachelor's degree	Postgraduate	Total
Ordu	N	1	46	46	8	0	101
	Local	1.0 %	45.5 %	45.5 %	7.9 %	0.0 %	100.0 %
Bingöl	N	1	9	18	6	2	36
	Local	2.8 %	25.0 %	50.0 %	16.7 %	5.6 %	100.0 %

Tab. 4: Number of Children

Province		None	1	2–3	4–5	6 and more	Total
Ordu	N	6	5	74	12	4	101
	Local	5.9 %	5.0 %	73.3 %	11.9 %	4.0 %	100.0 %
Bingöl	N	6	3	16	8	3	36
	Local	16.7 %	8.3 %	44.4 %	22.2 %	8.3 %	100.0 %

Tab. 5: Marital Status

Province		Married	Single	Total
Ordu	N	96	5	101
	Local	95.0 %	5.0 %	100.0 %
Bingöl	N	31	5	36
	Local	86.1 %	13.9 %	100.0 %

Number of children women entrepreneurs have, are presented in Tab. 4. The share of those having no child was 5.9 % in Ordu and 16.7 % in Bingöl. Women entrepreneurs having 1 child constitute 5 % of total in Ordu and 8.3 % in Bingöl. The share of those with 2–3 children was 73.3 % in Ordu and 44.4 % in Bingöl. Women entrepreneurs having 4–5 children constituted 11.9 % of total in Ordu and 22.2 % in Bingöl. The ratio of those with 6 and more children was 4 % in Ordu and 8.3 % in Bingöl.

The marital status of women entrepreneurs is presented in Tab. 5. It was found that 95 % of women entrepreneurs were married in Ordu and 5 % were single, whereas 86.1 % of women entrepreneurs in Bingöl were married and 13.9 % were single.

Tab. 6: Main Goal of Beekeeping

Province		Hobby	Additional income	Main source of income	Total
Ordu	N	9	18	74	101
	Local	8.9 %	17.8 %	73.3 %	100.0 %
Bingöl	N	5	10	21	36
	Local	13.9 %	27.8 %	58.3 %	100.0 %

Tab. 7: Activity Years in Beekeeping

Province		0–2	3–5	6–10	11–15	16 and more	Total
Ordu	N	8	13	16	13	51	101
	Local	7.9 %	12.9 %	15.8 %	12.9 %	50.5 %	100.0 %
Bingöl	N	2	16	3	2	13	36
	Local	5.6 %	44.4 %	8.3 %	5.6 %	36.1 %	100.0 %

3.2.2. Beekeeping Activities

The women entrepreneurs were asked about their main goals in beekeeping and the results are presented in Tab. 6. The ratio of those engaging in beekeeping as a hobby was 8.9 % in Ordu and 13.9 % in Bingöl. It was found that 17.8 % of women entrepreneurs in Ordu and 27.8 % of women entrepreneurs in Bingöl were engaged in beekeeping for an additional income. On the other hand, 73.3 % of women entrepreneurs in Ordu and 58.3 % of those in Bingöl were engaged in beekeeping as the main source of income.

Women entrepreneurs were asked about their activity years in beekeeping industry and the results are presented in Tab. 7. Among the women entrepreneurs, those having 0–2 years in beekeeping had the share of 7.9 % in Ordu and 5.6 % in Bingöl, whereas the ratio of those having 3–5 years in beekeeping was 12.9 % in Ordu and 44.4 % in Bingöl. The ratio of those having 6–10 years of experience in beekeeping was 15.8 % in Ordu and 8.3 % in Bingöl. The ones having 11–15 years of experience constituted 12.9 % of the total in Ordu and 5.6 % in Bingöl, whereas the share of those having the experience of 16 years or longer was 50.5 % in Ordu and 36.1 % in Bingöl. The beekeeping experience of women entrepreneurs in Ordu was longer than those in Bingöl.

The forms of beekeeping are presented in Tab. 8. It was found that 22.8 % of women entrepreneurs in Ordu and 58.3 % of women entrepreneurs in Bingöl are engaged in stationary beekeeping. On the other hand, migratory beekeepers

Tab. 8: Form of Beekeeping

Province		Stationary beekeeping	Migratory beekeeping	Total
Ordu	N	23	78	101
	Local	22.8 %	77.2 %	100.0 %
Bingöl	N	21	15	36
	Local	58.3 %	41.7 %	100.0 %

Tab. 9: Time Spent for Beekeeping per Year (Month)

Province		2–3–4	5	6	8	9–10	Total
Ordu	N	31	12	14	38	5	101
	Local	31.0 %	12.0 %	14.0 %	38.0 %	5.0 %	100.0 %
Bingöl	N	15	6	0	15	0	36
	Local	41.7 %	16.7 %	0.0 %	41.7 %	0.0 %	100.0 %

Tab. 10: Total Number of Employees Working at the Apiary

Province		1	2	3	4	5 and more	Total
Ordu	N	2	38	36	15	10	101
	Local	2.0 %	37.6 %	35.6 %	14.9 %	9.9 %	100.0 %
Bingöl	N	0	19	10	3	4	36
	Local	0.0 %	52.8 %	27.8 %	8.3 %	11.1 %	100.0 %

constitute 77.2 % of total in Ordu and 41.7 % of those in Bingöl. It can be stated that majority of women entrepreneurs in Ordu are engaged in migratory beekeeping, whereas the majority in Bingöl were engaged in stationary beekeeping.

Women entrepreneurs were asked an open-ended question about how long are they engaged in beekeeping every year and the grouped answers are presented in Tab. 9. In Ordu, 31 % of women entrepreneurs were spending 2–3–4 months, 12 % spend 5 months, 14 % spend 6 months, 38 % spend 8 months, and 5 % spend 9–10 months. In Bingöl, however, 41.7 % of women entrepreneurs spend 2–3–4 months, 16.7 % spend 5 months, and 41.7 % spend 8 months.

Women entrepreneurs were asked about how many employees -including themselves- were working in the apiary and the results are presented in Tab. 10. It was found that 2 % of women entrepreneurs in Ordu reported 1 person, 37.6 % reported 2 persons, 35.6 % reported 3 persons, 14.9 % reported 4 persons, and 9.9 % reported 5 and more employees. In Bingöl, 52.8 % of women entrepreneurs reported the number of employees to be 2, 27.8 % reported the number to be 3, and 8.3 % reported the number to be 4, and 11.1 % reported the number to be 5 and more.

Women entrepreneurs were asked about how many family members were working in their apiary. The results are presented in Tab. 11. In Ordu, 4 % of women entrepreneurs reported that none of family members were working in their apiary, whereas 41.6 % of women reported the number of family members to be 1, 34.7 % of participants reported this number to be 2, 12.9 % of participants reported the number to be 3, and 6.9 % reported the number to be 4 and more. In Bingöl, 2.8 % of women entrepreneurs reported none of their family members, 50 % reported the number of family members working in their apiary to be 1, 30.6 % reported this number to be 2, 8.3 % reported the number to be 3, and 8.3 % reported the number to be 4 and more.

The family members helping the women entrepreneur participants are presented in Tab. 12. It can be seen that 90.1 % of women entrepreneurs in Ordu were supported by their spouses, 48.5 % by children, 15.8 % by parents and siblings, 5 % by nephew and cousin, and 1 % reported that they receive no support from family. In Bingöl province, 77.8 % of women entrepreneurs were supported by spouse, 27.8 % by children by nephew and cousin, 41.7 % by parents and siblings, and 2.8 % by cousins or nephews. In Bingöl, there was no women entrepreneur not receiving support from her family.

Tab. 11: Number of Family Members Working at the Apiary

Province		None	1	2	3	4 and more	Total
Ordu	N	4	42	35	13	7	101
	Local	4.0 %	41.6 %	34.7 %	12.9 %	6.9 %	100.0 %
Bingöl	N	1	18	11	3	3	36
	Local	2.8 %	50.0 %	30.6 %	8.3 %	8.3 %	100.0 %

Tab. 12: Helping Family Members

Province		Spouse	Children	Mother/Father, sibling	Nephew/ cousin	Nobody
Ordu	N	91	49	16	5	1
	Local	90.1 %	48.5 %	15.8 %	5.0 %	1.0 %
Bingöl	N	28	10	15	1	0
	Local	77.8 %	27.8 %	41.7 %	2.8 %	0.0 %

In Tab. 13, the number of family members owning an apiary is presented. It was determined that none of the families of women entrepreneurs in Bingöl had an apiary, whereas 96 % of women entrepreneurs' families in Ordu had no apiary. In Ordu, 3 % of women entrepreneurs had 1 family member owning an apiary and 1 % of women had 2 family members having an apiary.

Women entrepreneurs were asked about how they have learned beekeeping and the results are presented in Tab. 14. Among the women entrepreneurs living in Ordu, 47.5 % learned beekeeping from father, 12.9 % from a course, 8.9 % from another beekeeper, 12.9 % by reading and experiencing oneself, and 17.8 % with other methods (spouse and Internet). Among the women entrepreneurs living in Bingöl, 38.9 % learned beekeeping from father, 13.9 % from a course, 19.4 % from another beekeeper, 13.9 % by reading and experiencing oneself, and 13.9 % with other methods (spouse).

The colony numbers of women entrepreneurs are presented in Tab. 15. Among the women entrepreneurs living in Ordu, 1 % had 0–10 colonies, 5.9 % had 11–30 colonies, 15.8 % had 31–100 colonies, 18.8 % had 101–150 colonies, and 58.4 % had 150+ colonies. Out of the women entrepreneurs living in Bingöl, 52.8 % had 31–100 colonies, 16.7 % had 101–150 colonies, and 30.6 % had 150+ colonies.

Tab. 13: Number of Family Members Owning an Apiary

Province		**None**	**1**	**2**	**Total**
Ordu	N	97	3	1	101
	Local	96.0 %	3.0 %	1.0 %	100.0 %
Bingöl	N	36	0	0	36
	Local	100.0 %	0.0 %	0.0 %	100.0 %

Tab. 14: Way of Learning Beekeeping

Province		**Father**	**Course**	**Another beekeeper**	**Reading and experiencing oneself**	**Other**	**Total**
Ordu	N	48	13	9	13	18	101
	Local	47.5 %	12.9 %	8.9 %	12.9 %	17.8 %	100.0 %
Bingöl	N	14	5	7	5	5	36
	Local	38.9 %	13.9 %	19.4 %	13.9 %	13.9 %	100.0 %

Tab. 15: Number of Colonies

Province		0–10	11–30	31–100	101–150	150 +	Total
Ordu	N	1	6	16	19	59	101
	Local	1.0 %	5.9 %	15.8 %	18.8 %	58.4 %	100.0 %
Bingöl	N	0	0	19	6	11	36
	Local	0.0 %	0.0 %	52.8 %	16.7 %	30.6 %	100.0 %

Tab. 16: Supporters in Beginning the Beekeeping

Province		Nobody	Mother	Father	Spouse	Children	Relatives	Total
Ordu	N	1	1	5	92	1	1	101
	Local	1.0 %	1.0 %	5.0 %	91.1 %	1.0 %	1.0 %	100.0 %
Bingöl	N	0	0	2	34	0	0	36
	Local	0.0 %	0.0 %	5.6 %	94.4 %	0.0 %	0.0 %	100.0 %

Tab. 17: Change in Beekeeping Revenues in the Last 5 Years

Province		Significantly decreased	Decreased	No change	Increased	Significantly increased	Total
Ordu	N	2	16	38	45	0	101
	Local	2.0 %	15.8 %	37.6 %	44.6 %	0 %	100.0 %
Bingöl	N	0	8	7	21	0	36
	Local	0.0 %	22.2 %	19.4 %	58.3 %	0 %	100.0 %

Women entrepreneurs were asked about whom they have received support from while beginning the beekeeping process. The entrepreneurs were provided with multiple options and the results are presented in Tab. 16. Among the women entrepreneurs living in Ordu, 1 % received no support, whereas 6 % received support from mother and father, 91.1 % from spouse, 1 % from children, and 1 % from relatives. Among the women entrepreneurs living in Bingöl, however, 5.6 % of participants received support from father and 94.4 % from spouse. It can be seen that, in both provinces, the women entrepreneurs received significant support from their husbands.

The changes in beekeeping revenues of women entrepreneurs in the last 5 years are presented in Tab. 17. It was determined that 17.8 % of the women entrepreneurs living in Ordu reported a decrease in their revenues and 44.6 % reported an increase, whereas 37.6 % reported no change in the last 5 years. Of the women entrepreneurs living in Bingöl, 22.2 % reported a decrease in

Tab. 18: Percentage of Beekeeping Revenues in the Total Revenues

Province		1–20 %	21–40 %	41–60 %	61–80 %	81–100 %	Total
Ordu	N	26	13	18	14	30	101
	Local	25.7 %	12.9 %	17.8 %	13.9 %	29.7 %	100.0 %
Bingöl	N	6	8	4	4	14	36
	Local	16.7 %	22.2 %	11.1 %	11.1 %	38.9 %	100.0 %

Tab. 19: Filling and Packaging

Province		Oneself	Beekeeper Unions	Beekeeping companies	Other	Total
Ordu	N	70	1	29	1	101
	Local	69.3 %	1.0 %	28.7 %	1.0 %	100.0 %
Bingöl	N	36	0	0	0	36
	Local	100.0 %	0.0 %	0.0 %	0.0 %	100.0 %

beekeeping revenue, whereas 58.3 % reported an increase. It can be seen that 19.4 % of women entrepreneurs living in Bingöl stated that their beekeeping revenues didn't change in the last 5 years.

The percentages of beekeeping revenues in the total revenues of women entrepreneurs are presented in Tab. 18. It was determined that the percentage of beekeeping revenues in the total revenues of women entrepreneurs in Ordu was 1–20 % in 25.7 % of women, 21–40 % in 12.9 % of women, 41–60 % in 17.8 % of women, 61–80 % in 13.9 %, and 81–100 % in 29.7 % of women. Considering the women entrepreneurs in Bingöl, it was determined that the percentage of beekeeping revenues in the total revenues was 1–20 % in 16.7 %, 21–40 % in 22.2 %, 41–60 % in 11.1 %, 61–80 % in 11.1 %, and 81–100 % in 38.9 %.

3.2.3. *Production*

The details of the filling and packaging process are presented in Tab. 19. It was found that 69.3 % of women entrepreneurs in Ordu were performing the filling and packaging process on their own, whereas this process was carried out in beekeeper unions for 1 %, in beekeeping companies in 28.7 %, and filling and packaging facility of Ordu Municipality in 1 %. In Bingöl, it was determined that all (100 %) of the women entrepreneurs were performing the filling and packaging process on their own. None of the women entrepreneurs have the filling and packaging process to be done in the provincial/district directorate of agriculture.

Tab. 20: Difficulty in Supplying Beekeeping Equipment and Material

Province		Very difficult	Difficult	Neutral	Not difficult	Not difficult at all	Total
Ordu	N	2	24	0	74	1	101
	Local	2.0 %	23.8 %	0.0 %	73.3 %	1.0 %	100.0 %
Bingöl	N	0	10	1	25	0	36
	Local	0.0 %	27.8 %	2.8 %	69.4 %	0.0 %	100.0 %

Tab. 21: Sources of Technical Support Regarding Production

Province		Provincial-District Directorate of Agriculture	Beekeeper Unions	University	Experienced beekeepers	Buyer companies	Total
Ordu	N	2	47	17	34	1	101
	Local	2.0 %	46.5 %	16.8 %	33.7 %	1.0 %	100.0 %
Bingöl	N	0	18	16	2	0	36
	Local	0.0 %	50.0 %	44.4 %	5.6 %	0.0 %	100.0 %

Tab. 20 shows the difficulty level of supplying beekeeping equipment and material. It can be seen that 25.8 % of women entrepreneurs living in Ordu stated that they had difficulty but 74.2 % reported no difficulty in supplying beekeeping equipment and material. In Bingöl, 27.8 % of women entrepreneurs stated that they had difficulty in supplying, 69.4 % reported no difficulty. Moreover, 2.8 % of women in Bingöl were undecided about determining the level of difficulty in supplying beekeeping equipment and material.

In Tab. 21, the women entrepreneurs' sources of production-related technical support are presented. It can be seen that 2 % of women entrepreneurs living in Ordu received technical support from the provincial/district directorate of agriculture, 46.5 % from beekeeper union, 16.8 % from university, 33.7 % from experienced beekeepers, and 1 % from the buyer companies they are selling their products. For Bingöl, it was found that 50 % of women entrepreneurs received technical support from beekeeper unions, 44.4 % from university, and 5.6 % from experienced beekeepers. None of the women entrepreneurs in Bingöl have received technical support from the provincial/district directorate of agriculture or the buyer companies they are selling their products.

Tab. 22 shows where the women entrepreneurs have the honey's quality control done. In Ordu, it was determined that 45.5 % of women entrepreneurs had no analysis for honey quality, whereas 32.7 % of entrepreneurs stated that the buyer company performs the quality analysis, 7.9 % have it done in universities,

Tab. 22: Quality Analysis of Honey

Province		No quality analysis	Buyer company	Universities	Agricultural Food Control Laboratory	Unions or Cooperatives	Total
Ordu	N	46	33	8	2	12	101
	Local	45.5 %	32.7 %	7.9 %	2.0 %	11.9 %	100.0 %
Bingöl	N	26	1	6	1	2	36
	Local	72.2 %	2.8 %	16.7 %	2.8 %	5.6 %	100.0 %

Tab. 23: Channels Used for Selling the Products

Province		Phone	Private website	E-commerce platforms	Store owned/ shared	Social Media
Ordu	N	88	2	0	5	6
	Local	87.1 %	2.0 %	0 %	5.0 %	5.9 %
Bingöl	N	36	1	0	3	3
	Local	100.0 %	2.8 %	0 %	8.3 %	8.3 %
Total	N	124	3	0	8	9
	Local	90.5 %	2.2 %	0 %	5.8 %	6.6 %

2 % in agricultural food control laboratory, and 11.9 % in unions or cooperatives. In Bingöl, 72.2 % of women entrepreneurs stated that they had no honey quality analysis done and 2.8 % reported that the buyer company performs the quality analysis of honey. The quality analysis was performed in universities in 16.7 %, in agricultural food control laboratory in 2.8 %, and unions or cooperatives in 5.6 %.

3.2.4. Sales and Marketing

Women entrepreneurs were asked about the channels they are using for sales, in case of selling the products by themselves. The participants were provided with multiple options and the results are presented in Tab. 23. It was found that 87.1 % of women entrepreneurs in Ordu sell their products via phone, 2 % via private website, 5 % in owned/shared store, and 5.9 % via social media. In Bingöl, it was found that 100 % of women entrepreneurs sell their products via phone, 2.8 % via private website, 8.3 % in owned/shared store, and 8.3 % via social media. It can be seen that all the women entrepreneurs in Bingöl and majority of them in Ordu use phone in selling their products. There was no women entrepreneur using e-commerce platforms in these provinces.

Tab. 24: Women Entrepreneurs Selling Their Honey under Their Own Brand

Province		With brand	Without brand	Total
Ordu	N	6	95	101
	Local	5.9 %	94.1 %	100.0 %
Bingöl	N	1	35	36
	Local	2.8 %	97.2 %	100.0 %

Tab. 25: Product Quality

Province		Low	Medium	High	Total
Ordu	N	4	40	57	101
	Local	4.0 %	39.6 %	56.4 %	100.0 %
Bingöl	N	0	7	29	36
	Local	0.0 %	19.4 %	80.6 %	100.0 %

Tab. 24 shows if the women entrepreneurs are selling their products under their own brand. In Ordu, 5.9 % of women entrepreneurs were selling their products under their brand, whereas 94.1 % were not. In Bingöl, 2.8 % of women entrepreneurs were found to sell their products under their own brand, whereas 97.2 % were not.

The qualities of products produced by women entrepreneurs are presented in Tab. 25. In Ordu, the quality of products was reported to be low by 4 % of women entrepreneurs, medium by 39.6 %, and high by 56.4 %. In Bingöl, the quality of products was reported to be medium by 19.4 % and high by 80.6 %. In Bingöl, there was no women entrepreneur producing a low-quality product.

In Tab. 26, the sales channels used in selling the bee products produced by women entrepreneurs are presented. For ease of reading, the sales channels used by women entrepreneurs were marked with bold digits. In Ordu, majority (77.2 %) of women entrepreneurs were selling their own products on their own at different ratios, followed by wholesaler with 51.5 %, retailer with 28.7 %, directly to consumer with 4 %, processor/national brand with 3 %, and union or cooperative with 1 %. In Bingöl, all (100 %) of the women entrepreneurs were selling their products on their own; the ratio of women entrepreneur selling 76–100 % of their product on their own was 80.6 %, followed by retailer with 14 %, wholesaler with 11.1 %, and union or cooperative with 2.8 %. In Bingöl, none of the women entrepreneurs was selling her products to processor/national brand or directly to consumer.

Tab. 26: Sales Channels of Bee Products

	Province		0 %	1–25 %	26–50 %	51–75 %	76–100 %	Total
Women entrepreneur by herself	Ordu	N	23	26	22	3	27	101
		Local	22.8 %	**25.7 %**	**21.8 %**	**3.0 %**	**26.7 %**	100.0 %
	Bingöl	N	0	4	3	0	29	36
		Local	0.0 %	**11.1 %**	**8.3 %**	0.0 %	**80.6 %**	100.0 %
Processor/ national brand	Ordu	N	98	3	0	0	0	101
		Local	97.0 %	**3.0 %**	0.0 %	0.0 %	0.0 %	100.0 %
	Bingöl	N	36	0	0	0	0	36
		Local	100.0 %	0.0 %	0.0 %	0.0 %	0.0 %	100.0 %
Retailer	Ordu	N	72	4	11	7	7	101
		Local	71.3 %	**4.0 %**	**10.9 %**	**6.9 %**	**6.9 %**	100.0 %
	Bingöl	N	31	2	0	1	2	36
		Local	86.1 %	**5.6 %**	0.0 %	**2.8 %**	**5.6 %**	100.0 %
Wholesaler	Ordu	N	49	2	10	11	29	101
		Local	48.5 %	**2.0 %**	**9.9 %**	**10.9 %**	**28.7 %**	100.0 %
	Bingöl	N	32	0	1	3	0	36
		Local	88.9 %	0.0 %	**2.8 %**	**8.3 %**	0.0 %	100.0 %
Union or cooperative	Ordu	N	100	1	0	0	0	101
		Local	99.0 %	**1.0 %**	0.0 %	0.0 %	0.0 %	100.0 %
	Bingöl	N	35	1	0	0	0	36
		Local	97.2 %	**2.8 %**	0.0 %	0.0 %	0.0 %	100.0 %
Directly to consumer	Ordu	N	97	0	0	2	2	101
		Local	96.0 %	0.0 %	0.0 %	**2.0 %**	**2.0 %**	100.0 %
	Bingöl	N	36	0	0	0	0	36
		Local	100.0 %	0.0 %	0.0 %	0.0 %	0.0 %	100.0 %

3.2.5. Support

Tab. 27 shows the sources of financial supports the entrepreneurs received while establishing their businesses. In Ordu, it was found that 11.9 % of women entrepreneurs received no support, whereas 86.1 % received support from family and 2 % used credit. In Bingöl, 100 % of women entrepreneurs received support only from family.

The women entrepreneurs were asked about if they were benefiting incentives and the results are presented in Tab. 28. It was determined that 36.6 % of women entrepreneurs in Ordu were receiving the colony incentives but 63.4 % were not.

Tab. 27: Financial Support while Establishing the Business

Province		No support	From family	Credit	Total
Ordu	N	12	87	2	101
	Local	11.9 %	86.1 %	2.0 %	100.0 %
Bingöl	N	0	36	0	36
	Local	0.0 %	100.0 %	0.0 %	100.0 %

Tab. 28: Status of Benefiting from Colony-based Incentives

Province		Benefiting	Not benefiting	Total
Ordu	N	37	64	101
	Local	36.6 %	63.4 %	100.0 %
Bingöl	N	7	29	36
	Local	19.4 %	80.6 %	100.0 %

The rate of those benefiting colony incentives was 19.4 % in Bingöl but 80.6 % of women entrepreneurs were not.

3.2.6. Problems

Women entrepreneurs were asked an open-ended question about the most important difficulty in beekeeping. The answers were grouped and results are presented in Tab. 29. It was determined that 49.5 % of women entrepreneurs in Ordu and 55.6 % of those in Bingöl stated that they had no difficulty. Distance was reported by 28.7 % of women in Ordu and 5.6 % of women in Bingöl. The ratio of women entrepreneurs reporting the heavy workload as the most important difficulty was 11.9 % in Ordu and 33.3 % in Bingöl, whereas the ratio of those reporting loneliness was only 1 % in Ordu and there was no women entrepreneur having difficulty of loneliness in Bingöl. The ratio of those having difficulty in accommodation was 5 % in Ordu and there wasn't any in Bingöl. Although none of women entrepreneurs had problem with security in Bingöl, 2 % of women reported a problem with accommodation. Climate was reported to be the most important problem by 1 % of women entrepreneurs in Ordu but none of women entrepreneurs in Bingöl specified the climate as a difficulty. Finally, marketing was specified as a difficulty by 1 % of women entrepreneurs in Ordu and 2.8 % of them in Bingöl.

Women entrepreneurs were asked an open-ended question about the second-most important difficulty in beekeeping. The answers were grouped

Tab. 29: The Most Important Difficulty in Beekeeping

Province		**Ordu**	**Bingöl**	**Total**
None	N	50	20	70
	Local	49.5 %	55.6 %	51.1 %
Distance	N	29	2	31
	Local	28.7 %	5.6 %	22.6 %
Heavy workload	N	12	12	24
	Local	11.9 %	33.3 %	17.5 %
Loneliness	N	1	0	1
	Local	1.0 %	0.0 %	0.7 %
Accommodation	N	5	0	5
	Local	5.0 %	0.0 %	3.6 %
Security	N	2	0	2
	Local	2.0 %	0.0 %	1.5 %
Climate	N	1	0	1
	Local	1.0 %	0.0 %	0.7 %
Marketing	N	1	1	2
	Local	1.0 %	2.8 %	1.5 %

and results are presented in Tab. 30. No difficulty was reported by 72.3 % of women entrepreneurs in Ordu and 91.7 % of those living in Bingöl. Distance was specified as a difficulty by 8.9 % in Ordu and 5.6 % in Bingöl, while loneliness was specified as a difficulty by 1 % of women entrepreneurs in Ordu and no women entrepreneur in Bingöl. While none of women entrepreneurs in Bingöl reported the heavy workload as difficulty in Bingöl, the ratio of those specifying it as difficulty was 7.8 % in Ordu. Electricity-water was specified as the second-most important difficulty by 1 % of women entrepreneurs in Ordu, whereas none of the women entrepreneurs in Bingöl specified it as a problem. Although none of women entrepreneurs in Bingöl considered accommodation as a problem, 4 % of women entrepreneurs in Ordu specified it as a difficulty. Security was specified as a difficulty by 5 % of women entrepreneurs in Ordu and 2.8 % of women in Bingöl.

3.2.7. Difference tests

In order to choose the difference test to be used in determining if there is a statistically significant difference between women entrepreneurs in Ordu and Bingöl in terms of various variables, the dataset was categorized first and then

Tab. 30: Second Most Important Difficulty in Beekeeping

		Ordu	Bingöl	Total
None	N	73	33	106
	Local	72.3 %	91.7 %	77.4 %
Distance	N	9	2	11
	Local	8.9 %	5.6 %	8.0 %
Loneliness	N	1	0	1
	Local	1.0 %	0.0 %	0.7 %
Heavy workload	N	8	0	8
	Local	7.9 %	0.0 %	5.8 %
Electricity-Water	N	1	0	1
	Local	1.0 %	0.0 %	0.7 %
Accommodation	N	4	0	4
	Local	4.0 %	0.0 %	2.9 %
Security	N	5	1	6
	Local	5.0 %	2.8 %	4.4 %

analyzed using the One-Sample Kolmogorov Smirnov test. After determining the variables were not normally distributed ($p = .00 < .05$), a non-parametric Mann-Whitney U test was used.

Mann-Whitney U test is used in investigating the presence of significant difference between 2 continuously measured (categorical) independent groups. It is a non-parametric alternative to the independent samples t-test. When comparing two groups, mean values of groups are used in t-test and median values are used in the Mann-Whitney U test. Mann-Whitney U statistics transforms the values of continuous variables in two groups into ordinal form. Thus, it is determined if the ordinals differ between the groups. Since the values have been transformed into ordinal form, the original distribution of values is not important (Durmuş et al., 2013). In this study, the categorical variable used for grouping was the province, where the women entrepreneurs are living. It was examined if there is a difference between women entrepreneurs operating in Ordu and Bingöl provinces. The variables used in analyses were measured using ordinal and interval scales.

In order to ensure the ease of reading in the tables, Ordu was categorized with "1" and Bingöl with "2." In case of a statistically significant difference between women entrepreneurs operating in Ordu and Bingöl ($p < .05$), the mean rank

Tab. 31: General Info

		N	Mean Rank	Sum of Rank	Mann-Whitney U	Wilcoxon W	Z	*p*-value
Age	1	101	**74.02**	7476.00	1311.000	1977.000	-2.565	**.010**
	2	36	54.92	1977.00				
Educational status	1	101	64.62	6526,50	1375.500	6526.500	-2.372	**.018**
	2	36	**81.29**	2926,50				
Size of the place of residence	1	101	68.82	6950.50	1772.000	6923.000	-0.242	.809
	2	36	69.51	2502.50				
Number of children	1	101	68.82	6950.50	1799.500	6950.500	-0.107	.915
	2	36	69.51	2502.50				

and *p* value of the variable were shown in bold. The sample consisted of 101 women entrepreneurs from Ordu and 36 women entrepreneurs from Bingöl.

The differences in demographic data of women entrepreneurs are presented in Tab. 31. It was found that there were statistically significant differences between women entrepreneurs living in Ordu and Bingöl in terms of age. When compared to Bingöl, women entrepreneurs in Ordu have higher ages but lower educational level. On the other hand, there was no statistically significant difference in terms of the number of children and the size of the place of residence.

In Tab. 32, the differences between women entrepreneurs regarding their enterprises are presented. Statistically significant differences were found between women entrepreneurs in Ordu and Bingöl in terms of the years in beekeeping and the number of colonies. When compared to women entrepreneurs in Bingöl, women entrepreneurs in Ordu have longer experience in beekeeping and have a higher number of colonies. On the other hand, no statistically significant difference was found between the women entrepreneurs living in Ordu and Bingöl in terms of the months of beekeeping per year, number of employees at apiary, number of family members working at apiary, number of family members owning an apiary, changes in beekeeping revenues in the last 5 years, and percentage of beekeeping in the total revenue.

The differences in various questions regarding the women entrepreneurs' enterprises are presented in Tab. 33. Statistically significant differences were found between women entrepreneurs in Ordu and Bingöl in terms of the product quality and the annual average amount of beekeeping credit used. Women entrepreneurs living in Ordu used more beekeeping credits when compared to those living in Bingöl, whereas they consider their product quality to

Tab. 32: Enterprise of the Women Entrepreneur

		N	Mean Rank	Sum of Rank	Mann-Whitney U	Wilcoxon W	Z	*p*-value
Years of beekeeping	1	101	**73.18**	7391.50	1395.500	2061.500	-2.197	**.028**
	2	36	57.26	2061.50				
Months of beekeeping per year	1	100	70.56	7055.50	1594.500	2260.500	-1.069	.285
	2	36	62.79	2260.50				
Number of employees at apiary	1	101	71.02	7173.50	1613.500	2279.500	-1.062	.288
	2	36	63.32	2279.50				
Number of family members working at the apiary	1	101	70.11	7081.50	1705.500	2371.500	-0.588	.557
	2	36	65.88	2371.50				
Number of family members owning an apiary	1	101	69.71	7041.00	1746.000	2412.000	-1.207	.227
	2	36	67.00	2412.00				
Number of colonies	1	101	**74.46**	7520.50	1266.500	1932.500	-2.936	**.003**
	2	36	53.68	1932.50				
Changes in the beekeeping revenues in the last 5 years	1	101	67.32	6799.50	1648.500	6799.500	-0.900	.368
	2	36	73.71	2653.50				
Percentage of beekeeping in total revenue	1	101	67.30	6797.00	1646.000	6797.000	-0.866	.387
	2	36	73.78	2656.00				

Tab. 33: Enterprise of the Women Entrepreneur – 2

		N	Mean Rank	Sum of Rank	Mann-Whitney U	Wilcoxon W	Z	*p*-value
Level of difficulty in supplying of beekeeping equipment and material	1	101	69.76	7046.00	1741.000	2407.000	-0.483	.629
	2	36	66.86	2407.00				
Product quality	1	101	64.52	6516.50	1365.500	6516.500	-2.622	**.009**
	2	36	**81.57**	2936.50				
Annual average amount of beekeeping credit used	1	101	**75.16**	7591.00	1196.000	1862.000	-3.407	**.001**
	2	36	51.72	1862.00				

Tab. 34: Support Requests from the Ministry

		N	Mean Rank	Sum of Rank	Mann-Whitney U	Wilcoxon W	Z	*p*-value
Product	1	101	71.75	7246.50	1540.500	2206.500	-1.789	.074
	2	36	61.29	2206.50				
Colony	1	101	**75.14**	7589.50	1197.500	1863.500	-3.381	**.001**
	2	36	51.76	1863.50				
Queen bee	1	101	67.23	6790.00	1639.000	6790.000	-1.024	.306
	2	36	73.97	2663.00				
Transportation	1	101	65.94	6660.00	1509.000	6660.000	-1.925	.054
	2	36	77.58	2793.00				
Nutrition	1	101	68.23	6891.00	1740.000	6891.000	-0.428	.669
	2	36	71.17	2562.00				
Technical training	1	101	68.62	6931.00	1780.000	6931.000	-0.524	.600
	2	36	70.06	2522.00				
New incentives and supports	1	101	65.75	6641.00	1490.000	6641.000	-1.968	**.049**
	2	36	**78.11**	2812.00				
Increasing the current supports	1	101	66.40	6706.00	1555.000	6706.000	-1.576	.115
	2	36	76.31	2747.00				

be lower. On the other hand, no statistically significant difference was found between women entrepreneurs living in Ordu and Bingöl in terms of difficulty in the supplying beekeeping equipment and material.

Women entrepreneurs were asked about subjects, for which they request support from the ministry. The differences between these subjects are presented in Tab. 34. There were statistically significant differences in terms of colony support and new incentives and supports. Women entrepreneurs living in Ordu requested more colony support but less new incentives and supports when compared to those living in Bingöl. On the other hand, women entrepreneurs living in Ordu and Bingöl showed similarities in terms of product, queen bee, transportation, nutrition, technical training, and increasing the current supports.

Women entrepreneurs were asked about the most important problems in beekeeping. The differences in terms of these questions are presented in Tab. 35. Statistically significant differences were found between women entrepreneurs in Ordu and Bingöl in terms of finding high-quality breeding bees, accommodation location and rent, and agricultural spraying. When compared to women entrepreneurs in Bingöl, the women entrepreneurs in Ordu specified finding high-quality breeding bees, accommodation location and rent, and agricultural

Tab. 35: Most Important Problems in Beekeeping

		N	Mean Rank	Sum of Rank	Mann-Whitney U	Wilcoxon W	Z	*p*-value
High prices of inputs	1	101	70.00	7069.50	1717.500	2383.500	-0.637	.524
	2	36	66.21	2383.50				
Honey cannot be sold or is sold at low prices	1	101	67.37	6804.00	1653.000	6804.000	-1.092	.275
	2	36	73.58	2649.00				
Lack of high-quality breeding bee	1	101	**72.38**	7310.00	1477.000	2143.000	-2.122	**.034**
	2	36	59.53	2143.00				
Accommodation location and rent	1	101	**73.20**	7393.50	1393.500	2059.500	-2.447	**.014**
	2	36	57.21	2059.50				
Agricultural spraying	1	101	**74.67**	7541.50	1245.500	1911.500	-3.311	**.001**
	2	36	53.10	1911.50				
Insufficient support policy	1	101	68.31	6899.00	1748.000	6899.000	-0.436	.663
	2	36	70.94	2554.00				
Educational deficiency	1	101	70.60	7131.00	1656.000	2322.000	-1.845	.065
	2	36	64.50	2322.00				

spraying as problems at a higher level. On the other hand, there wasn't any significant difference in terms of high prices of inputs, problems in selling the honey, selling the honey at low prices, deficiency of support policies, and educational deficiencies.

In Tab. 36, the differences between women entrepreneurs in terms of the problems in marketing the honey are presented. Significant differences were found between women entrepreneurs in Ordu and Bingöl in terms of fake honey in the market and unconscious customers. When compared to women entrepreneurs in Ordu, the women entrepreneurs in Bingöl specified the fake honey in market and the unconscious customers as problems at a higher level. On the other hand, the women entrepreneurs in Ordu and Bingöl gave similar answers about the lack of effective cooperatives in marketing, issues in selling the honey at the desired price, lack of price standardization, uncontrolled enter of foreign-origin products into market, lack of wholesale market, and packaging problems.

The differences related with products are presented in Tab. 37. Statistically significant differences were found between the women entrepreneurs in Ordu and Bingöl in terms of meat and dairy products, grains-cereals, and other production activities. When compared to women entrepreneurs in Ordu,

Tab. 36: Problems in Marketing the Honey

		N	Mean Rank	Sum of Rank	Mann-Whitney U	Wilcoxon W	Z	*p*-value
Lack of effective cooperatives in marketing	1	101	67.19	6786.00	1635.000	6786.000	-1.035	.301
	2	36	74.08	2667.00				
Not selling at the desired price	1	101	67.97	6865.00	1714.000	6865.000	-0.637	.524
	2	36	71.89	2588.00				
Lack of price standardization	1	101	70.89	7159.50	1627.500	2293.500	-1.519	.129
	2	36	63.71	2293.50				
Uncontrolled enter of foreign-origined products into the market	1	101	68.07	6875.50	1724.500	6875.500	-0.634	.526
	2	36	71.60	2577.50				
Fake honey in the market	1	101	64.40	6504.50	1353.500	6504.500	-3.054	**.002**
	2	36	**81.90**	2948.50				
Absence of wholesale market	1	101	69.61	7031.00	1756.000	2422.000	-0.444	.657
	2	36	67.28	2422.00				
Hesitation about the naturalness of products	1	101	70.32	7102.00	1685.000	2351.000	-1.443	.149
	2	36	65.31	2351.00				
Unconscious customers	1	101	61.71	6233.00	1082.000	6233.000	-3.834	**.000**
	2	36	**89.44**	3220.00				
Packaging problems	1	101	68.97	6966.00	1815.000	6966.000	-0.031	.975
	2	36	69.08	2487.00				

Tab. 37: Distribution of All the Products Produced

		N	Mean Rank	Sum of Rank	Mann-Whitney U	Wilcoxon W	Z	*p*-value
Bee products	1	101	69.77	7046.50	1740.500	2406.500	-0.410	.682
	2	36	66.85	2406.50				
Meat and dairy products	1	101	66.00	6666.00	1515.000	6666.000	-4.179	**.000**
	2	36	**77.42**	2787.00				
Fruits – vegetables	1	101	68.18	6886.50	1735.500	6886.500	-1.058	.290
	2	36	71.29	2566.50				
Grains – cereals	1	101	**76.84**	7761.00	1026.000	1692.000	-4.682	**.000**
	2	36	47.00	1692.00				
Others	1	101	65.04	6569.00	1418.000	6569.000	-2.013	**.044**
	2	34	**76.79**	2611.00				

Tab. 38: Distribution of Bee Products

		N	Mean Rank	Sum of Rank	Mann-Whitney U	Wilcoxon W	Z	p-value
Strained/	1	101	67.93	6861.00	1710.000	6861.000	-1.490	.136
honeycomb honey	2	36	72.00	2592.00				
Queen bee/cluster	1	101	**70.96**	7167.00	1620.000	2286.000	-2.056	**.040**
	2	36	63.50	2286.00				
Wax	1	101	69.75	7045.00	1742.000	2408.000	-0.915	.360
	2	36	66.89	2408.00				
Pollen	1	101	**71.97**	7269.00	1518.000	2184.000	-2.221	**.026**
	2	36	60.67	2184.00				
Propolis	1	101	71.39	7210.00	1577.000	2243.000	-1.889	.059
	2	36	62.31	2243.00				
Royal jelly	1	101	69.53	7023.00	1764.000	2430.000	-1.042	.298
	2	36	67.50	2430.00				
Bee venom	1	101	69.00	6969.00	1818.000	2484.000	0.000	1.000
	2	36	69.00	2484.00				
Beebread	1	101	69.00	6969.00	1818.000	2484.000	0.000	1.000
	2	36	69.00	2484.00				

the women entrepreneurs in Bingöl produced more meat and dairy products and other products (shoe, atelier, furniture, construction material) but less grains-cereals. On the other hand, there were similarities between women entrepreneurs in Ordu and Bingöl in terms of productions levels of bee products and fruits-vegetables.

The differences in bee product production are presented in Tab. 38. Statistically significant differences were found between women entrepreneurs in Ordu and Bingöl in terms of queen bee/cluster and pollen products. When compared to those in Bingöl, the women entrepreneurs in Ordu produce more queen bee/cluster and pollen. On the other hand, there were similarities between women entrepreneurs in Ordu and Bingöl in terms of strained/honeycomb honey, wax, propolis, royal jelly, bee venom, and beebread production.

The differences between women entrepreneurs in terms of the sales channels of bee products are presented in Tab. 39. Statistically significant differences were found between women entrepreneurs in terms of the levels of selling the products by the entrepreneur and selling the products to wholesaler. Women entrepreneurs in Bingöl sell their products on their own at a higher level, women

Tab. 39: Bee Product Sales Channels

		N	Mean Rank	Sum of Rank	Mann-Whitney U	Wilcoxon W	Z	*p*-value
Sold by entrepreneur	1	101	58.67	5925.50	774.500	5925.500	-5.348	**.000**
	2	36	**97.99**	3527.50				
Processor/ National brand	1	101	69.53	7023.00	1764.000	2430.000	-1.042	.298
	2	36	67.50	2430.00				
Retailer	1	101	71.66	7237.50	1549.500	2215.500	-1.733	.083
	2	36	61.54	2215.50				
Wholesaler	1	101	**76.71**	7747.50	1039.500	1705.500	-4.304	**.000**
	2	36	47.38	1705.50				
Union or cooperative	1	101	68.68	6936.50	1785.500	6936.500	-0.765	.444
	2	36	69.90	2516.50				
Directly to customer	1	101	69.71	7041.00	1746.000	2412.000	-1.207	.227
	2	36	67.00	2412.00				

Tab. 40: Regions of Selling the Bee Products

		N	Mean Rank	Sum of Rank	Mann-Whitney U	Wilcoxon W	Z	*p*-value
Local	1	101	56.52	5708.50	557.500	5708.500	-6.381	**.000**
	2	36	**104.01**	3744.50				
Regional	1	101	71.53	7224.50	156.500	2228.500	-1.616	.106
	2	36	61.90	2228.50				
Domestic	1	101	**81.24**	8205.00	582.000	1248.000	-6.450	**.000**
	2	36	34.67	1248.00				
Abroad	1	101	69.18	6987.00	1800.000	2466.000	-0.597	.550
	2	36	68.50	2466.00				

entrepreneurs in Ordu more frequently sell their products to wholesaler. On the other hand, there was no statistically significant difference in terms of selling the products to processor/national brand, retailer, union or cooperative, or directly to the consumer.

The differences in the sales location of bee products are presented in Tab. 40. Statistically significant differences were found between women entrepreneurs in Ordu and Bingöl in 2 of 4 regions, where the bee products are sold. When

Tab. 41: Regions of Supplying the Inputs Used in Beekeeping

		N	Mean Rank	Sum of Rank	Mann-Whitney U	Wilcoxon W	Z	*p*-value
Local	1	101	67.53	6820.50	1669.500	6820.500	-1.303	.193
	2	36	73.13	2632.50				
Regional	1	101	69.53	7023.00	1764.000	2430.000	-0.813	.416
	2	36	67.50	2430.00				
Domestic	1	101	69.77	7046.50	1740.500	2406.500	-0.773	.439
	2	36	66.85	2406.50				

compared to those in Ordu, women entrepreneurs in Bingöl sell their products locally at a higher level, whereas women entrepreneurs in Ordu sell their products domestically to a higher extent. On the other hand, no significant difference was found in terms of selling bee products in the region or abroad. There was no exporting women entrepreneur in any of the two provinces.

The differences in regions, where the inputs used in beekeeping have been supplied from, are presented in Tab. 41. No statistically significant difference was found between women entrepreneurs in Ordu and Bingöl in terms of the regions, where the inputs used in beekeeping have been supplied from. Women entrepreneurs in Ordu and Bingöl supply inputs locally, regionally, domestically, and internationally at similar levels.

The differences in women entrepreneurs' answers to questions about the environmental supportive conditions are presented in Tab. 42. Statistically significant differences were found between women entrepreneurs in Ordu and Bingöl in terms of encouragement of women entrepreneurs for entrepreneurship by the dominant culture of the region and the presence of sufficient supportive mechanisms. When compared to those operating in Bingöl, women entrepreneurs in Ordu stated more frequently that the dominant culture in their region encourages women for entrepreneurship and there are sufficient supportive mechanisms. On the other hand, women entrepreneurs in Ordu and Bingöl made similar statements regarding seeing appropriate opportunities for growth in beekeeping, thinking that beekeeping is very suitable for women entrepreneurs, thinking that she hasn't experienced problems that men entrepreneurs could only because she is a woman, being subjected to prejudiced attitudes and discrimination, and having difficulty in beekeeping.

Tab. 42: Environmental Supportive Conditions

		N	Mean Rank	Sum of Rank	Mann-Whitney U	Wilcoxon W	Z	*p*-value
I see appropriate opportunities to grow in beekeeping.	1	101	69.43	7012.00	1775.000	2441.000	-0.323	.747
	2	36	67.81	2441.00				
I think beekeeping is very suitable for women entrepreneurs.	1	101	65.56	6622.00	1471.000	6622.000	-1.947	.052
	2	36	78.64	2831.00				
I think the dominant culture in my region encourages women for engaging in entrepreneurship.	1	101	**73.92**	7466.00	1321.000	1987.000	-2.792	**.005**
	2	36	55.19	1987.00				
I think there are sufficient support mechanisms for women entrepreneurs in my region.	1	101	**76.66**	7743.00	1044.000	1710.000	-4.309	**.000**
	2	36	47.50	1710.00				
I do not think that I have difficulties more than men only because I'm a woman.	1	101	71.17	7188.50	1598.500	2264.500	1.506	.132
	2	36	62.90	2264.50				
I do not have any difficulty in beekeeping.	1	101	71.23	7194.00	1593.000	2259.000	-1.358	.174
	2	36	62.75	2259.00				
I haven't been subjected to prejudiced attitudes and discrimination in beekeeping only because I'm a woman.	1	101	71.20	7191.50	1595.500	2261.500	-1.397	.163
	2	36	62.82	2261.50				

4. Discussion and Conclusion

In the present study examining the regional differences between rural women entrepreneurs in terms of various variables, a field survey was conducted on 137 rural women entrepreneurs operating in the beekeeping industry in Ordu and Bingöl. In order to perform a comparative analysis, it was preferred to carry out the present study in Ordu and Bingöl regions, which have different climatic, geographical, social, cultural, and economic characteristics and where beekeeping activities are intensely performed. The survey results are believed to contribute to the literature on rural women entrepreneurship and the programs to be designed for supporting rural women entrepreneurship.

4.1. Differences

The analysis results showed that there were differences between women entrepreneurs operating in Ordu and Bingöl in 22 of 60 variables. When compared to those in Bingöl, women entrepreneurs in Ordu have a lower educational level and higher mean age. On the other hand, women entrepreneurs in Bingöl have larger families.

Women entrepreneurs in Bingöl are engaged in stationary beekeeping more than those in Bingöl and they spend maximum 8 months in beekeeping annually. Women entrepreneurs in Ordu are mainly engaged in migratory beekeeping and they spend almost entire year in beekeeping. Majority of women entrepreneurs in Ordu have large-scale apiaries as the main source of income, whereas women entrepreneurs in Bingöl have medium-scale apiaries. All the women entrepreneurs in Bingöl receive support from their families and they have no family member owning an apiary. Majority of women entrepreneurs in both provinces received support from their husbands when starting their beekeeping business. All the women entrepreneurs in Bingöl were found to fulfill honey filling and packaging processes on their own, whereas women entrepreneurs in Ordu had these processes done, besides fulfilling on their own, in beekeeper unions, beekeeper companies, and Ordu Municipality's filling and packaging facilities.

Women entrepreneurs in Ordu use more beekeeping credits and have longer years of experience in beekeeping. They have higher numbers of colonies and request more colony support from the ministry. Moreover, they produce more grains-cereals. The women entrepreneurs in Ordu were also found to have a higher level of queen bee/cluster and pollen production. They sell these products domestically and to wholesalers.

When compared to those in Ordu, women entrepreneurs in Bingöl consider their products to have a higher level of quality and they primarily request new incentives and supports from the ministry. Vast majority of women entrepreneurs in Bingöl and almost half of women entrepreneurs in Ordu have not done any quality analysis of honey. Women entrepreneurs in Bingöl were found to gain income from meat and dairy products and other production activities (shoe, atelier, furniture, construction materials). Moreover, they generally sell their products locally and on their own. In both provinces, women entrepreneurs were found to not use e-commerce platforms in selling their products. These findings corroborate the results reported by Rezaei-Moghaddam et al. (2019). According to their study, the authors reported that women entrepreneurs widely used marketing methods such as face-to-face advertising, phone calls, exhibitions, SMS advertisement, etc. On the other hand, these results are also in parallel with those reported by Pocol and McDonough (2015) for the field survey on women beekeepers in Someş region of Romania. In their study, authors determined that women continued their agricultural activities as subsistence farming and beekeeping were at a small scale. They also observed that beekeeping yielded improvements in household incomes and women's participation in the beekeeping industry. Moreover, this study is in parallel with literature from the aspects of women's role in beekeeping, contribution of honey production to improving the household income sources, and revenues earned by women by producing value-added products and selling honey in markets by women despite the fact that beekeeping is considered as a men's job (Ejigu et al., 2008; Olana & Demrew, 2018).

In both Ordu and Bingöl, almost half of women entrepreneurs stated that they had no problem during their beekeeping activities. The most important problem of those reporting that they had issues is the distance for women entrepreneurs in Ordu and heavy workload for those in Bingöl.

When compared to those in Bingöl, the women entrepreneurs in Ordu had more problems in finding high-quality breeding bees, accommodation place and rent, and agricultural spraying. Regarding the marketing of honey, women entrepreneurs in Bingöl have problems with fake honeys in market and unconscious consumers. Regarding their opinions about environmental and supportive conditions, in comparison to those in Bingöl, women entrepreneurs in Ordu more frequently stated that the dominant culture in their region encourages women for entrepreneurship and there are sufficient supportive mechanisms.

4.2. Similarities

It was determined that there was no statistically significant difference between rural women entrepreneurs in Ordu and Bingöl in 38 variables including the size of place of residence, number of children, months spent in beekeeping per year, total number of employees in apiary, number of family members working in apiary, changes in beekeeping revenues from beekeeping in the last 5 years, percentage of beekeeping in total income, level of difficulty in the supply of equipment and materia used in beekeeping, and requests from the ministry about product, queen bee, nutrition, technical training, and increasing current supports.

There were similarities between women entrepreneurs operating in Ordu and Bingöl in terms of the distribution of bee products and fruits-vegetables in the total products and distribution of strained/honeycomb honey, wax, royal jelly, bee venom, and beebread in the total bee products. In Ordu and Bingöl, women entrepreneurs sell their products to processor/national brand, retailer, union or cooperative, and directly to consumer at similar levels. Moreover, the levels of regional and international sales of bee products, and the levels of local, regional, and domestic supply of inputs used in beekeeping were found to be similar. In both provinces, there was no women entrepreneur importing input or exporting product. A small percentage of women entrepreneurs were found to sell their products under their own brand names.

No difference was found between rural women entrepreneurs in Ordu and Bingöl in terms of 4 out of 7 statements regarding the problems in beekeeping. These statements were high prices of inputs, honey marketing issues or low prices, insufficiency support policy, and educational deficiencies. Moreover, no difference was found in 7 out of 9 statements about marketing the honey: lack of effective cooperatives in marketing, issues in selling the honey at the desired price, lack of price standardization, uncontrolled enter of foreign-origined products into market, lack of wholesale market, concerns of consumers about the naturalness of products, and packaging.

Moreover, women entrepreneurs made similar statements in 5 out of 7 statements regarding the environmental and supportive conditions: appropriate opportunities for growth in beekeeping, thinking that beekeeping is very suitable for women entrepreneurs, thinking that women entrepreneurs face forms of problems that men do not face, being subjected to prejudiced attitudes and discrimination because of being a woman, and having difficulties in beekeeping. These results are corroborated by those reported by studies in the literature on problems in rural women entrepreneurship (Goyal & Parkash,

2011; Patel & Chavda, 2013; Pharm & Sritharan, 2013; Nguyen et al., 2014; Limbu & Bordoboloi, 2015; Gautam & Mishra, 2016; Muhammad et al., 2016; Ghouse et al., 2017; Li et al., 2019).

References

Afrin, S., Islam, N., & Ahmed, S. (2008). A multivariate model of micro credit and rural women entrepreneurship development in Bangladesh. *International Journal of Business and Management*, *3*(8), 169–185. https://doi.org/10.5539/ijbm.v3n8p169

Austin, A., Schouten, C. N., Hinton, J., & Lloyd, D. J. (2020). Barriers to women's participation in beekeeping in Papua New Guinea. *Bee World*, *98*(1), 27–31. https://doi.org/10.1080/0005772X.2020.1818465

Behara, S. R., & Niranjan, K., (2012). Rural women entrepreneurship in India. *IJCEM International Journal of Computational Engineering & Management*, *15*(6), 6–15. https://doi.org/10.24941/ijcr.34451.06.2019

Choudhary, A. S. (2015). Economic empowerment of rural women entrepreneurs in Rajasthan through self-help group: A case of SAKHI. *Advances in Economics and Business Management*, *2*(3), 287–292. http://www.krishisanskriti.org/aebm.html

Dastourian, B., Kesim, H. K., Seyyedamiri, N., & Moradi, S. (2016). Women entrepreneurship: Effect of social capital, innovation and market knowledge. *AD-Minister*, *30*, 115–130. https://doi.org/10.17230/ad-minister.30.6

Driga, O., Lafuente, E., & Vaillant, Y. (2009). Reasons for the relatively lower entrepreneurial activity levels of rural women in Spain. *Sociologia Ruralis*, *49*(1), 70–96. https://doi.org/10.1111/j.1467-9523.2008.00475.x

Durmuş, B., Yurtkoru, E.S., & Çinko, M. (2013). *Sosyal Bilimlerde SPSS'le Veri Analizi* (5. Baskı). Beta Yayınevi.

Dutta, K. (2018). Women entrepreneurs in rural India: Challenges and opportunities. *International Journal of Humanities and Social Science*, *6*(4), 215–220. http://www.thecho.in

Edirisinghe, A. (2013). Issues of using new technology in young rural women entrepreneurship in Sri Lanka. *Patima Jinnah Women University – Ruwalpindi Pakisthan*, 1–10.

Egyir, I. S. (2010). Rural women and microfinance in Ghana: Challenges and prospects. *Contributed Paper Presented at the Joint 3rd African Association of Agricultural Economists (AAAE) and 48th Agricultural Economists Association of South Africa (AEASA) Conference, Cape Town, South Africa, September 19–23.* https://doi.org/10.22004/ag.econ.95782

Ejigu, K., Adgaba, N., & Bekele, W. (2008). The role of women and indigenous knowledge in Ethiopian Beekeeping. *Bees for Development Journal*, *86*, 4–6.

Gautam, R. K., & Mishra, K. (2016). Study on rural women entrepreneurship in India: Issues and challenges. *International Journal of Applied Research*, *2*, 33–36.

Ghouse, S., McElwee, G., Meaton, J., & Durrah, O. (2017). Barriers to rural women entrepreneurs in Oman. *International Journal of Entrepreneurial Behavior & Research*, 1355–2554. https://doi.org/10.1108/IJEBR-02-2017-0070

Goyal, M., & Parkash, J. (2011). Women entrepreneurship in India-problems and prospects. *International Journal of Multidisciplinary Research*, *1*(5), 195–207. http://dx.doi.org/10.2139/ssrn.3110340

Gürbüz, I. B., & Özkan, G. (2020). Integrated environmental impact and risk assessment in rural women entrepreneurs. *Environmental Science and Pollution Research*, *27*(31), 1–12. https://doi.org/10.1007/s11356-020-08753-w

Hashemi, S. M., Schuler, S. R., & Riley, A. P. (1996). Rural credit programs and women's empowerment in Bangladesh. *World Development*, *24*(4), 635–653. https://doi.org/10.1016/0305-750X(95)00159-A

Healey, K. (2012). *Global entrepreneurship monitor 2012 women's report*. Global Entrepreneurship Monitor (GEM). http://docshare01.docshare.tips/files/24036/240361101.pdf

Iakovidou, O., Koutsou, S., & Partalidou, M. (2009). Women entrepreneurs in the Greek countryside: A typology according to motives and business characteristics. *Journal of Developmental Entrepreneurship*, *14*(02), 165–179. https://doi.org/10.1142/S1084946709001211

Jyoti, J., Sharma, J., & Kumari, A. (2011). Factors affecting orientation and satisfaction of women entrepreneurs in rural India. *Annals of Innovation & Entrepreneurship*, *2*(1), 5813. https://doi.org/10.3402/aie.v2i1.7371

Khan, T. A., Khan, F. A., Violinda, Q., Aasir, I., & Jian, S. (2020). Microfinance facility for rural women entrepreneurs in Pakistan: An empirical analysis. *Agriculture*, *10*(3), 54. https://doi.org/10.3402/aie.v2i1.7371

Kumari, S., Kaushik, V., & Lodha, N. (2010). Problems faced by rural women entrepreneurs of Rajasthan. *Studies on Home and Community Science*, *4*(2), 115–119. https://doi.org/10.1080/09737189.2010.11885308

Kungwansupaphan, C., & Leihaothabam, J. K. S. (2016). Capital factors and rural women entrepreneurship development. *Gender in Management: An International Journal*, *31*(3), 207–221. https://doi.org/10.1108/GM-04-2015-0031

Lashgarara, F., & Ghashghaei, F. (2014). Identifying factors affecting on the development of rural women entrepreneurship in Tehran province. *Agriculture Science Developments*, *3*(11), 351–353.

Lawatre, J. (2016). Women entrepreneurship and rural development. *International Journal of Recent Trends in Engineering & Research*, *2*(11), 238–242.

Li, C., Ahmed, N., & Qalati, S. A. (2019). Impact of gender-specific causes on women entrepreneurship: An opportunity structure for entrepreneurial women in rural areas. *Journal of Entrepreneurship & Organization Management*, *8*, 270.

Limbu, S., & Bordoloi, N. (2015). Women entrepreneurship: Problems and prospects in rural Assam. *International Journal of Interdisciplinary Research in Science Society and Culture (IJIRSSC)*, *1*(1), 117–125.

Manjunatha, K. (2013). The rural women entrepreneurial problems. *IOSR Journal of Business and Management (IOSR-JBM)*, *14*(4), 18–21.

Marangoz, M., Gülay, H. I. Z., & Aydin, A. E. (2016). Kırsal alandaki kadınların girişimcilik eğilimi üzerine bir araştırma. *ASSAM Uluslararası Hakemli Dergi*, *3*(5), 24–44. https://dergipark.org.tr/tr/pub/assam/issue/31573/346055

Maru, L., & Chemjor, R. (2013). Microfinance interventions and empowerment of women entrepreneurs rural constituencies in Kenya. *Research Journal of Finance and Accounting*, *4*(9), 84–95.

Mburu, P., Affognon, H., Irungu, P., Mburu, J., & Raina, S. (2015). Beekeeping for women empowerment: Case of commercial insect programme in Kitui County, Kenya. *Proceedings of the The International Association for Feminist Economics Conference, Berlin, Germany*, 1–19. https://doi.org/10.13140/RG.2.1.1452.4245

Mennakanti, J. P. (2017). Rural women entrepreneurship: Problems and challenges. *International Journal of Research in Applied Management, Science & Technology*, *2*(4). https://zenonpub.com/images/pdf-files/Vol2/Issue4/2JohnPaulMennakanti.pdf

Mishra, G., & Kiran, U. V. (2014). Rural women entrepreneurs: Concerns & importance. *International Journal of Science and Research*, *3*(9), 93–98.

Muhammad, N., McElwee, G., & Dana, L. P. (2016). Barriers to the development and progress of entrepreneurship in rural Pakistan. *International Journal of Entrepreneurial Behavior & Research*, *23*(2), 279–295. https://doi.org/10.1108/IJEBR-08-2016-0246

Mujuni, A., Natukunda, K., & Kugonza, D. R. (2012). Factors affecting the adoption of beekeeping and associated technologies in Bushenyi District, Western Uganda. *Livestock Research for Rural Development*, *24*(08), 1–19.

Muya, B. I. (2014). *Determinants of adoption of modern technologies in beekeeping projects: The case of women groups in Kajiado County, Kenya* [Unpublished doctoral dissertation]. University of Nairobi.

Muya, B. I. (2018). *Stakeholder Participation Process, Leadership Styles And Performance of Beekeeping Projects: A Case of Women Beekeeping Groups in Kajiado County-Kenya* [Unpublished doctoral dissertation]. University Of Nairobi.

Mwakatobe, A. R. (2001). Participation of women and the youth on beekeeping activities in Arumeru Homegardens, Arumeru District, Arusha Tanzania. *Proceedings of the 37th International Apicultural Congress, 28 October – 1 November 2001, Durban, South Africa.*

Mwakatobe, A. R., Ntalwila, J. A., Kohi, E. M., Kipemba, N., & Mrisha, C. (2016). Income generation promote the participation of youth and women in beekeeping activities in Western Tanzania. *Journal of Entomology and Zoology Studies, 4*(4), 718–721.

Nguyen, C., Frederick, H., & Nguyen, H. (2014). Female entrepreneurship in rural Vietnam: An exploratory study. *International Journal of Gender and Entrepreneurship, 6*(1), 50–67. https://doi.org/10.1108/IJGE-04-2013-0034

Nukpezah, J. A., & Blankson, C. (2017). Microfinance intervention in poverty reduction: A study of women farmer-entrepreneurs in rural Ghana. *Journal of African Business, 18*(4), 457–475. https://doi.org/10.1080/15228916.2017.1336915

Olana, T., & Demrew, Z. (2018). The role of women in beekeeping activities and the contribution of bee-wax and honey production for livelihood improvement. *Livestock Research for Rural Development, 30*(7), 118.

Padmavathi, D. (2011). Sustainable development of rural women entrepreneurs. *International Conference on Business, Economics and Tourism Management, 24*, 67–70.

Parveen, K. (2014). Development of rural women entrepreneurs through workshop training. *Research Journal of Management Sciences, 3*(2), 15–18.

Patel, B., & Chavda, K. (2013). Rural entrepreneurship in India: Challenge and problems. *International Journal of Advance Research in Computer Science and Management Studies, 1*(2), 28–37.

Petridou, E., & Glaveli, N. (2008). Rural women entrepreneurship within co-operatives: Training support. *Gender in Management: An International Journal, 23*(4), 262–277. https://doi.org/10.1108/17542410810878077

Pharm, A. D., & Sritharan, R. (2013). Problems being faced by women entrepreneurs in rural areas. *The International Journal of Engineering and Science, 2*(3), 52–55.

Pocol, C. B., & McDonough, M. (2015). Women, apiculture and development: Evaluating the impact of a beekeeping project on rural women's livelihoods. *Bulletin of University of Agricultural Sciences and Veterinary Medicine Cluj-Napoca. Horticulture*, *72*(2), 487–492. https://doi.org/10.15835/buasvmcn-hort:11423

Poon, J. P., Thai, D. T., & Naybor, D. (2012). Social capital and female entrepreneurship in rural regions: Evidence from Vietnam. *Applied Geography*, *35*(1–2), 308–315. https://doi.org/10.1016/j.apgeog.2012.08.002

Rathee, V., & Yadav, R. (2017). Role of women entrepreneurs in economic empowerment of rural areas. *International Journal of Emerging Research in Management & Technology*, *6*(12), 1–8. https://doi.org/10.23956/ijermt.v6i12.29

Rezaei-Moghaddam, K., Karami, O., & Fatemi, M. (2019). The comparative analysis of marketing activities among rural women entrepreneurs in Fars province, Iran. *Journal of Global Entrepreneurship Research*, *9*(1), 1–20. https://doi.org/10.1186/s40497-019-0189-8

Sharma, A., Dua, S., & Hatwal, V. (2012). Micro enterprise development and rural women entrepreneurship: Way for economic empowerment. *Arth Prabhand: A Journal of Economics and Management*, *1*(6), 114–127.

Sidhu, K., & Kaur, S. (2006). Development of entrepreneurship among rural women. *Journal of Social Sciences*, *13*(2), 147–149. https://doi.org/10.1080/09718923.2006.11892543

Sosyal, A. (2013). Kırsal alanda kadın girişimciliği: Türkiye için durum değerlendirmesi. *Eskişehir Osmangazi Üniversitesi İktisadi ve İdari Bilimler Dergisi*, *8*(1), 163–190. https://dergipark.org.tr/en/pub/oguiibf/issue/5715/76503

Survey System. (2020). *Sample Size Calculator.* (Retrieved, November 2020), https://www.surveysystem.com/sscalc.htm

Vosta, L. N., & Jalilvand, M. R. (2014). Examining the influence of social capital on rural women entrepreneurship. *World Journal of Entrepreneurship, Management and Sustainable Development*, *10*(3), 209–227. https://doi.org/10.1108/WJEMSD-10-2013-0054

Yu, H., & Cui, L. (2019). China's e-commerce: Empowering rural women. *The China Quarterly*, *238*, 418–437. https://doi.org/10.1017/S0305741018001819

Wernerfelt, B. (1984). A resource-based view of the firm, *Strategic Management Journal*, *5*(2), 171–180. https://doi.org/10.1002/smj.4250050207

Zin, M. L. M., & Ibrahim, H. (2020). The influence of entrepreneurial supports on business performance among rural entrepreneurs. *Annals of Contemporary Developments in Management & HR (ACDMHR)*, *2*(1), 31–41. https://doi.org/10.33166/ACDMHR.2020.01.004

Berrak YELLİCE[1]

Differences in Prejudices, Pressures, and Problems of Women Entrepreneurs

Besides the achievements and supports they receive, women entrepreneurs also are subjected to various obstacles and problems in their entrepreneurship pathway that they have started with various motivations (Çelik & Özdevecioğlu, 2001; Soysal, 2010). These problems include lack of role models and access to funds and qualified personnel while establishing their businesses and the role conflict and gender discrimination while running the business (Cooper & Artz, 1995; Papatya, 2013; Bakay et al., 2020). Continuity of these problems or these problems' differentiation triggering other problems may reach the level discouraging women from entrepreneurial activities. The difficulties of women entrepreneurs are not limited to establishing and managing businesses but they also have to struggle with pressures and prejudices arising from the traditional and patriarchal social structure (Özkaya, 2009; Özçatal, 2009; Öztürk, 2016; Elam et al., 2019).

In this chapter, a comprehensive literature review is made on the problems, pressures, and prejudices women entrepreneurs face with and the results are presented with country emphasis. It was aimed to investigate if the women entrepreneurs' problems and the pressures and prejudices, which they face, vary by the countries.

1. Women Entrepreneurs' Problems on a Country Basis

In addition to the motivations encouraging women for entrepreneurship throughout the world, there also are factors preventing their entrepreneurial activities. These factors cause women entrepreneurs to have problems in their entrepreneurial activities. Social prejudices and pressures, gender discrimination, role conflict arising from the lack of work-life balance, absence of time-management skills, lack of role model and leader, and lack of established organizational culture among women are some of the women entrepreneurs' problems (Papatya, 2013). When these problems cannot be overcome, women

1 Lecturer, Ağrı İbrahim Çeçen University, Vocational School, Department of Foreign Trade, byellice@agri.edu.tr, ORCID ID: 0000-0001-9991-5689.

entrepreneurs may waver and even surrender. This situation leads women entrepreneurs to have a lower share when compared to men (Batı & İnel, 2015).

The obstacles in women's entrepreneurial activities can be categorized in various ways. These categories can be listed as obstacles preventing women from entrepreneurship, obstacles women face with while establishing their businesses, and obstacles they face with while running their businesses (Türko, 2016). Moreover, some of women entrepreneurs also have difficulties as a result of sociocultural obstacles (Arıkan, 2016). The difficulties that women entrepreneurs face with are widely discussed by the researchers within the scope of investigating the gender discrimination and role conflict. It was reported that women entrepreneurs face with most of the problems due to gender discrimination during their entrepreneurial activities (Bruni et al., 2004).

In a study carried out in order to determine the obstacles to women entrepreneurship in Turkey, Soysal (2010) discussed the gender-based obstacles and the obstacles arising from organizational and environmental factors. According to the results achieved, Soysal reported that social beliefs and taboos, verbal, physical or emotional abuse, glass ceiling syndrome, distrust, role conflict, and lack of education are considered as gender-based obstacles, whereas lack of leadership potential, lack of holistic perspective and organizational skills, and lack of politic behavior development and implementation are considered as obstacles arising from organizational and environmental factors.

Similarly, Naktiyok (2013) also emphasized that gender discrimination poses a problem in presence of women in business life and this problem must be resolved. Moreover, stating that the problem that women have are based on the lack of education and counseling, the author also emphasized that receiving support on these subjects would play a key role in resolving the problems. With reference to a study of Padmavathi (2011), Soysal (2013) tabulated the difficulties, which women entrepreneurs face with, and focused on the solutions to these problems. According to Soysal, eight problems that women entrepreneurs face with at most are the lack of self-esteem, increased workload due to double role, hard conditions of the male-dominated market, lack of sociability, lack of financial support, lack of qualified education, lack of knowledge on educational programs, and lack of access to resources. Moreover, various studies also asserted that women entrepreneurs' leadership deficiencies pose an important obstacle (Henry et al., 2015; McGowan et al., 2015).

In literature, various studies reported that, besides the gender discrimination, women entrepreneurs also have difficulties about topics such as the management process of their businesses, funding, marketing activities, determining which product will be produced at which amount, how to resolve the problems in the production process, sales, and procurement of qualified personnel and, besides these problems, they may also have problems due to their personal issues such as customer relations, coping with rivals in the industry, and lack of self-esteem and courage (Garg & Agarwal, 2017; Tulan & Türko, 2018). Brush et al. (2020) also emphasized that, like other entrepreneurs, women entrepreneurs also had difficulties due to the global crises and they are subjected to gender discrimination.

The results of field studies carried out in Turkey can be summarized as follows:

In their analyses on 4 cities in the Southern Anatolia region, Memiş et al. (2007) determined the most important factors that might cause women entrepreneurs, who participated in the survey, to leave their entrepreneurial activities. These factors were found to be intense workload, failure in activities, and irregular work hours. The sample of study carried out by Bedük et al. (2016) involved 43 women entrepreneurs. Among the participating women entrepreneurs, 13 women reported bureaucratic obstacles, 23 reported capital insufficiencies, 2 reported taxes, and 5 reported personal insufficiencies as the most important problems they have faced with during their entrepreneurial activities. When categorizing the problems into those in establishing the business and those while running the business, it can be stated that environmental factors, bureaucratic obstacles, male dominance, and lack of information can be considered in both categories, whereas customer relations, lack of qualified personnel, and unfair competition are the problems observed only during the activities (Bakay et al., 2020). Similar results were also reported in a study carried out in Elazığ on 100 women entrepreneurs and it was reported that capital procurement, lack of knowledge, and familial factors pose significant problems (Demir & Sezgin, 2020).

Arslan and Toksoy (2017) reported that, while establishing their businesses, 96.7 % of women have problems in the employment of qualified personnel, followed by the procurement of suitable material (87.8 %). Moreover, according to the results achieved, 84.5 % of women entrepreneurs reported that they have had bureaucratic obstacles. Hancı (2004) carried out a study on the region around Adapazarı and Kocaeli and reported that women entrepreneurs had problems with educational insufficiencies and coping with customers and competitors. Another subject, in which women entrepreneurs have problem with from financial aspect, is the rent of business places. In their study carried out in Sivas province, Erol and Çiçek (2020) reported that women had problem with rents at most. Besides that, they also faced with problems of flotation, lack of experience, bureaucratic obstacles, and family-business conflicts. Similar problems were also reported in the thesis of Öztürk (2016) and it was reported that the remarkable problems were bureaucratic obstacles, patriarchal structure, and employment of qualified personnel. Çelik and Özdevecioğlu (2001) emphasized that the women entrepreneurs had problems due to the irregularity of market conditions, followed by the political irregularities. In the same study, other problems that women entrepreneurs were specified to be sexual expectations, not being considered equivalent to their male peers, being underrated due to inexperience, and pressures.

Özkaya (2009: 67) emphasized that women entrepreneurs have lack of knowledge on funding and organization and specified the major problems as familial pressure, region-oriented pressures, lack of education, lack of self-esteem, gender inequality, not being taken seriously, prejudices, and responsibility of taking care of children and elders. Sayın (2011) specified the problems of women entrepreneurs as lack of education on entrepreneurship, opportunity inequality, no membership to women organizations, and lack of support to members of these organizations, and also provided solution suggestions.

Role conflicts constitute another problem that women entrepreneurs face with. Cooper and Artz (1995) reported that, although they may overcome the financial risks in their businesses, they would have problems with establishing a balance between home and business. Kutanis and Alparslan (2006) carried out a study on Sakarya, Düzce, and Kocaeli provinces from the perspective of a woman and determined that the most important problem of women entrepreneurs is to establish a balance between private and professional lives. Moreover, it was also emphasized that men entrepreneurs are more objective in the management process but women entrepreneurs' more emotional approach poses a problem. In a study, Ödemiş (2018) stated that work-life balance is affected by various factors such as age, marital status, having child(ren), working time, and industry. In that study, considering from the aspect of marital status, it was determined that single women entrepreneurs are more successful in establishing work-life balance since they are exposed to less pressure arising from the inability to establish a balance between private and professional lives and causing a role conflict. On the other hand, both married and divorced women entrepreneurs had problems in establishing the balance between family and business lives but the married women entrepreneurs make effort to overcome the problems by receiving support from their spouses.

At this point, the studies considering the problems of women entrepreneurs will be presented on a country basis.

In a study carried out on the South Korean economy, which is an advanced economy, it was determined that men are not keen about working with women entrepreneurs, that there is a general distrust that women would fail in running a business efficiently enough, that women have difficulties in access to funding and financial services, and that they have problems in terms of leadership and business culture (Cho et al., 2020). In another study carried out in South Korea, it was observed that, when compared to men, women had more problems regarding the access to funds while establishing their businesses (Chun, 2016).

In a study carried out on women entrepreneurs operating in online sales in England, it was determined that women entrepreneurs working online and having flexible working hours had similar problems with women entrepreneurs operating in other sectors. Although they work online, they are exposed to pressures due to problems in accessing to funds and financial services, role conflicts arising from family and friends, and not being taken seriously in business. It is a factor that might cause women to give up becoming an entrepreneur (Forson & Özbilgin, 2003). In their study carried out on Ireland, McGowan et al. (2012) focused on providing solutions for the role conflict arising from women entrepreneurs' problems between private and professional lives.

In a study carried out on the efficiency of women entrepreneurs in farming tourism in Switzerland, the authors focused on the gender discrimination in this sector and the problems in establishing a balance between private and business lives (Cassel & Pettersson, 2015). In addition to these problems, also the difficulties in access to financial services and the management difficulties are observed in France. However, the governmental support in France positively contributes to resolving these problems (Vial & Richomme-Huet, 2017).

In Spain, it was determined that women have a lack of qualified education required for the sector, that they have difficulties in the management process, and that they are subjected to problems arising from gender discrimination. Moreover, they also have problems by being subjected to role conflict because they cannot establish a balance between business responsibilities and responsibilities arising from taking care of their families, besides the bureaucratic and financial difficulties (Huarng, 2012).

In studies carried out on women entrepreneurs in Romania, it was determined that they face with problems such as gender discrimination, having no spare time due to working at office and home, inability to manage time, receiving no approval and appreciation in private and business lives, and need for proving themselves to be as successful in business as men (social prejudice) (On, 2011; Pocol & Moldovan-Teselios, 2014).

Polish women entrepreneurs consider it as a problem that they do not have qualified education. Moreover, they reported that they have difficulties with bank credits and lack of funding, as well as not being supported by the community (Elam et al., 2019). Women entrepreneurs are exposed to role conflict in both Czech Republic and Poland. At this point, they receive the support of their families regarding the solution of this problem and it positively affects their achievements (Lituchy & Reavley, 2004).

In Russia, social structure, laws, and tax systems lay the foundation of problems that women entrepreneurs face with. Moreover, role conflict arising from the lack of balance between family and business lives, lack of qualified knowledge, appreciation expectance, inability to take risks, and limited access to financial services are the other obstacles posing problem for women entrepreneurs (Ylinenpaa & Chechuriana, 2000; Satre, 2016).

In a study carried out on Turkey, Germany, and Iran, Mohamadi (2020) reported that the most common problems of women entrepreneurs in these countries were financial problems. According to Mohamadi, the reason for women entrepreneurs in Germany and Iran to desist from entrepreneurship was generally the wrong partner selection, whereas the work-life balance is the first reason in Turkey. Moreover, in all three countries, future uncertainty, gender discrimination, and long working hours were the other problematic areas.

In a study carried out on Northern Cyprus Turkish Republic, it was determined that the most prominent problem of women entrepreneurs was the ongoing Cyprus problem, followed by exchange market instability and governmental planning problems. Moreover, the other problems reported by women entrepreneurs in Northern Cyprus Turkish Republic were reported to be lack of qualified personnel and funding problems (Toros & Altınay, 2018).

In order to examine the problems and opportunities of women entrepreneurs in developing countries, Jamali (2009) carried out a study in Lebanon and determined that patriarchal structure and normative pressures in the region pose important problems in entrepreneurial activities.

Examining the problems of women entrepreneurs in Egypt with a legal basis, Sarhan (2019) found that women entrepreneurs have problems arising from gender discrimination and they prefer female lawyers in terms of expressing themselves better in legal procedures.

In Algeria, it was determined that, besides the cultural limitations on women, women entrepreneurs have problems in their entrepreneurial activities also because of the lack of familial support, male-dominant structure, lack of education and experience, prioritizing the marriage, and inability to take a risk (Bouguesri et al., 2019).

In a study, Tlaiss (2015) investigated the Muslim women entrepreneurs in United Arab Emirates, Kuwait, Oman, and Lebanon and determined that women have problems with social pressure and prejudices due to the patriarchal social structure, management process due to long working hours, and gender discrimination. Moreover, they also take Muhammad the Prophet's first wife, who has been a tradeswoman, as a role model and they can cope with problems thanks to their belief.

In a previous study, Hashim (2012) determined that women entrepreneurs have difficulties in establishing a balance between family and business lives. Moreover, Malaysian women entrepreneurs also have managerial and financial difficulties in business life.

In a study carried out in Nagpur-India, women entrepreneurs have financial problems such as obtaining credit, as well as problems in establishing a balance between family and business lives. Moreover, an interesting point here is that women do not want to be more successful than their spouses, they receive no support from their spouses while establishing their business, and they consider it as a psychological obstacle (Sangode & Vakhariya, 2013). Again, in a study carried out in India, it was reported that women entrepreneurs working in Gulbarga province of Karnataka state have to cope with illiteracy and difficult living conditions. Women living in this province had to engage in entrepreneurship in order to maintain their lives. They are not really aware of opportunities (Sangolagi & Alagawadi, 2016). Funding and marketing problems are important points, at which women entrepreneurs in this region have problems with (Velmurugan, 2015).

In a study carried out in Japan and Bangladesh, it was emphasized that women entrepreneurs have problems with not receiving support as a result of social pressure. In that study, it was also emphasized that women entrepreneurs in Bangladesh also have problems with access to resources, as well as infrastructure-related problems (Ahamed et al., 2020). Moreover, it was also determined that women entrepreneurs in Bangladesh have limited access to financial services and financial resources (Ghosh et al., 2018).

A previous study reported that the patriarchal structure in Indonesia has negative effects on women entrepreneurs (Wahdiniwaty & Rustam, 2019). Again, in another study carried out in Indonesia, women entrepreneurs reported that they significantly feel the glass ceiling effect and, besides that, they also have role conflicts in family and business lives. In that study, glass ceiling effect refers to the obstacles that women entrepreneurs are exposed to while running their businesses with farmers, merchants, and other shareholders in male-dominant industries. Within this context, the glass ceiling does not affect how they manage their businesses but how they see themselves as a women and entrepreneur, as well as their decisions and strategies about their businesses (Rita et al., 2019).

In another study carried out on a global scale, it was observed that the women entrepreneurs in advanced economies such as the USA and Canada have problems in technology-oriented business sectors due to their lack of technical education. The women entrepreneurs in regions such as Asia, Africa, and Latin America were found to begin their entrepreneurial activities at elderly ages and, thus, they may have funding and role conflict problems. In both developed and developing countries, women entrepreneurs have difficulties in funding and using bank credits. From the aspect of making use of the opportunities, women entrepreneurs living in developed countries are luckier when compared to women entrepreneurs living in developing countries. Similarly, although gender discrimination problem is observed in any country, the rate of exposure is higher in developing countries (Pandey et al., 2013).

In this section, the problems of women entrepreneurs living in 45 countries were classified and graded using the results of 97 studies and the results are presented in Tab. 1. The women entrepreneurs' problems, which have been reported in the literature to be frequently observed, are presented in Tab. 1. using the main titles: role conflict, gender discrimination, social pressure, lack of support, lack of technical education, difficulties in funding, bureaucratic obstacles, and management process. The presence of problems, which were examined in studies, was graded. If the problem was reported in a single study for a country, then the grade was labeled with L referring to low frequency, whereas the problems reported in 2–3 studies were labeled with M referring to moderate and the problems reported in 4 or more studies were labeled with H referring to high. The most important limitation of the table is that the studies published in the native language of that country were not included and only the studies published in Turkish or English languages were reviewed. While some of the studies focused on a single country, some studies focused on multiple countries.

In Tab. 1, it can be seen that the problems that women entrepreneurs have most frequently were gender discrimination and social pressure, followed by funding difficulties and difficulties in the management process. Women entrepreneurs' problems in finding qualified personnel and problems in relationships with customers and rivals while running their businesses were gathered under the title of "management process." It can be seen that women entrepreneurs have more problems of lack of support, role conflict, lack of technical education, and bureaucratic obstacles more frequently than the problems of social pressure, gender discrimination, and funding difficulties.

Examining the studies by the countries, it was found that, besides the social pressure and gender discrimination, the women entrepreneurs in the USA are also subjected to the racial discrimination having significant effects (Santos,

Tab. 1: Problems of Women Entrepreneurs by the Countries*

Countries	***Problems***							
	Role Conflict	**Gender Discrimination**	**Social Pressure**	**Lack of Support**	**Lack of Technical Education**	**Funding Difficulties**	**Bureaucratic Obstacles**	**Management Process**
USA	H		H	H	H	H		
Germany	M	M	M	M		M		M
Australia		M	M	M	M			M
Bangladesh			M	M				
United Arab Emirates		L	L	L				L
Brazil	L	L	L			L		
Bulgaria		L	L	L		L		
Czech Republic	L		L					
Algeria	L	L	L	L	L			
China		M		M		M	M	M
Denmark		L	L	L		L		
Indonesia	M		M					
Ethiopia	L	L	L	L	L	L		L
Finland		L	L	L		L	L	L

(*continued on next page*)

Tab. 1: Continued

Countries	*Problems*							
	Role Conflict	**Gender Discrimination**	**Social Pressure**	**Lack of Support**	**Lack of Technical Education**	**Funding Difficulties**	**Bureaucratic Obstacles**	**Management Process**
France	M	M		M		M		M
South Korea		H				H		H
India	H	H	H	H	H	H		H
England	H	H	H		H	H		H
Iran	M	M	M		M	M	M	M
Ireland		M	M	M		M		
Spain	M	M	M	M	M	M		
Switzerland	L	L				L		L
Italy	M	M		M		M		M
Japan	L					L		L
Canada		M			M	M		M
Kuwait		L	L	L				L
North Ireland	M	M	M	M		M		
Northern Cyprus Turkish Republic						L	L	L
Lebanon		M	M	M				M
Malaysia	L		L			L		L
Egypt	M	M	M	M	M	M		M

Nigeria	M	M	M		M	M		M
Norway		L	L	L		L		
Pakistan		L		L		L		L
Poland	M		M	M	M	M		M
Romania	M		M	M				
Russia	M		M	M		M	M	M
Sub-Saharan Africa	M	M	M	M	M	M		M
Singapore	L	L			L	L		L
Slovenia		L		L				L
Tanzania	L		L			L		L
Tunisia		L	L		L			L
Turkey	H	H	H	H	H	H		H
Oman		L	L	L				L
New Zealand		M	M	M		M		

Source: Prepared by the researcher.

* L – Low, M – Medium, H – High.

2009; Zincir & Tunç, 2019) and the funding difficulties (Starcher, 1996; Lee & Denslow, 2005). In Germany, financial problems and social pressure are the prominent problems in women entrepreneurs' activities (Welter, 2006). The common problems of women entrepreneurs operating in countries with different size and development levels such as Australia, Canada, Denmark, Finland, Norway, Spain, Slovenia, Bulgaria, Ireland, England (Carter & Peter, 1998), and New Zealand are the social pressure, gender discrimination, and funding problems (McClelland et al., 2005; Pardo-del-val, 2009). In studies carried out on women entrepreneurs operating in China, it was emphasized that women entrepreneurs are subjected to gender discrimination, social pressure, funding difficulties, bureaucratic obstacles, and management process problems (Kitching & Woldie, 2004; Tan, 2008).

Similarly, women entrepreneurs in Pakistan have problems of gender discrimination and funding problems, as well as receiving no support (Roomi & Parrott, 2008). Women entrepreneurs in Tanzania (Kapinga & Montero, 2017) and Ethiopia (Hundera, 2020) were found to be subjected to the problems of role conflict and the problems in access to funding, as well as social pressures. In India and Sub-Saharan Africa, which are seen in Tab. 1 to be most studied, women entrepreneurs have problems in gender discrimination, role conflict, and funding difficulties (Lyn & Karin, 2009; Goyal & Parkash, 2011; Kumbhar, 2013).

It can be seen in Tab. 1 that women entrepreneurs in Northern Cyprus Turkish Republic (Toros & Altınay, 2018), Iran (Elam, et al., 2019), China (Tan, 2008), France (Orhan, 2001), and Russia have problems due to bureaucratic obstacles. Especially in Northern Cyprus Turkish Republic, women entrepreneurs have problems since Northern Cyprus Turkish Republic is not officially recognized due to the Cyprus Problem.

Examining the countries over Tab. 1, women entrepreneurs in both developed and developing countries have similar problems regardless of development level. In entire world, women entrepreneurs are subjected to pressure due to traditional social characteristics or patriarchal structure and they reported that they are subjected to gender discrimination and social support at most. Similarly, another important problem having an effect on entrepreneurial activities is the funding difficulty while establishing their businesses. Moreover, inability of using bank credits, inability of finding qualified personnel, and not being taken seriously by customers and rivals negatively affect the management process. When combined with prejudices and pressures addressing the women entrepreneurship, these factors might be deterrent. However, although women entrepreneurs have difficulties due to pressure and prejudices, they may find a solution to overcome these problems and maintain their activities as entrepreneurs.

2. Pressures on Women Entrepreneurs

American Psychology Association (APA) defines the term "pressure" as "*Excessive or stressful demands, imagined or real, made on an individual to think, feel, or act in particular ways.*" Moreover, the pressure experience is described as "*The experience of pressure is often the source of cognitive and affective discomfort or disorder, as well as of maladaptive coping strategies, the correction of which may be a mediate or end goal in psychotherapy.*" (American Psychological Association, n.d.). Sullivan et al. (2009), however, defined the pressure concept as "*A social demand or force that can compel a person to behave in a certain way or to adopt certain characteristics.*" The authors identified the sources of pressure and exemplified the possible effects as "*Sources of the pressure include family members and peers, and media images. For example, people may feel social pressure to be married or have children by a certain age. Adolescent girls and boys may feel social pressure to match a given body type, even if unrealistic. Social pressure can then lead to stress or strain, such as when teenage girls become anorexic or teenage boys take steroids to alter their bodies*" (Sullivan et al., 2009: 481).

The pressure, which is generally discussed focusing on the individual in psychological and sociological studies, can be seen in forms of "social pressure" or "channelization" in nations with strong social and familial bonds. The orientations made explicitly or implicitly in form of encouragement or enforcement have a fundamental effect in the formation of societies. As in examples provided by Sullivan et al. (2009), the external factors may form the thoughts generally accepted in social, economic, and political theories in both modern and conservative ways (Gruen, 2012).

Against psychological pressure or intimidation, individuals develop coping skills and seek for the ways of surviving and increasing their success performance. This is named resilience. Resilience can be defined as abilities to adapt and resisting to characteristics, which can change by the individuals or time, or the negative experiences of individuals (Miceli, 2012). Moreover, the performance of individuals in keeping their mental health strong against negative experiences can also be named "resistance" or "resilience" (Herrman et al., 2011; Ryff et al., 2012).

These psychological pressure or intimidation factors, which may cause significant negative effects in daily and business lives, have also significant effects on the women in terms of maintaining their entrepreneurial activities. Beyond limiting the entrepreneurial activities of women, these pressure factors may be dissuasive (Türko, 2016).

The social expectations emphasizing that women should only be good spouses, mothers, or sisters but not participate in business life nowadays started to disappear. Thus, women started playing effective roles in business life and being entrepreneurs. Although the approach to women has changed in recent years, it was reported in studies that women still have problems in family and business lives due to role conflict, gender discrimination, and pressures on them. Especially in the families with traditional social structure, these problems become more remarkable (Kumbhar, 2013).

The problems examined in the previous section can also be considered as factors creating pressure on women entrepreneurs. The problems such as role conflict, gender issues, gender discrimination, social pressure, lack of support, and being underrated can be considered as factors causing pressure on women entrepreneurs.

Women entrepreneurs facing role conflict are subjected to pressure emphasizing that they may have problems in fulfilling their responsibilities in private and business lives just because they passed beyond the roles attributed to them and participate in business life rather than just being a good spouse, a good mother, or a good housewife. This pressure makes entrepreneurship more difficult by causing focusing problems and creates a perception that they are not sufficient for their families and they neglect them. These negative thoughts may even dissuade women from entrepreneurship (Kutanis & Alparslan, 2006; McGowan et al. 2012; Cassel & Pettersson, 2015; Rita et al., 2019; Wahdiniwaty & Rustam, 2019; Erol & Çiçek, 2020; Mohamadi, 2020).

Considering from the aspect of social pressure, the patriarchy (traditional social structure) draws attention. Rawat (2014) defined the patriarchal structure as follows: "Patriarchy is a social and ideological construct which considers men (who are the patriarchs) as superior to women." Moreover, the author also emphasized that patriarchy reinforces the inequality between men and women (gender discrimination) (p. 43). Based on the financial aspects, patriarchy is defined as the whole of social relationships emphasizing that men are superior to women, based on the male-dominance, and creating mutual dependencies (Öztürk & Dedeoğlu, 2010; Bakıcı & Aydın, 2020). In studies investigating women entrepreneurs, it was determined that, as a result of the patriarchal structure, women have problems because they are exposed to the educational limitations and the pressures preventing them from participating in business life and working in jobs that men can do (Jamali, 2009; Öztürk, 2016; Bouguesti et al., 2019; Wahdiniwaty & Rustam, 2019).

Women entrepreneurs are subjected to pressures such as inability to participate in the male-dominant structure of society and inability to act without the permission of a man. Participation of women in business life as entrepreneurs is considered as a threat for men, an authority conflict for dominance in family, and a destabilizing factor. For this reason, women are taken under pressure in many societies (Weiler & Bernasek, 2001; Soysal, 2010; Bouguesti et al., 2019). Moreover, in cases that women entrepreneurs have better working conditions, performances, and incomes than men, society may create pressure on women keeping them away from getting past men and forcing them to prioritize men. Women have to adapt to these pressures (Özkaya, 2009; Sangode & Vakhariya, 2013).

Another result of traditional social structure and cultural background is gender discrimination and underestimation (not being approved). Since time immemorial, women-men discrimination has been one of the main problems of societies. Men are defined as the party earning the livelihood for family, meeting the financial need of household, and naturally being the decision-making unit of the family, whereas women are defined as the party raising children, cooking meals, ensuring the order in house, being unable to take care of themselves, and needing supervision of a man. This role triggered the social pressure on women and, only because they were women, the society aimed to limit or prevent them from having an education, participate in business life, being entrepreneur, and playing a role in social activities (Koray, 2000; Bedük, 2005).

In a previous study, Bayraktaroğlu and Uluköy (2014) investigated how the participation of women entrepreneurs in business life in Turkey is perceived by men and which types of pressures women entrepreneurs are exposed to. The results showed that, on the contrary with literature, women were not subjected to a pressure preventing them from establishing or running a business. This is a finding motivating the women, who want to be an entrepreneur (Bayraktaroğlu & Uluköy, 2014).

Religious beliefs may also be used as a pressure instrument by society. In Malaysia, it is thought that the main role of women entrepreneurs is to take care of their families and fulfill their religious responsibilities. On this subject, Hashim (2012) reported that "As a woman who is a wife and mother, it is unavoidable that her primary role clashes with her secondary role as an entrepreneur. In the private and domestic domain, although a woman entrepreneur is a manager in the company, she is still bound by the norms and principles of being a Malay Muslim woman who must show obedience to the head of the family, her husband."

In many countries, although they engage in entrepreneurial activities in the same sector with men, women have problems regarding acceptance in the sector only because they are women. Only because they are women, they are exposed to gender-based prejudices such as distrust, sexual expectations, traditional pressure, failure expectation, and perception of insufficiency. Moreover, again only because they are women, they have difficulties in finding a partner, they face with barriers to funding their businesses, as well as finding qualified personnel and managing the business. These pressures may cause a problem in engaging entrepreneurial activities in new business areas. Many women entrepreneurs reported that they had difficulties because of these pressures while establishing their businesses (Çelik & Özdevecioğlu, 2001; On, 2011; Henry et al., 2015; McGowan et al., 2015; Bedük et al., 2016; Ghosh et al., 2018; Bouguesri et al., 2019).

3. Prejudices that Women Entrepreneurs Face

Prejudice is defined as negative and hostile definitions or behaviors of society towards individuals coming to the forefront with their characteristics such as racial origin, ethnic structure, sex, occupation, and educational status (Budak, 2003). Prejudices are generally not created by the real cases and they are shaped by the emotions and thoughts of the person having the prejudice (Marshall, 1999; Vatandaş, 2007). As in the pressure concept, prejudice is a concept generally discussed from the aspect of social psychology and having effects on society, besides the individual. In the shortest definitions, the prejudice refers to the negative behaviors and thoughts of individuals or groups towards another individual or society in parallel with wrong information and without accurate information about the individual or group (Vatandaş & Erdoğan, 2020). Vescio and Weaver (2013) discussed the prejudice with the concept of stereotype and explained the difference. The authors reported that "Prejudice and stereotyping are biases that work together to create and maintain social inequality. Prejudice refers to the attitudes and feelings that people have about members of other groups. In contrast, stereotypes have traditionally been defined as specific beliefs about a group, such as descriptions of what members of a particular group look like, how they behave, or their abilities. As such, stereotypes are cognitive representations of how members of a group are similar to one another and different from members of other groups."

Prejudices are among the factors having the highest effect on the formation of discrimination in societies. Especially the gender-related prejudices are of significant importance within the context of this study. Considering the gender discriminations specify which behaviors, physical characteristics, or personality traits belong to men and which ones belong to women and how these two groups should differ from each other. Moreover, gender prejudices shape how women should treat women and which rights women should have and, thus, women are subjected to pressure through these perceptions (Vatandaş, 2007).

Considering the prejudices as gender prejudices suggests the discriminations that women are subjected to. Especially in patriarchal societies, the effect of gender prejudices on the oppressive attitudes towards women. Moreover, these prejudices may play a significant role in problems of women entrepreneurship. In their field surveys, researchers include items aiming to understand and determine these prejudices (İlter, 2008; Jamali, 2009; Özkaya, 2009; Türko, 2016; Arslan & Toksoy, 2017; Ghosh et al., 2018; Tulan & Türko, 2018; Türko & Tulan, 2019; Erol & Çiçek, 2020).

Especially in sectors such as banking, software, computer, and automotive industry in which there is a "men's job – women's job" categorization, these prejudices towards women entrepreneurs may appear in form of perceptions expressed as "women cannot do this job, they cannot be successful." These perceptions create distrust towards women. In a study, Özkaya (2009) asked women entrepreneurs if "they have experienced a gender discrimination in their business lives" and 25 % of participants responded "yes" and listed that: "men prefer men in the shopping process and avoid working with women," "entrepreneurship of women is not accepted yet," "certain sectors belong to men," "women will never be enough to be an entrepreneur," and "men believe that processes would progress faster when contact with a man." Similarly, Türko (2016) reported the stereotypes about women entrepreneurs' lives in Turkey as follows: "women are emotional they can't handle the stress of work," "women cannot manage business planning with complex manufacturing processes," "employees would not respect women entrepreneurs' authority," "women get less risk" and "women are easily cheated and get fraud by suppliers and customers."

Women entrepreneurs are also subjected to prejudices from their families or friends. Emphasizing that women entrepreneurs are involved in business life, these prejudices turn into a pressure factor. In a study, Türko (2016: 60) discussed the stereotypes leading these prejudices as "women's primary responsibility is to care for family and children," "women's economic independence will reduce their commitment to home," and "according to our religion values women should not start up their own business and work." Batı and İnel (2015) stated that the prejudices addressing the women entrepreneurs focus on neglecting the family and failing in business. However, the authors also emphasized that women found solutions to overcome these prejudices.

For women entrepreneurs living in either developed or developing countries, the most frequently seen problems while establishing their businesses were funding difficulties and banking services. Gender-based prejudices also accompany the problems on these subjects (Carter & Peter, 1998; Ghosh et al., 2018; Brush et al., 2020; Cho et al., 2020). Several studies in literature reported that financial institutions consider women entrepreneurs not as reliable as men. This is claimed to be because women entrepreneurs have lack of experience and knowledge, besides the lack of financial history. Furthermore, there also are many studies reporting that men also consider working with women not reliable in many fields, especially in financial procedures. According to the results reported, when compared to women entrepreneurs, these prejudices led men entrepreneurs to benefit from banking and funding services and to have an advantage in establishing their businesses. Moreover, many studies reported that women entrepreneurs mainly used their own savings while establishing a business and request more financial support from their families, spouses, and friends (Toksöz, 2007; Kutanis & Karakiraz, 2013; Soysal, 2013; Arıkan, 2016).

Because of the prejudices towards them, women entrepreneurs have a feeling of insecurity and they are scared of failure. According to the report of Global Entrepreneurship Monitor (GEM), the fear of failure has a negative effect on entrepreneurial skills and may cause withdrawal from entrepreneurial activities. Although the fear of failure does not prevent the entrepreneurs from continuing their businesses in high-income countries, the fear of failure is a factor discouraging the entrepreneurs in low-income countries from maintaining their operations. In Iran, Madagascar, Poland, Qatar, the Russian Federation, and Sweden, min. 5 % of women have more fear of failure than men (Elam et al., 2019: 30). In Year 2010 Report of GEM, it was emphasized that women have a fear of failure at a higher level when compared to men. In Sub-Saharan Africa and Latin America – Caribbean regions, women's level of fear of failure is generally low and there is a statistically significant difference between sexes. In Turkey, women have a low level of fear of failure, whereas men have a much lower level. In Brazil, it was determined that women have a high level of fear of failure, whereas men have a moderate level of fear (Kelley et al., 2011: 14).

Beginning with the prejudice that marriage poses an obstacle for women entrepreneurship, Türko and Tulan (2019) investigated the difference between married and single women entrepreneurs in terms of various variables. The results they achieved showed that there was a statistically significant difference in only 4 of 32 variables. In 28 variables, there was no significant difference between married and single entrepreneurs and they were found to have similar problems while establishing and managing their businesses.

In a study carried out on 244 women entrepreneurs from Kayseri, Yozgat, and Sivas provinces of Turkey, it was determined that the prejudices towards women were defined by women entrepreneurs as "being alienated by their friends." In their analysis, it was also found that women entrepreneurs were exposed to gender discrimination. Even though it doesn't force women, who want to contribute to their families, to quit entrepreneurship, they have significant difficulties (Filizöz & Yaraş, 2020).

Bedük et al. (2016: 12) asked men entrepreneurs a question in order to measure their level of perception about the women's entrepreneurial activities and aimed to determine the perception levels by the educational status. The analysis results showed that prejudices towards women entrepreneurs decreased as the educational status increased.

In a study carried out on stereotypes of women entrepreneurship in Turkey, Türko (2016) suggested that entrepreneurship educations can be used as important instruments for eliminating such stereotypes. The context of entrepreneurship education was revised and applied with a special emphasis on gender. Statistically significant differences were found between experimental group and control group in terms of stereotypes; it was found that university students in experimental group exhibited stereotypes at a lower level.

Developed as a result of no reason regarding a person or a group, prejudices may have very limiting effects on especially the lives of women. Since these prejudices address the women entrepreneurs, women entrepreneurs having personality traits arising from entrepreneurial spirit (resilient, risk-taking, and solution-oriented women entrepreneurs) find a way to cope with these prejudices. However, especially the prejudices limiting the financial transactions over the gender discrimination lay the foundation of the most of problems of women entrepreneurs.

4. Conclusion

Despite the increasing number of women entrepreneurs throughout the world and the positive advancements, women entrepreneurs still face with problems because of the social pressure and biased attitudes. The main question here is if the problems, pressures, and prejudices that women entrepreneurs face with differ by the countries. For this purpose, the applied field studies investigating the problems, pressures, and prejudices that women entrepreneurs face with were reviewed, the most frequent problems were categorized, and the results were grouped by the countries investigated. The most frequently observed problems were found to be social pressure in 34 countries, gender discrimination in 34 countries, funding difficulties in 33 countries, difficulties in management process in 31 countries, lack of support in 29 countries, role conflict in 26 countries, lack of technical education in 16 countries, and bureaucratic obstacles in 5 countries. Moreover, these studies were examined focusing on the country.

The familial and social structure and belief system of women entrepreneurs play an important role in which type of prejudice or pressure the women entrepreneurs will be subjected to. Examining the studies by the countries, it was determined that there was no significant difference between developed and developing countries in terms of the frequency of problems. Despite that, while the problems arising from gender discrimination are observed in funding and management processes in developed countries, the problems originating from social pressure due to the patriarchal social structure are observed in developing countries. Field studies showed that the opinions supporting the entrepreneurship of women increased with an increase in educational level, the prejudices are overcome, and supports of government and women associations might yield positive outcomes (Cooper & Artz, 1995; Forson & Özbilgin, 2003; Hancı, 2004; Kutanis & Alparslan, 2006; Welter, 2006; Soysal, 2010; Hashim, 2012; Pandey et al., 2013; Tlaiss, 2015; Elam et al., 2019; Ahamed et al., 2020; Bakay et al., 2020).

In previous studies, it was observed that women entrepreneurs have problems in the effective use of time within the scope of role conflict between their roles in house and business. The studies emphasized that women are subjected to prejudiced attitudes in family and business lives. It can be perceived as a negative effect on the balance of power in family, especially in patriarchal societies. Studies reported that one of the most frequent problems of women is the inability to establish a work-life balance but they resolve these problems with the support of their families and they became successful when receiving familial support.

Examining the problems that women entrepreneurs face with, studies reported that the most frequent problems that women entrepreneurs are subjected to were social pressure, gender discrimination, role conflict, and funding problems. It was also determined that they are subjected also to prejudices related with having education and working outside the house and they have to cope with various pressures. In conclusion, it can be seen that women entrepreneurs do not give up even if they have problems, and that they find a way to cope with problems (Weiler & Bernasek, 2001; Bruni et al., 2004; Jamali, 2009; Özçatal, 2009; On, 2011; McGowan et al. 2012; Huarang, 2012; Papatya, 2013; Rawat, 2014; Pocol & Moldovan-Teselios, 2014; Ödemiş, 2018; Bouguesri et al., 2019; Wahdiniwaty & Rustam, 2019).

References

Ahamed, T., Noguchi, R., & Muhsin, N. (2020). Sustainable agricultural development: A micro-level GIS-based study on women's perceptions of environmental protection and entrepreneurship in Japan and Bangladesh. *Geo Journal*, 1–33. https://doi.org/10.1007/s10708-020-10169-5

American Psychological Association. (n.d.). Pressure. In *APA dictionary of psychology*. https://dictionary.apa.org/pressure.

Arıkan, C. (2016). Kadın girişimcilikte başarı ve başarıyı etkileyen faktörler: Bursa örneği. *Yönetim ve Ekonomi Araştırmaları Dergisi*, *14*(3), 138–156. http://dx.doi.org/10.11611/JMER193784

Arslan, K., & Toksoy, M. D. (2017). Türkiye'de kadınları girişimciliğe yönelten faktörler karşılaştıkları sorunlar ve çözüm önerileri. *İstanbul Ticaret Üniversitesi Girişimcilik Dergisi*, *1*(1), 123–148. https://dergipark.org.tr/tr/pub/tje/issue/55613/760879

Bakay, M., Müftüoğlu, M., Naltbantoğlu, A., & Çoçan, E. (2020). Kırsal kesimlerdeki kadın girişimciliği ve girişimci kadınların karşılaştıkları sorunlar üzerine nitel bir araştırma: Manisa-demirci örneği. *Journal of Yaşar University, Special Issue on Business and Operations Research*, March, *15*, 295–306. https://dergipark.org.tr/tr/pub/jyasar/issue/53734/631264

Bakıcı, C., & Aydın, E. (2020). Türkiye'de kadın çalışanların iş yaşam dengesini şekillendirmede ataerkilliğin rolü. *Economics, Business and Organization Research*, *2*(2), 82–98. https://dergipark.org.tr/tr/pub/ebor/issue/58609/796844

Batı, G. B., & İnel M. N. (2015). Kadın girişimcilerin profili bağlamında çatışma düzeyleri ve yatırım tercihleri: Yalova ili üzerine inceleme. *Marmara Üniversitesi Öneri Dergisi*, *11*(44), 101–119. https://doi.org/10.14783/od.v11i44.5000080006 http://hdl.handle.net/11424/5723

Bayraktaroğlu, S., & Uluköy, M. (2014). A field research about oppression incurred of women entrepreneurs in patriarchal societies, *Yönetim Ekonomileri Araştırmaları Dergisi*, *12*(24), 356–369. https://dx.doi.org/10.11611/JMER507 https://hdl.handle.net/20.500.12462/4247

Bedük, A. (2005). Türkiye'de çalışan kadın ve kadın girişimciliği. *Elektronik Sosyal Bilimler Dergisi, 3*(12), 106–117. https://dergipark.org.tr/tr/pub/esosder/issue/6126/82170

Bedük, A., Eryeşil, K., & Oğuz, H. (2016). Kadın ve erkek girişimcilerin algılama farklılıkları. *Selçuk Üniversitesi Sosyal Bilimler Meslek Yüksekokulu Dergisi, 19* (41st Year Special Issue), 1–15. https://dergipark.org.tr/tr/pub/selcuksbmyd/issue/26854/282433

Bouguesri, S., Azouz, A., & Beradia, S. (2019). The status of women entrepreneurs in Algeria. *Journal of Entrepreneurship and Sustainable Development (JESD) 1*(1), 03–12. https://www.researchgate.net/publication/343500762_THE_STATUS_OF_WOMEN_ENTREPRENEURS_IN_ALGERIA

Bruni, A., Gherardi, S., & Poggio, B. (2004). Entrepreneur-mentality, gender and the study of women entrepreneurs. *Journal of Organizational Change Management, 17*(3), 256–268. https://doi.org/10.1108/09534810410538315

Brush, C. G., Greene, P.G., & Welter, F. (2020). The Diana project: A legacy for research on gender in entrepreneurship. *International Journal of Gender and Entrepreneurship, 12*(1), 7–25. https://doi.org/10.1108/IJGE-04-2019-0083

Budak, S. (2003). *Psikoloji sözlüğü*. Ankara: Bilim ve Sanat Yayınları.

Carter, S., & Peter, R. (1998). The financing of male- and female-owned businesses. *Entrepreneurship & Regional Development, 10*(3), 225–242, https://doi.org/10.1080/08985629800000013

Cassel, S. H., & Pettersson, K. (2015). Performing gender and rurality in Swedish farm tourism. *Scandinavian Journal of Hospitality and Tourism, 15*(1–2), 138–151. https://doi.org/10.1080/15022250.2015.1005333

Cho, Y., Park, J., Han, S.J., Sung, M., & Park, C. (2020). Women entrepreneurs in South Korea: Motivations, challenges, and career success. *European Journal of Training and Development*. https://doi.org/10.1108/EJTD-03-2020-0039

Chun, H. (2016). Factors that explain the lag in building high-growth firms in women. *The Journal of the Korea Contents Association, 16*(7), 300–308. https://doi.org/10.5392/JKCA.2016.16.07.300

Cooper, A. C., & Artz, K. W. (1995). Determinants of satisfaction for entrepreneurs. *Journal of Business Venturing, 10*(6), 439–457. https://doi.org/10.1016/0883-9026(95)00083-K

Çelik C., & Özdevecioğlu, M. (2001). Kadın girişimcilerin demografik özellikleri ve karşılaştıkları sorunlara ilişkin Nevşehir ilinde bir araştırma. *1. Orta Anadolu İşletmecilik Kongresi*, Nevşehir, 487–498. https://www.researchgate.net/publication/292152726_Kadin_Girisimcilerin_Demografik_Ozellikleri_ve_Karsilastiklari_Sorunlara_Iliskin_Nevsehir_Ilinde_Bir_Arastirma

Demir, Ö., & Sezgin, E. E. (2020). Kadın girişimciliği ve karşılaştıkları sorunlar: Elazığ, Türkiye'den yerel bir bulgu. *Inönü University International Journal of Social Sciences (INIJOSS), 9*(1), 236–254. https://dergipark.org.tr/tr/pub/inijoss/issue/55622/694103

Elam, A. B., Candida, G. B., Patrica, G. G., Baumer, B., Dean, M., & Heavlow, R. (2019). *Global Entrepreneurship Monitor 2018/2019.* Women's Entrepreneurship Report GEM. https://www.gemconsortium.org/report/gem-20182019-womens-entrepreneurship-report

Erol, Y., & Çiçek, A. (2020). Kadın girişimcilerin iş kurma süreçlerinde karşılaştığı sorunlar ve demografik faktörlerle ilişkisi: Orta Anadolu örneği. *International Journal Entrepreneurship and Management Inquiries, Journal EMI, 4*(1), 72–94. https://dergipark.org.tr/tr/pub/ijemi/issue/57585/787807

Filizöz, B., & Yaraş, D. (2020). Kadın girişimci profilinin belirlenmesine yönelik TR72 bölgesinde bir araştırma. *Journal of Research in Entrepreneurship Innovation and Marketing, 4*(8), 179–196. https://doi.org/10.31006/gipad.785310

Forson, C., & Özbilgin, M. F. (2003) Dot-com women entrepreneurs in the UK. *International Journal of Entrepreneurship and Innovation, 4*(1), 13–25. https://doi.org/10.5367/000000003101299366

Garg, S., & Agarwal, P. (2017), Problems and prospects of woman entrepreneurship – A review of literature. *IOSR Journal of Business and Management, 19*(1), [Ver. VI], 55–60. https://doi.org/10.9790/487X-1901065560

Ghosh, P. K., Ghosh, S. K., & Chowdhury, S. (2018). Factors hindering women entrepreneurs' access to institutional finance- an empirical study. *Journal of Small Business & Entrepreneurship, 30*(4), 279–291. https://doi.org/10.1080/08276331.2017.1388952

Goyal, M., & Parkash, J. (2011). Women entrepreneurship in India-problems and prospects. *International Journal of Multidisciplinary Research, 1*(5), 195–207. https://www.academia.edu/7505511/14_Vol_01_Issue_05_MEENU_GOYAL_women_paper

Gruen, A. (2012). *Empatinin yitimi -kayıtsızlık politikası üzerine* (İ. İgan Translation). Çitlembik Yayınları.

Hancı, A. (2004). *Girişimcilikte cinsiyet faktörü ve kadın girişimciler üzerine bir araştırma* [Unpublished master's thesis]. Sakarya Üniversitesi.

Hashim, R. S., Ho-Abdullah, I., Raihanah, M.M., Noraini, M. D. Y., Hamdan, S. I., & Jamsari. E. A. (2012). Construction of a Muslim woman entrepreneur in Malay fiction. *Advances in Environment, Computational Chemistry and Bioscience (Proceedings of the 3rd International Conference on Arts and*

Culture ICAC 2012). https://www.academia.edu/3128985/Construction_of_A_Muslim_Woman_Entrepreneur_in_Malay_Fiction

Henry, C., Foss, L., Fayolle, A., Walker, E., & Duffy, S. (2015). Entrepreneurial leadership and gender: Exploring theory and practice in global contexts. *Journal of Small Business Management, 53*(3), 581–586. https://doi.org/10.1111/jsbm.12174

Herrman, H., Stewart, D. E., Diaz-Granados, N., Berger, E. L., Jackson, B., & Yuen, T. (2011). What is resilience? *Canadian Journal of Psychiatry, 56*(5), 258–265. https://doi.org/10.1177/070674371105600504

Huarng, K. H., Mas-Tur, A., & Yu, T. H. (2012). Factors affecting the success of women entrepreneurs. *International Entrepreneurship and Management Journal, 8*, 487–497. https://doi.org/10.1007/s11365-012-0233-4

Hundera, M. B., Duysters, G., Naude, W., & Dijkhuizen, J. (2020). How do role conflict intensity and coping strategies affect the success of women entrepreneurs in Africa? Evidence from Ethiopia. *Journal of Small Business Management*, https://doi.org/10.1080/00472778.2020.1756121

İlter, B. (2008). *Girişimcilik sürecinde kadın girişimcilerin karşılaştıkları sorunların analizi: KAGİDER örneği* [Unpublished doctoral dissertation]. Afyon Kocatepe University.

Jamali, D. (2009). Constraints and opportunities facing women entrepreneurs in developing countries a relational perspective. *Gender in Management: An International Journal, 24*(4), 232–251. https://doi.org/10.1108/17542410910961532

Kapinga, A. F., & Montero, C. S. (2017). Exploring the socio-cultural challenges of food processing women entrepreneurs in Irınga, Tanzanıa and strategies used to tackle them. *J Glob Entrepr Res, 7*(17), 2–24. https://doi.org/10.1186/s40497-017-0076-0

Kelley, D. J., Brush, C. G., Greene, P. G., & Litovsky, Y. (2011). *Global entrepreneurship monitor; 2010 women's report*. Global Entrepreneurship Research Association GEM. https://www.gemconsortium.org/report/gem-2010-womens-report

Kitching, B., & Woldie, A. (2004). Female Entrepreneurs in Transitional Economies: A comparative study of Businesswomen in Nigeria and China. *Proceedings of the Hawaii International Conference on Business, Honolulu*, https://core.ac.uk/download/pdf/10873453.pdf

Koray, M. (2000). *Sosyal Politika*, Ezgi Kitapevi.

Kumbhar, V. (2013). Some critical issues of women entrepreneurship in rural India. *European Academic Research, 1*(2), 192–200. https://doi.org/10.2139/ssrn.2043821

Kutanis, R. Ö., & Alpaslan, S. (2006). Girişimci ve yönetici kadınların profilleri farklı mıdır? *Afyon Kocatepe Üniversitesi İktisadi ve İdari Bilimler Fakültesi Dergisi, 8*(2), 139–153. https://dergipark.org.tr/tr/pub/akuiibfd/issue/1632/20471

Kutanis, R. Ö., & Karakiraz, A. (2013). Girişimcilikte cinsiyet faktörü. In Kaygın, E. & Güven, B. (Eds.), *Farklı Boyutlarıyla Kadın Girişimcilik* (pp. 15–27), Veritasakademi. https://www.academia.edu/37234319/Farkli_Boyutlariyla_Kadin_Girisimcilik

Lee, S., & Denslow, D. (2005). A study on the major problems of U.S. women-owned small busınesses. *Journal of Small Business Strategy, 15*(2), 77–89. https://core.ac.uk/download/pdf/236084073.pdf

Lituchy, T. R., & Reavley, M. A. (2004). Women entrepreneurs: A comparison of ınternational small business owners in Poland and the Czech Republic. *Journal of International Entrepreneurship 2*, 61–87. https://doi.org/10.1023/B:JIEN.0000026906.28190.df

Lyn, S. A., & Karin M. S. (2009). Women entrepreneurs in Sub-Saharan Africa: An institutional theory analysis from a social marketing point of view. *Entrepreneurship and Regional Development, 21*(2), 183–211. https://doi.org/10.1080/08985620802182144

Marshall, G. (1999). *Sosyoloji Sözlüğü*, İstanbul: Bilim ve Sanat.

McClelland, E., Swail, J., Bell, J., & Ibbotson, P. (2005). Following the pathway of female entrepreneurs: A six-country investigation. *International Journal of Entrepreneurial Behaviour & Research, 11*(2), 84–107. https://doi.org/10.1108/13552550510590527

McGowan, P., Cooper, M., Durkin, M., & O'Kane, C. (2015). The influence of social and human capital in developing young women as entrepreneurial business leaders. *Journal of Small Business Management, 53*(3), 645–661. https://doi.org/10.1111/jsbm.12176

McGowan, P., Redeker, C. L., Cooper, S. Y., & Greenan, K. (2012). Female entrepreneurship and the management of business and domestic roles: Motivations, expectations and realities. *Entrepreneurship & Regional Development, 24*(1–2), 53–72. https://doi.org/10.1080/08985626.2012.637351

Memiş, H., Paksoy, M., & Paksoy, S. (2007). Bölgesel kalkınmada kadın girişimciliğinin önemi: GAP bölgesinde bir araştırma. *Girişimcilik ve Kalkınma Dergisi, 2*(2), 137–152. http://acikerisim.lib.comu.edu.tr:8080/xmlui/handle/COMU/969

Miceli, P. L. (2012). *The acceptance of complexity: Effects on psychological well-being and resilience* [Unpublished doctoral dissertation]. University of North Carolina. https://doi.org/10.17615/fn7f-b388

Mohamadi, K. (2020). *In Depth Analysis of women entrepreneurs in Turkey, Germany and Iran* [Unpublished master's thesis]. Yıldız Technical University.

Naktiyok, A. (2013). Türkiye'de kadın girişimciliği ve önündeki engeller. *I. Uluslararası Katılımlı Kadın Girişimcilik Çalıştayı,* 16–17 Mayıs 2013, Bildiri Kitabı, 80–86. http://kentarsivi.corum.bel.tr/wp-content/uploads/2017/12/%C3 %87al%C4 %B1 %C5 %9Ftay-Kitap.pdf

On, A. (2011). Women entrepreneurship in Romania. *Revista Romana de Economie (Romanian Journal of Economics), 42*(2), 138–145. https://revecon.ro/articles/2011-2/2011-2-8.pdf

Orhan, M. (2001). Women business owners in France: The issue of financing discrimination. *Journal of Small Business Management, 39*(1), 95–102. https://doi.org/10.1111/0447-2778.00009

Ödemiş, G. (2018). *Kadın girişimcilerin iş-yaşam dengesi üzerine bir araştırma: İzmir ili örneği* [Unpublished master's thesis]. Kâtip Çelebi University. http://acikerisim.ikc.edu.tr:8080/xmlui/bitstream/handle/11469/327/215-YLT%20Gizem%20 %C3 %96demi%C5 %9F%202018 %20-YOK.pdf?sequence=1&isAllowed=y

Özçatal, Ö. E. (2009). Kadınların işgücü piyasasına katılımını ve çalışma koşullarını etkileyen sosyo-demografik ve kültürel faktörler. *Uluslararası-Disiplinlerarası Kadın Çalışmaları Kongresi Bildiriler Kitabı, Sakarya,* 45–54. http://www.kadinkongre.sakarya.edu.tr/kadin_calismalari_kongresi_cilt_1.pdf

Özkaya, M. O. (2009). Kadın girişimcilere yönelik "strateji geliştirmede" yerel yönetimlerle işbirliği içinde olmak, mümkün mü? *Yönetim ve Ekonomi Araştırmaları Dergisi, 7*(11), 56–72. https://dergipark.org.tr/tr/pub/yead/issue/21820/234552

Öztürk, M. D. (2016). *Türkiye'de kadın girişimcilik: Kadınları girişimciliğe yönelten faktörler, karşılaştıkları sorunlar ve çözüm önerileri* [Unpublished master's thesis]. İstanbul Ticaret University. http://acikerisim.ticaret.edu.tr/xmlui/handle/11467/2241

Öztürk, M. Y., & Dedeoğlu, S. (2010). Kapitalizm, ataerkillik ve kadın emeği: Türkiye örneği. In Kurt, S. (Eds.), *Sosyal Araştırmalar Vakfı Yayınları Küreselleşme Dizisi* (pp. 11–26). Sosyal Araştırmalar Vakfı İktisadi İşletmesi. https://www.academia.edu/35474904/Kapitalizm_Ataerkillik_ve_Kad%C4 %B1n_Eme%C4 %9Fi_T%C3 %BCrkiye_%C3 %96rne%C4 %9Fi

Padmavathi, D. (2011). Sustainable development of rural women entrepreneurs. *2nd International Conference on Business, Economics and Tourism Management, IPEDR, 24,* 67–72. IACSIT Press, Singapore. http://www.ipedr.com/vol24/14-CBETM2011-M10017.pdf

Pandey, A., Raman, A. V., & Kaul, V. K. (2013). Women entrepreneurship from a global perspective. *International Journal of Research in Commerce, Economics & Management, 3*(6), 10–16. https://www.academia.edu/4194970/Women_Entrepreneurship_from_a_Global_Perspective

Papatya, G. (2013). Yeni İş/İşletmecilik Dünyasında Kadın Liderliği: Girişimci Kadınlar İçin Genişletilmiş Okumalar ve Notlar. In Kaygın, E. & Güven, B. (Eds.), *Farklı Boyutlarıyla Kadın Girişimcilik* (pp. 213–239), Veritasakademi. https://www.academia.edu/37234319/Farkli_Boyutlariyla_Kadin_Girisimcilik

Pardo-del-Val, M. (2009). Growth-oriented women entrepreneurs and their businesses. *International Entrepreneurship and Management Journal, 5,* 117–120. https://doi.org/10.1007/s11365-008-0107-y

Pocol, C. B., & Moldovan-Teselios, C. (2014). Women entrepreneurship in Romania: A regional evaluation. *Bulletin of University of Agricultural Sciences and Veterinary Medicine Cluj-Napoca. Horticulture, 71*(2), 408–416. http://dx.doi.org/10.15835/buasvmcn-hort:10607

Rawat, P. (2014). Patriarchal beliefs, women's empowerment and general well-being. *Vikalpa: The Journal for Decision Makers, 39*(2), 43–55. https://doi.org/10.1177/0256090920140206

Rita, R., Rabiah, A., & Fahlevi, M. (2019). Women entrepreneurs in Indonesia. *Journal of Research in Business, Economics and Management, 13*(2), 2416–2425. http://www.scitecresearch.com/journals/index.php/jrbem/article/view/1728.

Roomi, M. A., & Parrott, G. (2008). Barriers to development and progression of women entrepreneurs in Pakistan. *International Journal of Entrepreneurship, 17*(1), 59–72. https://doi.org/10.1177/097135570701700105

Ryff, C. D., Friedman, E. M., Morozink, J. A., & Tsenkofa, V. (2012). Psychological resilience in adulthood and later life: Implications for health. *Annual Review of Gerontology and Geriatrics, 32*(1), 73–92. https://doi.org/10.1891/0198-8794.32.73

Sangode, P., & Vakhariya, S. (2013). Barriers for women entrepreneurs in Nagpur region. *Elk Asia Pacific Journal of Marketing and Retail Management, 4*(3). https://www.elkjournals.com/MasterAdmin/UploadFolder/7.%20BARRIERS%20FOR%20WOMEN%20ENTREPRENEURS%20IN%20NAGPUR%20REGION-2/7.%20BARRIERS%20FOR%20WOMEN%20ENTREPRENEURS%20IN%20NAGPUR%20REGION-2.pdf

Sangolagi, K., & Alagawadi, M. (2016). Women entrepreneurs. *International Journal of Advancement in Engineering Technology, Management & Applied Science. 3*(1), 216–222. https://www.researchgate.net/publication/316430274_Women_Entrepreneurs

Santos, F.J. (2009). Women entrepreneurs across racial lines: Issues of human capital, financial capital and network structures. *International Entrepreneurship and Management Journal, 5*, 341–344. https://doi.org/10.1007/s11365-007-0067-7

Sarhan, N. (2019). *Women entrepreneurs access to justice in Egypt* [Unpublished master's thesis]. University of Sussex. https://www.academia.edu/41672656/Women_entrepreneurs_access_to_justice_in_Egypt

Satre, A. M., (2016). Women's entrepreneurship in Russia: Impacts from the Soviet system. *Journal of Enterprising Communities: People and Places in the Global Economy, 10*(1), 53–69. http://dx.doi.org/10.1108/JEC-08-2015-0045

Sayın, E. (2011). Kadın Girişimcilerin Sorunlarının Betimleyici Analizi. *Organizasyon ve Yönetim Bilimleri Dergisi. 3*(1), 23–32. https://dergipark.org.tr/tr/pub/oybd/issue/16337/171040

Soysal, A. (2010). Türkiye'de kadın girişimciler: Engeller ve fırsatlar bağlamında bir değerlendirme. *Ankara Üniversitesi SBF Dergisi, 65*(1), 83–114. https://doi.org/10.1501/SBFder_0000002153

Soysal, A. (2013). Kırsal alanda kadınların girişimcilik faaliyet ve yeteneklerini etkileyen ve engelleyen faktörler. In Kaygın, E. & Güven, B. (Eds.), *Farklı Boyutlarıyla Kadın Girişimcilik* (pp. 93–111). Veritasakademi. https://www.academia.edu/37234319/Farkli_Boyutlariyla_Kadin_Girisimcilik

Starcher, D. C. (1996). Women entrepreneurs: Catalysts for transformation. *European Baha'i Business Forum*. http://www.ebbf.org/woman.htm

Sullivan, L. E., Johnson, R. B., Mercado, C. C., & Terry, K. J. (Eds.). (2009). *The sage glossary of the social and behavioral sciences*. Sage Publications, Inc. https://doi.org/10.4135/9781412972024

Tan, J. (2008). Breaking the "bamboo curtain" and the "glass ceiling": The experience of women entrepreneurs in high-tech industries in an emerging market. *Journal of Business Ethics, 80*, 547–564. https://doi.org/10.1007/s10551-007-9454-9

Tlaiss, H. A. (2015). How Islamic business ethics impact women entrepreneurs: Insight from four Arab Middle Eastern Countries. *Journal of Business Ethics, Special Issue on Globalization, Development and Islamic Business Ethics, 129*(4), 859–877. https://www.jstor.org/stable/24702982, https://doi.org/10.1007/s10551-014-2138-3

Toksöz, G. (2007). İşgücü piyasasının toplumsal cinsiyet perspektifinden analizi ve bölgeler arası dengesizlikler. *Çalışma ve Toplum, 4*(15), 57–79. https://www.calismatoplum.org/makale/isgucu-piyasasinin-toplumsal-cinsiyet-perspektifinden-analizi-ve-bolgeler-arasi-dengesizlikler

Toros, E., & Altınay, M. (2018). Women entrepreneurs as employers. *Open Access Peer-Reviewed Chapter.* http://doi.org/10.5772/intechopen.80309

Tulan D., & Türko, E. S. (2018). Kadın girişimciliği: Erzurum ilinde bir uygulama. *Finans Ekonomi ve Sosyal Araştırmalar Dergisi. 3*(1), 285–306. https://doi.org/10.29106/fesa.364291

Türko, E. S. (2016). Can entrepreneurship education reduce stereotypes against women entrepreneurship? *International Education Studies, 9*(11), 53–65. http://dx.doi.org/10.5539/ies.v9n11p53

Türko, E. S. & Tulan, D. (2019). Evlilik neyi değiştirir? Kadın girişimciler üzerine karşılaştırmalı bir uygulama. *Anemon Muş Alparslan Üniversitesi Sosyal Bilimler Dergisi, 7*(2) 245–256. https://doi.org/10.18506/anemon.461971

Vatandaş, C. (2007). Toplumsal cinsiyet ve cinsiyet rollerinin algılanışı. *Sosyoloji Konferansları, 0*(35), 29–56. https://dergipark.org.tr/tr/pub/iusoskon/issue/9517/118909

Vatandaş, C., & Erdoğan, M. (2020). Bireysel ve toplumsal dışlanma pratiği: Önyargı ve ayrımcılık. *İnsan ve Sosyal Bilimler Dergisi, 3*(1), 474–485. https://dergipark.org.tr/tr/pub/johass/issue/54512/724821

Velmurugan, R. (2015). Problems of women entrepreneurship. *Intercontinental Journal of Human Resource Research Review, Print Impact Factor, 3*(1), 101–104. https://www.researchgate.net/publication/322852130_PROBLEMS_OF_WOMEN_ENTREPRENEURSHIP

Vescio, T., & Weaver, K. (2013). Prejudice and stereotyping. *Oxford Bibliographies.* http://dx.doi.org/10.1093/obo/9780199828340-0097

Vial, V., & Richomme-Huet, K. (2017). Women entrepreneurs in France. *International Journal of Entrepreneurship and Small Business, 30*(1), 80–109. http://dx.doi.org/10.1504/IJESB.2017.081034

Wahdiniwaty, R., & Rustam D. A. (2019). Patriarchy as a barrier to women entrepreneurs in Indonesia. *IOP Conference Series Materials Science and Engineering. 662*(3), 1–4. http://dx.doi.org/10.1088/1757-899X/662/3/032042 https://iopscience.iop.org/article/10.1088/1757-899X/662/3/032042

Weiler, S., & Bernasek, A. (2001). Dodging the glass ceiling? Networks and the new wave of women entrepreneurs. *The Social Science Journal, 38*(1), 85–103. https://doi.org/10.1016/S0362-3319(00)00111-7

Welter, F. (2006). Women's entrepreneurship in Germany: Progress in a still traditional environment. In Brush, C., Carter, N., Greene, P., Gatewood, B., & Hart, M. (Eds), *Growth Oriented Women Entrepreneurs and Their Businesses,* A Global Research Perspective. https://www.researchgate.net/publication/235966771_Women's_entrepreneurship_in_Germany_Progress_in_a_still_traditional_environment

Ylinenpaa, H., & Chechuriana, M. (2000). Perceptions of female entrepreneurship in Russia. *Lulea: Lulea Tekniska Universitet*, 1–16. https://www.diva-portal.org/smash/record.jsf?pid=diva2 %3A995380&dswid=-8412

Zincir, O., & Tunç, A. Ö (2019). "Kendi yolumu kendim çizdim": ABD'nin ilk Afrika kökenli kadın milyoneri Madam CJ Walker'ın girişimci kariyerinin incelenmesi. *Marmara Üniversitesi İktisadi ve İdari Bilimler Dergisi, 41*(2), 556–582. https://doi.org/10.14780/muiibd.665808

Hasan GÜNEŞ[1]

Women Exporters

The entrepreneurial activities of women have significant importance for the regional and national economic developments (Türko, 2016: 53). The increasing number of women entrepreneurs in economy throughout the world had significant contributions (Kelly et al., 2011). One of the terms widely used regarding the promotion of economic growth through individual efforts in compliance with neo-liberal thoughts since 1980s has been the women entrepreneurship (Chitsike, 2000: 71). The advancement in information technologies and the improvements in communication networks and platforms, and in education opportunities as well, allowed women to be more frequently seen in any field of business life. Within this context, entrepreneurship has become one of the most inviting fields in women's career plans (Güney, 2006: 26).

Constituting almost more than 40 % of the global labor force, women provided the labor market with new productive skills. There are more than 126 million women entrepreneurs founding and managing businesses throughout the world. Besides that, there also are more than 98 million businesses founded by women. These women in business life provide innovation and new employment opportunities (GEM, 2015: 10). For this reason, women entrepreneurship recently started drawing interest of policymakers and academic circles (Jennings & Brush, 2013; Henry et al., 2015).

As stated by the studies dating far back, the export activity has been identified as a market entry behavior (Welch et al., 2008: 114) and this type of behavior has strengthened with the concept of export entrepreneurship (Etemad, 2005; Ibeh & Young, 2001; Welch et al., 2008: 115). In today's economies, where the outward-oriented export models increased, participation of women entrepreneurs in export activities constitutes an important part of the economic growth. Women entrepreneurs' engagement in export incorporates many dynamics from both social and economic aspects. The activities of exporter women entrepreneurs play important role for the involvement of more women entrepreneurs in export since they are seen as role models. Since

1 Research Assistant, Erzurum Technical University, Faculty of Economics and Administrative Sciences, Department of Economics, hasan.gunes@erzurum.edu.tr, ORCID ID: 0000-0001-9924-0167

the benefits obtained from export are spread through different segments of the society, it plays an important role in the economic development (Can & Karataş, 2007: 253).

Besides the fact that women are an important part of economic development, the entrepreneurial opportunities of women are also limited by the obstacles that they face. These obstacles also limit the export activities of women entrepreneurs (WTO, 2017a). For instance, as stated by the International Trade Center (ITC, 2017), even though 40 % of the businesses worldwide belong to women or are managed by women, only 15 % of the businesses engaging in export activities are managed by women entrepreneurs. For this reason, it is very important to guarantee a better adaptation alignment of women to the foreign trade system (WTO, 2017a). Within this context, the International Trade Center aimed to integrate a minimum of 1 million new women entrepreneurs as of the year of 2002 (ITC, 2015).

There are several factors confining the involvement of women entrepreneurs in export activities; these factors can be summarized as social restrictions, financial difficulties, lack of knowledge and experience, diplomatic and bureaucratic obstacles, and social anti-feminine biases and norms (ITC, 2015: 21–25).

Entrepreneur and Exporter Women

Being one of the most important shareholders contributing to the international trade, women offer significant support to the development of foreign trade as manufacturer, entrepreneur, employee, and consumer. From this aspect, the most important contribution of women occurs through the businesses they own or run (ITC, 2015: 2).

In most of developed economies, women draw more interest as the new pioneers of the economic development (In Hyeock Lee et al., 2016). The benefits of women exporters' economic activities for the foreign trade and global economy come forward as an idea that is gradually more accepted. However, the women have a limited participation in the foreign trade activities. Besides that, women exporters' activities significantly vary by the countries and regions (ITC, 2015: 24).

Low level of women's representation in international trade is also one of the subjects remarkably occupying the political agenda. Within this context, as stated in the Buenos Aires Declaration on Trade and Women's Economic Empowerment approved in Buenos Aires WTO Ministerial Conference in 2017, it was adopted that empowering the women entrepreneurs, reducing the gender inequality, and establishing more inclusive trade policies would allow achieving the economic growth more effectively. In parallel with this idea, several international organizations developed programs in order to eliminate the obstacles to women's trade activities, support their economic empowerment, and help them with their involvement in foreign trade activities (WTO, 2017a: 71).

The increase in the number of women entrepreneurs actively engaging in export activities became one of the subjects drawing attention in recent years. The trend that is accepted at global scale, besides in the developed countries, is to ensure more women establishing and managing their own businesses (Adler, 2004). Furthermore, another notion is the globalization. Together with the increasing interconnection of markets and the competition exceeding beyond the borders, the number of exporter businesses also started increasing (UNCTAD, 2004: 5).

The economic opportunities enabling women to participate in export activities have positive effects also on the economic development. This is true especially when it allows women to participate in international trade. According to the results reported in a study carried out in the United States of America, the economic benefits of the exports of women-owned businesses is more than the non-exporter businesses (ITC, 2015: 2).

As stated in a study carried out by Dana and Wright (2004), regardless of their locations, the businesses have to face the fact that they have to compete in the globalizing market. Thus, together with the more businesses penetrating the foreign markets, the more women become exporters owning a business (Dana & Wright, 2004: 11)

In the first studies on export activities, it can be seen that the women exporters were rarely seen. However, despite the increase in their number, the women exporters have a small share in the total exporters even in the recent period. This causes the women exporters to be a statistical noise in the studies carried out on this subject (Welch et al., 2008: 114). For instance, it can be stated that Westhead et al. (2001) excluded the gender variable from their study on the export because the authors considered it as an exception.

Even though the gender variable was found to be not significant, previous studies incorporate the hypothesis that the men entrepreneurs' possibility of being exporter was higher than that of women entrepreneurs (Welch et al., 2008: 114). However, in their studies on the export behavior of women, Grondin and Grondin (1994) and Grondin and Schaefer (1995) examined the exporter and non-exporter women entrepreneurs (Grondin & Grondin, 1994; Grondin & Schaefer, 1995).

Another one of the fields incorporating the largest gender gap in business administration and foreign trade super-cluster is the ownership or management of businesses. When compared to women, the exporter businesses are generally owned or managed by men. According to the results of a survey conducted with approx. 19,000 businesses in 99 developing countries, it was concluded that only 36 % of businesses were partially or completely owned by women (Davies & Mazhikeyev, 2015). For the exporters, this ratio decreases down to 15 %. Since it is related with several development indictors such as GDP per capita, low ratio of women entrepreneurs poses an important problem for the economic development (Amin, 2014).

1. Profile and Characteristics of Women Exporters

They are willing to take risks, have high self-confidence, and are assertive and courageous about penetrating the distant markets. Besides that, the individuals avoiding taking risk tend to trade in familiar markets that are closer to their locations. Accordingly, the exporting market targets of women entrepreneurs are the near or neighbor markets that they can easily access (van Staveren, 2013: 110).

When compared to the men-owned businesses, the women-owned businesses exhibit more timid behaviors in terms or taking risk and engaging in new entrepreneurial activities. As a result of this, the location selection made by women-owned foreign trade companies differs from their rivals. Moreover, when compared to women exporters, men exporters tend to take more risk and be more ambitious and assertive (Williams & Best, 1990; Lee at al. 2016). Women exporters are, however, more inclined to guiding when compared to men.

With the freedom and flexibility of managing a business rather than being motivated by financial gains, women business administrators are able to combine their families and career plans (Fischer et al., 1993; Marlow, 1997; Burt, 1998; Fasci & Valdez, 1998; DeMartino & Barbato, 2003; Hughes, 2005, Lee et al., 2016). However, the need for achieving the work-life balance poses extra obstacles and difficulties for women exporters in their decisions about entering new markets (Chelekis & Mudambi, 2010: 418). The reasons of women exporters for establishing their export enterprises in near countries include the need for establishing the balance between family and business at the same time (Lee et al., 2016).

In their study, Davies & Mazhikeyev (2015) emphasized that, rather than the trade barriers, women exporters have problem with learning from export. A limitation of their study was that they didn't directly test the selection of learning from or towards export (Davies & Mazhikeyev, 2015: 2).

Chiu and Froman (2018) reported that the businesses, which are managed by women, engage in export activities much less than their rivals. Considering the positive effects of businesses managed by women on economy and society, this finding seems very surprising. Moreover, D'Espallier (2011) stated that the businesses managed by women paying their credits and debts faster and more reliably than their rivals; according to WTO (2017a), the debt discharging ratio of women entrepreneurs is very high (98 %) (D'Espallier, 2011: 7). Besides that, the women-owned businesses have positive effect on the women employment by employing more women employees (ITC, 2015).

According to an interesting result reported for exporter women entrepreneurs, the women exporters have a higher educational level than non-exporter women business managers (Canadian Trade Commissioner, 2016: 4). Encouraging the women entrepreneurs for export positively affects the economy and society. Since women have important investments in fields such as child education and health, a high level of income that they would gain is accepted as one of the most important instruments needed for reducing the poverty in developing world (ITC, 2015).

The research carried out using ITC's company-level data revealed 7 fundamental findings about the women exporters:

* The women-owned exporter businesses constitute only one-fifth of the total of exporter businesses. The highest level of this ratio was observed in Latin America and Caribbean, whereas the lowest ratio was found in Western Africa.
* It was determined that women tend to work at large-scale exporter companies rather than small-scale companies.
* Large-scale exporter businesses employ more women employees when compared to small-scaled businesses.
* It was concluded that women tend to own small-scaled businesses, which are at lower level also in terms of employment opportunities. However, small-scale businesses generally do not have the sources needed for export.
* Women exporters engage in different sectors than men. The sectors, where the export activities of businesses owned or managed by women are at the highest level, are textile and clothing sectors. Besides that, the ratio of ownership by women entrepreneurs in sectors such as computer, telecommunication, and consumer electronics that are generally associated with men is 23 %.
* As with the women exporters, women employment is also at a higher level in traditional sectors of women exporters. Women generally prefer businesses

in fabric and textile, leather, and leather products sectors for working. Women exporters and employees avoid the businesses operating in transportation equipment, electrical machine, and main manufacturing sectors.

* The geographical characteristics of the countries play effective role in the industries, in which women exporters have businesses and engage in (ITC, 2015: 7).

The export efficiency of businesses owned by women entrepreneurs is lower when compared to those owned by men entrepreneurs. One of the reasons for this difference is the insufficiency of women entrepreneurs in using communication technologies in contacting new buyers and providers in their export operations. One of the most apparent examples is that the use of e-mail in women-managed businesses is 12 % lower than in men-owned businesses. Besides that, the discrimination at the border during the export operations can be an important factor restricting the benefits of foreign trade for the women. The digital instruments such as single window might hinder or decrease the personal interaction in trade and it might sometimes complicate the transportation of goods exported by women exporters (WTO, 2017a: 232).

The previous studies concluded that the rate of technology usage was low in women-owned businesses. Policymakers developed various actions and programs in order to promote the access to digital technologies that might increase the competitive power of women exporters. Some of these actions include special programs developed for teaching certain skills to girls, promoting the participation of women entrepreneurs by improving the online context, and integrating the women into trade strategies (WTO, 2017b: 233).

The studies on export entrepreneurship generally focused on determining the personality traits of entrepreneur, which is one of the major determinants of entrepreneurial activities. However, the studies overlooked the psychological and demographic characteristics that are specific to entrepreneur (Mitchell et al., 2002: 95). Besides that, in addition to the export studies, also investigating the characteristics including the gender-related variables arises as an alternative.

The studies examining the women entrepreneurship, which draws more attention than women's export behaviors, focused on measuring the effects of gender-based differences. One of the subjects focused on is the relationship between gender and risk-taking. Within this context, some of the studies pointed out that exporter women entrepreneurs and administrators tend to take less risk (Zinkhan & Karande, 1991). Besides that, men and women entrepreneurs may vary in terms of the desire to grow. Bird and Brush (2002) claimed that women entrepreneurs tend to prefer longevity rather than growth fast (Bird & Brush, 2002).

Weiler and Bernasek pointed out that women attach importance to proving themselves rather than making profit (Weiler & Bernasek, 2001: 100). Cliffs stated that the criterion of success for women entrepreneurs, in comparison to their peers, is a controlled and manageable growth (Cliffs, 1998: 535).

2. Export Barriers to Women Entrepreneurs

There are numerous obstacles and barriers that women exporters are subjected to. These obstacles can be summarized as;

- Difficulty of access to finance and capital,
- Difficult of access to information and networks,
- Diplomatic problems that women exporters have in using their assets,
- Their social and familial commitments,
- Anti-feminine norms in the society,

Although these barriers that women exporters face also influence the non-exporter women entrepreneurs, export operations place great demands on the women exporters since they require more capital, access to market networks, foreign trades skills, travel activities, and more time for more intense working tempo (ITC, 2015: 21–25).

The barriers that women exporters face with can be categorized as demand-side and supply-side barriers. The demand-side barriers can be exemplified with preferring men exporters and businessmen over women exporters and lack of information about women exporters' skills and knowledge. This approach also embodies the business networks alienating the women or complicating their participation into business life. The supply-side obstacles include non-flexible working hours of women, their possibility of suspending their careers due to familial reasons, and their responsibilities such as housework and childcare. Besides that, the few number (numbers) of women exporters, who can be a role model, and the preferences or requests arising from lack of knowledge can be referred as supply-side barriers (Pande & Ford, 2011: 7).

Moreover, women's access to important trade networks can be inhibited much more easily. Given the time-consuming trade procedures, paper works, and time they spend for family and housework, it can be seen that women are subject to time deficiency. When compared to their rivals, women working in the production of goods and services required for export have less competencies regarding providing the inputs that will improve their productivity and increase their competitive power in cross-border markets (Brenton et al., 2013: 60).

Moreover, there is a comprehensive literature on the wage differences between women and men in exporter and non-exporter businesses, besides the women exporters (Goldin, 2014: 1098). In literature, a large body of studies focused on explaining the relationship between foreign trade, gender, productivity, and wages.

Using a dataset covering the business owners and workers, Boler investigated the gender-based wage differences in exporter Norwegian businesses. Because of their families and childcare responsibilities, women have less time for business life when compared to men. Besides that, exporting businesses face with intense competition conditions and they may require longer working hours. Under these conditions, the wages of male employees promising longer working hours increase to the detriment of female employees. Women expressed that they would be more successful in working at exporter businesses when supporting the child care in addition to business (Boler et al., 2018: 123).

The women-owned businesses have insufficient appearance in foreign trade because of various factors. These factors can be summarized as social, cultural, and regulatory barriers. These barriers prevent or hinder women from founding and managing businesses. The pressure of childbearing and housework, which are among the social barriers and considered as the duties of women in many countries worldwide, are seen among the factors placing a burden on the women in business life. Given the studies carried out on this subject, it can be seen that cultural and regulatory barriers, educational opportunities, and workload in the family play an important role in women entrepreneurs' integration to the foreign trade. Based on these points, the factors influencing the motivation of women exporters can be classified as follows;

* Time limitations arising from the responsibilities of women entrepreneurs;
* Difficulty of access to productive resources;
* Difficulty of access to foreign trade networks and information;
* Incompliance between women's skills and foreign trade;

Besides the factors specified above, the women-owned businesses have a smaller scale and are less productive when compared to an average business engaged in foreign trade. For this reason, they have problems in affording the fixed costs they face in foreign trade. In women-owned businesses, this disadvantage causes them to be affected by the costs such as non-tariff barriers more than other businesses.

Besides that, decreasing the cultural barriers negatively affecting the women exporters and facilitating the women's access to markets for trade activities might yield a strong influence (ITC, 2015: 14).

In her study, Dr. Linda Scott concluded that there is a consistent positive relationship between country's competitiveness and women's economic advantage at the national level. Thus, the countries offering higher level of economic advantages and opportunities to women have a more competitive position in the foreign trade (Scott, 2014).

Vast majority of the studies addressing the administrative effects on the export behavior do not specifically include the gender of exporter as an independent variable. There are few studies using the gender of exporter as a demographic variable and incorporate the biological sex (i.e., asking if the responder is woman or man). In a study carried out by Manolova, Brush, Edelman, and Green, the gender was categorized and defined as a demographic variable. Moreover, the authors also highlighted that this gender-based negligence might be as effective as the other factor influencing the internationalization and it should be considered together with other factors (Manolova et al., 2002: 14–15).

When facing with the same trade barriers with men-owned businesses, the women-owned businesses bear higher costs to overcome these trade barriers. For this reason, the effect to arise from the growth of businesses owned by women exporters would be more effective in meeting the costs (Davies & Mazhikeyev, 2015: 4).

The effect of advanced network-based trade supports on decreasing the barriers to women exporters might not be explicitly understood (Davies & Mazhikeyev, 2015: 2). However, network connections eliminate the face-to-face interactions or the electronic systems masking the gender of export operation's parties may sweep the hindering factors arising from the gender discrimination. For instance, the women exporters making effort to comply with standards and regulations have to involve in a process requiring multiple face-to-face communications and they are subject to authorities' discriminative behaviors (ITC, 2016: 50).

Besides posing a disadvantage, the face-to-face interaction is also an effective factor for the women-managed businesses since the digital solutions offer benefits by eliminating the causes of discriminations. For example, it is important that women exporters face with significant barriers in cross-border trade. These barriers may range from high bribes to gender-based violence (WTO, 2017a). For instance, it was reported by UNECA, AU, and AfDB that 37 % of women merchants are subject to gender-based violence in cross-border trade and 15 % of women merchants are forced to sexual intercourse in Liberia. There are several problems arising from the face-to-face interactions that women entrepreneurs have while requesting the licenses required for cross-border trade or continuing the export operations. From this aspect, the use of digital solution networks may help with decreasing the negative effects on women exporters while executing their operations (UNECA, 2010: 441).

Single window, an electronic system that can help women exporters, has been designed as a part of 2013 WTO Trade Facilitation Agreement. This system allows the procurement of regulatory documents and certificates for the merchants and removes the need for visiting multiple officers to export a product (WTO, 2017a). This system and similar ones support the women-owned businesses aiming to enter the international markets and having an export potential (WTO, 2017b: 234).

Besides establishing the trade networks, it might provide the women exporters or the women managers of exporter businesses with important benefits because reducing the number of intermediaries in export operations would reduce the number of face-to-face interactions. There are many online platforms allowing the women entrepreneurs to directly contact with international buyers. ITC's "SheTrades" platform is one of the most effective and successful platforms. This platform enables thousands of women exporters to establish connection with buyers at the same time and introduce their products to the international market. Establishing direct connection with buyers enables women to have higher shares from foreign trade profits and decreases the income inequality (WTO, 2017b: 234).

There are evidences proving that women exporters face with social and structural barriers and even an explicit discrimination. These barriers are related with access to financial, communicational, and human capitals. The difficulty in access to financial capital is the most widely accepted barrier among them. As reported in a study carried out on the service businesses in the USA, women-owned businesses are subject to higher interest rates and have to pay higher amounts of deposits. This finding indicates that women face with difficult conditions in access to financial capital (Coleman, 2000: 49).

Rothstein, Burke, and Bristor concluded that women have weaknesses in terms of having strong organizational networks and they receive more support from their connections with other women when compared to the men (Rothstein et al., 2001). In their study, Smeltzer and Fann (1989) examined the participation in foreign trade networks and reported that women want to communicate with women as a source of information and that they regard this communication as both social and instrumental trade support (Welch et al., 2008).

The increasing participation of women-owned businesses in export did not progress synchronously with the studies on their experience and behaviors. This causes the lack of information and data. Thus, it concerns policymakers aiming to encourage more women entrepreneurs for exporting.

3. Conclusion – Being Women Exporters in Different Countries and Regions

The women-owned businesses increased their cross-border trade in the recent period. The enterprises established by women exporters have 3 % share in developing Asian countries but this ratio increases to 27 % in developed European countries (Kelley et al., 2013: 8–27). Furthermore, the studies carried out on women entrepreneurs showed that women entrepreneurs are likely subjected to barriers in business process. Thus, the performance of women-owned businesses might be worse than that of men-owned businesses because the entrepreneurship is a process that incorporates gender differences (Eddleston & Powell, 2008: 247).

As in many regions, women are important trade partners in Africa too; they produce especially the food products and own or manage trade-oriented businesses. Manufacturer and merchant women in Africa generally face with certain barriers confining their trade activities. African women merchants operating in shadow sectors are generally exposed to abuse and robbery at the border.

The studies carried out by World Bank prove that the operations of women exporters are at small-scale (Amin, 2014: 4). Sabarwal and Terrell carried out a study on 26 transition economies. The authors concluded that women-owned businesses are at small scale in terms of employment and sales (Sabarwal & Terrell, 2008).

Examining the country group consisting of Tunisia, Cambodia, Senegal, United Republic of Tanzania, and Jamaica comprehensively, it was found that the exporter businesses owned or managed by women entrepreneurs have differences:

- The idea of ownership is more common among the businesses managed by women in Tunisia, Cambodia, and Senegal.
- In Jamaica and United Republic of Tanzania, women entrepreneurs tend to own an exporter business rather than working as a manager in such companies.

- When compared to the women in other countries, Jamaican women have a higher share in terms of owning and managing an exporter business.

There are some interesting details in the NTM Survey. In Jamaica, many businesses employing women in top management team are also owned by women. However, very few businesses are managed by women but owned by men. On the other hand, the situation is different in Cambodia. Many exporter businesses in Cambodia are managed but not owned by women. The situation in Tunisian exporter businesses is quite different; even though almost all of the exporter businesses are managed by women, almost none of them is owned by women (ITC, 2015: 7–8).

In recent years, the connections linking the countries' foreign trade activities have significantly grown and deepened. This advancement facilitates women-owned or women-managed businesses' communication with clients and providers at different locations of the world (WTO, 2017b: 220).

Although there are few experimental data, the results obtained from the studies suggest that the women-owned businesses' potential to export is lower than that of men-owned businesses. In a study carried out on the businesses in Australia, Harcourt reported that only 9 % of women-managed businesses engaged in export, the same ratio was 14 % for the businesses managed by men (Harcourt, 2006).

References

Adler, N.J. (2004). Women in international entrepreneurship. In Paul, L. (Ed.), *Handbook of Research on International Entrepreneurship*. Edward Elgar. https://doi.org/10.4337/9781845420512.00010

Amin, M., & Islam, A. (2014). *Presence of Woman in Top Managerial Positions*. World Bank Group Enterprise Note, 29. Washington D.C.

Bird, B., & Brush, C. (2002). A gendered perspective on organizational creation. *Entrepreneurship Theory and Practice*, *26*(3), 41–65. https://doi.org/10.1177/104225870202600303

Boler, E.A., Javorcik, B., & Ulltveit-Moe, K.H. (2018). Working across time zones: Exporters and the gender wage gap. *Journal of International Economics*, *111*, 122–133. https://doi.org/10.1016/j.jinteco.2017.12.008

Brenton, P., Gamberoni, E., & Sear, C. (2013). *Women and Trade in Africa: Realizing the Potential*. World Bank.

Burt, R.S. (1998). The gender of social capital. *Rationalty and Society*, *10*(1), 5–46. https://doi.org/10.1177/104346398010001001

Can, Y., & Karataş, A. (2007). Yerel ekonomilerde kalkınmanın itici gücü olarak kadın girişimcilerin rolü ve mikro finansman: Muğla ili örneği. *Selçuk Üniversitesi Karaman İ.İ.B.F. Dergisi Yerel Ekonomiler Özel Sayısı*, 251–261. http://hdl.handle.net/20.500.11857/329

Canadian Trade Commissioner (2016). *Majority-Female owned exporting SMEs in Canada*, 1–16. https://www.tradecommissioner.gc.ca/businesswomen-femmesdaffaires/2016-MFO_SMES-PME_EDMF.aspx?lang=eng

Chelekis, J., & Mudambi, S.M. (2010). MNCs and micro-entrepreneurship in emerging economies: The case of Avon in the Amazon. *Journal of International Management, 16*(4), 412–424. https://doi.org/10.1016/j.intman.2010.09.010

Chitsike, C. (2000). Culture as a barrier to rural women's entrepreneurship: experience from Zimbabwe. *Gender & Development*, *8*(1), 71–77. https://doi.org/10.1080/741923408

Chiu, B. (2018). Women-run businesses aren't exporting enough – but things are changing. *Forbes*. https://www.forbes.com/sites/bonniechiu/2018/10/05/female-entrepreneurs-are-going-global-new-policy-attention-may-close-the-gap/?sh=762975002df7

Cliffs, J.E. (1998). Does one size fit all? Exploring the relationship between attitudes towards growth, gender and business size. *Journal of Business Venturing, 13*, 523–542. https://doi.org/10.1016/S0883-9026(97)00071-2

Coleman, S. (2000). Access to capital and terms of credit: A comparison of men- and women-owned small businesses. *Journal of Small Business Management, 38*(3), 37–52.

Dana, L.P., & Wright R.W. (2004). Emerging paradigms of international entrepreneurship. *Handbook of Research on International Entrepreneurship*. https://books.google.com.tr/books?hl=tr&lr=&id=bmiusiqCuMQC&oi=fnd&pg=PR1&dq=emerging+paradigms+of+international+entrepreneurship+pdf&ots=AKtPvgM2F4&sig=Lm9uC-WkHsr3KexcigzFsa9XKiU&redir_esc=y#v=onepage&q&f=false

Davies, R. B., & Mazhikeyev, A. (2015). The glass border: Gender and exporting in developing countries. *UCD Centre for Economic Research Working Paper Series,* 2015(25).

DeMartino, R., & Barbato, R. (2003). Differences between women and men MBA entrepreneurs: Exploring family flexibility and wealth creation as career motivators. *Journal of Business Venturing, 18*(6), 815–832. https://doi.org/10.1016/S0883-9026(03)00003-X

D'Espallier, B., Guerin, I., & Mersland, R. (2011). Women and repayment in microfinance: A global analysis. *World Development*, *39*(5), 758–772. https://doi.org/10.1016/j.worlddev.2010.10.008

Eddleston, K.A., & Powell, G.N. (2008). The role of gender identity in explaining sex differences in business owners' career satisfier preferences. *Journal of Business Venturing, 23*, 244–256. https://doi.org/10.1016/j.jbusvent.2006.11.002

Etemad, H. (2005). Entrepreneurial internationalization or international entrepreneurship. *Management International Review, 45*, (Special Issue 3), 3–11.

Fasci, M. A., & Valdez, J. (1998). A performance contrast of male-and female-owned small accounting practices. *Journal of Small Business Management, 36*(3), 1–7.

Fischer, E.M., Reuber, A.R., & Dyke, L.S. (1993). A theoretical overview and extension of research on sex, gender, and entrepreneurship. *Journal of Business Venturing, 8*(2), 151–168. https://doi.org/10.1016/0883-9026(93)90017-Y

GEM. (2015). *Special report-women's entrepreneurship.* http://www.babson.edu/Academics/centers/blankcenter/globalresearch/gem/Documents/GE%20 2015 %20Womens%20 Report.pdf

Goldin, C. (2014). A grand gender convergence: Its last chapter. *American Economic Review, 104*(4), 1091–1119. http://dx.doi.org/10.1257/aer.104.4.1091

Grondin, D., & Grondin, C. (1994). The export orientation of Canadian female entrepreneurs in New Brunswick. *Women in Management Review, 9*(5), 21–30.

Grondin, D., & Schaefer, N. (1995). Differences in the export activities of female and male-owned small and medium-sized enterprises. *Women in Management Review, 10*(8), 4–10.

Güney, S. (2006). Kadın girişimciliğine genel bir bakış. *Girişimcilik ve Kalkınma Dergisi, 1*(1), 25–43.

Harcourt, T. (2006). The sisters are exporting for themselves presentation in Austrade. *Women in Export Series.*

Henry, C., Foss, L., & Ahl, H. (2015). Gender and entrepreneurship: A review of methodological approaches. *International Small Business Journal, 34*(3), 217–241. https://doi.org/10.1177/0266242614549779

Hughes, K.D. (2005). *Female enterprise in the new economy.* Toronto, Canada: University of Toronto Press.

Ibeh, K. I. N., & Young, S. (2001). Exporting as an entrepreneurial act. *European Journal of Marketing, 35*(5/6), 566–586. https://doi.org/10.1108/03090560110388114

ITC. (2015). *Unlocking markets for women to trade.* Geneva. https://www.intracen.org/uploadedFiles/intracenorg/Content/Publications/women_in_trade_web.pdf

ITC. (2016). *SME competiveness outlook 2016: Meeting the Standard for Trade.* Geneva. https://www.intracen.org/uploadedFiles/SMECO2016.pdf

ITC. (2017). *Closing the small-business and gender gap to make trade more inclusive.* Aid for Trade at a Glance 2017, 19–238. https://doi.org/10.1787/aid_glance-2017-en

Jennings, J. E., & Brush, C. G. (2013). Research on women entrepreneurs: Challenges to (and from) the broader entrepreneurship literature? *The Academy of Management Annals, 7,* 661–713.

Kelley, D. J., Brush, C. G., Greene, P. G., & Litovsky, Y. (2011). *Global entrepreneurship monitor 2010 women's report.* Babson College.

Kelley, D. J., Brush, C. G., Greene, P. G., & Litovsky, Y. (2013). *Global Entrepreneurship Monitor 2012 Women's Report.* Babson College.

Lee, H., Paik, Y., & Uygur, U. (2016). Does gender matter in the export performance of international new ventures? Mediation effects of firm-specific and country-specific advantages. *Journal of International Management, 22*(4), 365–379. http://dx.doi.org/10.1016/j.intman.2016.05.004

Manolova, T. S., Brush, C. G., Edelman, L. F., & Green, P. G. (2002). Internationalization of small firms: Personal factors revisited. *International Small Business Journal, 20*(1), 9–31. https://doi.org/10.1177/0266242602201003

Marlow, S. (1997). Self-employed women — new opportunities, old challenges? *Entrepreneurship & Regional Development, 9,* 199–210. https://doi.org/10.1080/08985629700000011

Mitchell, R. K., Busenitz, L., Lant, T., McDougall, P. P., Morse, E. A., & Smith, J. B. (2002). Toward a theory of entrepreneurial cognition: Rethinking the people side of entrepreneurship research. *Entrepreneurship Theory and Practice, 27*(2), 93–104. https://doi.org/10.1111/1540-8520.00001

Pande, R., & Ford, D. (2011). *Gender quotas and female leadership: A review.* Background paper for the World Development Report on Gender, Washington, DC, World Bank.

Rothstein, M. G., Burke, R. J., & Bristor, J. M. (2001). Structural characteristics and support benefits in the interpersonal networks of women and men in management. *The International Journal of Organizational Analysis,* 9(1), 4–25. https://doi.org/10.1108/eb028926.

Sabarwal, S., & Terrell, K. (2008). *Does gender matter for firm performance? Evidence from Eastern Europe and Central Asia.* World Bank Policy Research Working Paper, No:4705. Washington, DC, World Bank.

Scott, L. (2014). *Why we should all care about the women's economy.* Forbes. https://www.forbes.com/sites/forbeswomanfiles/2014/04/15/why-we-all-should-care-about-the-womens-economy/?sh=2c24dd1238bd.

Smeltzer, L. R., & Fann, G. L. (1989). Gender differences in external networks of small business owner/managers. *Journal of Small Business Management, 27*(2), 25–32.

Türko, E. S. (2016). Can entrepreneurship education reduce stereotypes against women entrepreneurship. *International Education Studies, 9*(11), 53–65. http://dx.doi.org/10.5539/ies.v9n11p53

UNECA. (2010). *Assessing regional integration in Africa IV. Enhancing Intra-African trade.* https://unece.org/DAM/trade/TF_JointUNRCsApproach/ECA_IntraAfricanTrade.pdf

United Nations Conference on Trade and Development. (2004). *Promoting the export competitiveness of SME.* https://digitallibrary.un.org/record/533904#record-files-collapse-header

van Staveren, I. (2013). An exploratory cross-country analysis of gendered institutions. *Journal of International Development, 25*(1), 108–121. https://doi.org/10.1002/jid.1850

Weiler, S., & Bernasek, A. (2001). Dodging the glass ceiling? Networks and the new wave of female entrepreneurs. *The Social Science Journal, 38*, 85–103. https://doi.org/10.1016/S0362-3319(00)00111-7

Welch, C. L., Welsch, D. E., & Hewerdine, L. (2008). Gender and export behaviour: Evidence from women-owned enterprises. *Journal of Business Ethics, 83*(1), 113–126. https://doi.org/10.1007A10551-007-9652-5

Westhead, P., Wright, M., & Ucbasaram, D. (2001). The internationalization of new and small firms: A resource-based view. *Journal of Business Venturing, 16*, 333–358. https://doi.org/10.1016/S0883-9026(99)00063-4

Williams, J. E., & Best, D. L. (1990). *Sex and psych: Gender and self viewed cross-culturally.* SAGE Publications.

WTO. (2017a). *Aid for trade global review 2017.* https://www.oecd.org/development/aid-for-trade-global-review-2017.htm

WTO. (2017b). *Gender aware trade policy: A springboard for women's economic empowerment.* https://www.wto.org/english/news_e/news17_e/dgra_21jun17_e.pdf

Zinkhan, G. M., & Karande, K. W. (1991). Cultural and gender differences in risk-taking behavior among American and Spanish decision makers. *The Journal of Social Psychology, 131*(5), 741–742. https://doi.org/10.1080/00224545.1991.9924657

Burak BAŞKAN[1]

Gender and Politics: The Structural Hegemony of Popular Culture over Women

In human society, nothing is natural and that woman, like much else, is a product elaborated by civilization.

Simone de Beauvoir[2]

The issue of women's entrepreneurship, which is the main topic of this book, inevitably necessitates a debate on women's position in everyday life as well as in their workplace. Such a necessity directs us to explore the political face of female labor and entrepreneurship, in other words, the power relations, inequality and dominance between the genders. A politics-based analysis will take the issue of women's entrepreneurship out of its narrow agency-based boundaries and enable it to be explained with more sophisticated fundamental structural factors. The following questions provide the starting point for a discussion of the topic:

> Which barriers determine the existence and action of women in work life?
> What are the structural bases of such barriers? and
> What are the discursive roots of such barriers?

In order to provide satisfactory answers to these questions, popular culture and its relation to the issue of gender were chosen as the main focus of this study. The primary reason for directing the study towards the field of popular culture is the power of popular culture to reflect the prevailing mainstream value judgments, preferences, perceptions and tastes in a society. In this sense, it is possible to understand the basic characteristics and dynamics of the existing production and power relations in society by analyzing the internal processes of popular culture. On the other hand, the content of popular culture, that is, the face of popular culture which is visible to ordinary people, explains how gender is constructed and how these constructed gender assumptions determine the

---

1 Assistant Professor Dr., Erzurum Technical University, Faculty of Economic and Administrative Sciences, Department of Political Science and Public Administration, burak.baskan@erzurum.edu.tr, ORCID ID: 0000-0002-2885-5911

2 Beauvoir, 1953: 681.

limits of women's action in everyday and work life. It can be said that popular culture is a structure which contributes greatly to the construction of gender and gender roles and reflects the social gender perception of a society.

"Popular culture" is a term which can have many different meanings depending on the perspective of the definition provider. The word "popular" refers to the people; its root is from the word *populus* in Latin (Kidd, 2018: 5). A very wide definition of popular culture might be "culture that is widely favoured or well-liked by many people" (Storey, 2009: 5). Although such a definition is successful in emphasizing the numerical size of popular culture, it is not successful in explaining the qualitative characteristics of this type of culture. In order to better understand the influence of popular culture on society and its success in constructing discourse, the definition should contain other distinctive elements.

On the other hand, mass culture theorists have gone beyond a quantitative understanding of popular culture and brought the concepts of "mass culture" and "mass society" into the popular culture debate. As a consequence of urbanization and industrialization, people have become atomized individuals, that is, their relationship with each other has been transformed by them losing their meaning and moral base. This atomization process has triggered the collapse of mediating social organizations such as the family, the village and religious institutions. As a result of the lack of social institutions, individuals have become more exposed to exploitation and manipulation by institutions such as popular culture and the mass media (Strinati, 2004: 5–6). Based on these discussions, mass culture corresponds to a popular culture produced by industrial techniques for the masses and marketed for profit to its masses who are completely transformed into customers. Therefore, popular culture is a commercial culture produced by the mass for the market of the mass (Strinati, 2004: 10).

For structuralism, which is not generally regarded as a part of the mass culture perspective, popular culture is also a type of ideological machine by which prevailing power structures are reproduced (Storey, 2009: 9). The semiological/structural perspective focuses on the structure of signs, whereas Marxist structural tradition emphasizes popular culture's ideological structures. However, both structuralist perspectives share the common point of devoting themselves to tracing the meaning of objects by emphasizing their deeper structural meaningfulness, rather than emphasizing their surface features (Mukerji & Schudson, 1986). In this sense, both perspectives shed light on the issue of gender inequality caused by deeply rooted structural constraints embedded within society, which forms a great contribution to the primary aim of this study.

Bennett (2006: 96), on the other hand, brought Gramsci's perspective on cultural hegemony to the issue of popular culture. For him, popular culture is a field shaped by the attempts of the ruling class to gain hegemony on the one hand, and the struggles of those who oppose these attempts on the other. In this regard, popular culture is not a form of culture which consists solely of the unilateral imposition of mass culture shaped by the influence of the dominant ideology and not merely a terrain of opposing cultures. It is, however, a terrain on which dominant, oppositional, subordinate, ideological and cultural elements and values of the two are mixed in varying permutations and negotiated.

Based on the discussions above regarding what popular culture is, it is possible to extract several significant points from each definition in order to develop a useful perspective within the frame of this study regarding what popular culture exactly is. First, popular culture is a culture which is shared by as many people as possible in a society or on a global scale. The concept therefore possesses a quantitative dimension. Second, people cannot be active and conscious creators of popular culture but, more importantly, are most of the time unconsciously exposed to it. As mass culture theorists and structuralists argue, therefore, popular culture possesses manipulative, exploitative as well as ideological dimensions. Third, popular culture possesses a hegemonic dimension, that is, it is based on gaining the consent of people as well as making negotiations with them.

In considering popular culture's complex structure and sophisticated way of constructing the "popular," however, we should avoid reducing popular culture to a very centrally planned and fully controlled hegemonic project of particular actors. On this point, the distinction between hegemonic projects and structural hegemonies made by Joseph (2000; 2001; 2002; 2008) becomes vital in order to avoid reductionism when endeavoring to understand the effect of the hegemonic character of popular culture on gender. Consequently, the originality of this current study stems from its acknowledgment of the distinction between deeper structural hegemonies and surface hegemonic projects and its reading of the gender issue with reference to that distinction.

1. The Structure/Agency Debate and the Concept of Structural Hegemony

Do women possess full control of the realization of their intentions, goals and attempts in social, economic and political life? Or are they restricted by social, economic, political and cultural structures? Such questions direct our attention to the structure/agency debate which is key to understanding the structural hegemonic character of popular culture and its determinative effect on the issue of women's labor and entrepreneurship. The structure/agency debate deals with the questions of the extent to which people as actors possess the capacity to shape their own destiny, the extent to which people's lives are structured without their control, and the extent to which people's future is designed by external forces (McAnulla, 2002: 271). The debate is therefore directly related to women's power of control over their destiny.

"Structure" can be simply defined as the context which corresponds to "the setting within which social, political and economic events occur and acquire meaning" (Hay, 2002: 94). It determines the material conditions which specify the range of actions available to the actors (McAnulla, 2002: 271). On the other hand, "agency" means action and can be described, basically, "as the ability or capacity of an actor to act consciously and, in doing so, to attempt to realize his or her intentions" (Hay, 2002: 94). Structure and agency therefore reciprocally necessitate each other in order for existence (Hay, 1995: 189–190). Structure creates opportunities for, or constraints on, agency.

A key concept which is useful in order to position the issue of "popular culture" on the terrain of the structure/agency debate is Gramsci's (1971) concept of cultural hegemony. This can simply be defined as "the ideal representation of the interests of the privileged groups as universal interests, which are then accepted by the masses as the natural political and social order" (Orlowski, 2011: 1). As Giroux (1981: 94) clarified, "hegemony functions to define the meaning and limits of common-sense as well as the form and content of discourse in a society. It does so by positing certain ideas as natural and universal." From this point of view, the concept is significant for enabling us to comprehend how the representation of women in popular culture is accepted as natural and universal. It also explains how the gender roles within society are reproduced and perpetuated.

Turning back to the structure/agency debate, the following questions map the discussion on popular culture's role in reproducing and perpetuating the current gender roles within society: Is popular culture the product of a conscious endeavor by particular actors in order to reproduce patriarchy? Or is it a deeper structure which draws the limits of women's action? Joseph's (2000; 2001; 2002; 2008) distinction between two aspects (or types) of hegemony, namely "structural hegemony" and "surface hegemony of actual hegemonic projects," is significant for finding a true answer to these questions. Structural hegemony is about "the deep, underlying conditions within society and the unity of the social formation" and its role is to reproduce structural ensembles and social structures. On the other hand, surface hegemony is about agency-based actual and conscious hegemonic projects which emanate from underlying deeper structures but have their own dynamics and powers (Joseph, 2002: 131).

Based on this distinction, hegemony should not be merely regarded as a struggle between different actors, but those actors should also be regarded in the context of wider social relations (Joseph, 2000: 181). The success of social groups in terms of ensuring domination and leadership in a society is directly related to the operation of dominant forces vis-à-vis dominant social structures and contexts (Joseph, 2001: 266). Therefore, deeper social structures provide a terrain for hegemonic actors where surface hegemonic projects can be actualized. Those structural conditions, however, cannot be said to consist of conscious and centrally planned processes. On the contrary, they are largely passive and unconscious (Joseph, 2002: 131). In this respect, they are the unconscious facilitators or restrictors of conscious hegemonic projects.

2. Popular Culture as a Deeper Structure Perpetuating Gender Roles

Recognizing popular culture as a structure, rather than an actual and specific hegemonic project on the surface without deeper roots, is significant for unveiling the conditions which create and consistently recreate such a deeper structure. It is unrealistic to imagine a very centralized decision-making process and definite decision makers with full control over popular culture. Popular culture is so vast that a single or several agents cannot produce and shape it in today's globalized world. Moreover, although people are exposed to it, they also unconsciously contribute to the reproduction of it by means of their preferences and demands. In other words, they are both shaped by and shape popular culture. Such circularity stems from the structural character of popular culture.

When seeking to comprehend the reasons behind a group's achievement in terms of establishing hegemony, solely emphasizing the group's dominance (in other words, a group's active effort to be dominant) over other groups is not explanatory. It is important to unveil the political, cultural and economic conditions which create a convenient context for that group to ensure dominance and leadership over other groups (Joseph, 2000: 183). Structural conditions not only give hegemonic struggles their meaning, but also restrict and even undermine the hegemonic struggles (Joseph, 2008: 121). Thus, popular culture emerges as a deeper structure which creates the conditions and determines the possibility of success for hegemonic projects reproducing male domination within a society.

Any effort to comprehend male domination in any sector of everyday life inevitably necessitates an emphasis on the conditions which create and reproduce such a domination. Within this framework, the conditions which constitute popular culture's role as a deeper structure are discussed here under the sub-topics of *Processes in Popular Culture* and *Content in Popular Culture*, both of which reveal underlying conditions which draw limits for women in their everyday life and particularly in their work life.

2.1. Processes in Popular Culture

The products of popular culture (written, auditory and visual products, images, tangible goods; and discourses embedded within those products) which are visible, audible or usable by ordinary people in their everyday life are produced and disseminated through specific male-dominated processes embedded within popular culture. Those processes include the organizational, representational and productional aspects of popular culture and constitute the structural conditions which draw the boundaries of hegemonic projects reproducing an historical male-dominated social order and of counter-hegemonic projects which seek to raise a challenge to those patriarchal projects.

Discussing popular culture by solely focusing on its outcomes (its products and discourses) might hinder us from seeing the deeper economic relations within it. The distinction made by Marx and Engels ([1932]1998: 98) between the base (the economic structure of society and relations of production) and the superstructure (social consciousness) becomes significant for comprehending popular culture's interior face which sets a barrier against women's counter-hegemonic challenges against settled male domination from the base to the surface of popular culture. Marx ([1859]1904: 11) described production relations as the real foundation (and economic structure) of society and highlighted that "The mode of production of material life determines the general character of the social, political and spiritual (intellectual) processes of life." According to this perspective, a superstructure (social consciousness) does not autonomously exist, in other words it does not exist by itself, but it is embedded within the social relations of production (Larrain, 1991: 45). This perspective regards cultural and thereby popular cultural terrain as an outcome of economic and productional relations. Thus relations of production and capital ownership embedded within the different sectors of popular culture are significant determiners of the cultural/discursive upper levels (or the exterior sphere) of popular culture.

Acknowledging the importance of Marx's distinction between base and superstructure, but disagreeing with his one-sided determinism from base to superstructure Marx ([1859]1904: 11–12), we can trace Gramsci's perspective in which he better appreciated the value of society's cultural and intellectual life. Unlike Marx, Gramsci highlighted interactivity between culture and the processes of production and human labor. He suggested that there is no one-sided determination of "material infrastructure" over "cultural superstructure," but the two levels of societal institutions co-determine one another (Fulton, 1987: 198). This perspective is important for comprehending the discursive power of popular culture and deeply rooted value judgments in determining the conditions of women in economic life.

The representation of women is a political matter, and because it is a political matter, women's representation in popular culture becomes directly related to power relations. Unless women are sufficiently involved in the decision-making mechanisms which affect them and have the power to define their own interests, they will be exposed to the decisions and definitions of others (men, in gender issues), who will make decisions and definitions in line with their own interests rather than the interests of women (Marshment, 1997: 125). In order to trace the underlying reasons for power and domination, Van Dijk (1995: 86) asked "*Who may speak or write to whom about what, when, and in what context?*," and "*Who may participate in such communicative events in various recipient roles?*" Returning to the base and superstructure distinction, the question becomes "*Who possesses the power to influence the superstructural level, in other words the level of social consciousness?*" Power is gained by privilege when accessing valued social resources like status, wealth and occupation, or when accessing communication opportunities and public discourse. Access to communication events and discourse, which is crucial for the discursive reproduction of power and domination, is unequally distributed (Van Dijk, 1995: 85–86). Both access to valued social resources and access to public discourse are related to the extent to which a person masters or possesses control over, or at least has the capability to influence, the instruments as well as the relations of production and economy.

Economic relations in popular culture occur within the production processes of popular culture such as the fashion industry, the media industry, the entertainment industry, the culture industry, the sports industry and print houses. The dissemination channels of popular culture by which the discursive outcomes of production processes become visible to the public are television and radio channels, newspapers, magazines, music, cinema and advertisements. As Marx ([1867]1981: 953) underlined, possessing capital means possessing the means of production. Therefore, ownership of capital in popular culture endows someone with the opportunity to be the master of the whole production process. So, private ownership relations in the industries listed above are a significant determinant which creates the conditions which set limits on the actions of women within the boundaries of popular culture.

In the Fortune 500 list which shows the largest corporations of the US, the number of female CEOs was only 37 in 2020. This corresponds to 7.4 % compared with the percentage of male CEOs which was 92.6 %. The number of female CEO's was only two in 2000 and then fifteen in 2010 (Fortune, 2020; Hinchliffe, 2020). The representation of women in top management positions of more than 100,000 private corporations around the globe reached only 18 % in 2019 (World Bank, 2019). A significant proportion of those corporations operate in sectors which are directly or indirectly related with popular culture and so are able to construct what is "popular." Second, those corporations spend significant amounts of money on advertising and they possess the power to shape gender images with their share in the advertisement sector.

Considering the significance of having control of the most fundamental instruments of constructing and shaping public discourse, namely the media (with television and radio channels and newspapers) and cinema, the top 100 international media corporations across the globe have a male-dominated management structure and 94 % of them have a male CEO. The proportion of men in the top management positions of these corporations was 83 % in 2018 (Nordicom, 2018). In the cinema sector, the richest film producers and directors in the Hollywood film industry were white men whose combined personal wealth had reached $US20 billion by 2015 (Fox, 2015). So the entry standards seen on media instruments are determined and the decisions to be included in or excluded from popular culture are made through male-dominated processes within the sectors of popular culture. Such a situation results in the uneven distribution of power for discourse construction between genders.

The fashion industry, which sets the appearance standards for genders and by this means makes a great contribution to the construction of gender roles, is also composed of male-dominated processes. A *Business of Fashion* survey revealed that 86 % of the 50 most valuable fashion brands were led by a male executive in 2015 (Pike, 2016). Across the globe, only 40.2 % of the 371 fashion designers working in the 313 most prestigious brands were women, according to another survey conducted in September 2016 by *Business of Fashion* during the world's four most popular fashion weeks (Ahmed, 2017). A first female designer was appointed by Dior in 2016 and then by Givenchy in 2017 (Danziger, 2019). What is more dramatic about gender inequality is that the British beauty and fashion brands, whose audiences and consumers are predominantly women, were the worst lawbreakers in terms of the gender pay gap (Paton, 2018).

In addition to these gender problems such as being disadvantaged in production relations and being excluded from the decision-making mechanisms of popular culture, the dominant standards and values within those sectors also create a structural barrier against the inclusion of women in the processes of popular culture. According to the feminist critique, men in Western societies have sustained privilege as a result of the normalization of competitive and aggressive behaviors. The most visible instances of this have been competitive power struggles which hinged on direct physical male dominance over women and tough competitive standards which caused disadvantages for women vis-à-vis men (Karlberg, 2005: 5). Although it is possible to encounter such competitive power struggles in every sector of popular culture, they are particularly apparent in the area of organized sports. Organized sport has emerged as a cultural field which has been perpetuating the ideology of male dominance and superiority. It has constructed a homo-social cultural area which provides tragic symbolic ideological confirmation of men's "natural superiority" over women (Messner, 1988: 199–200). Thus, the sports industry, with its standards which attribute superiority to masculinity and so-called inferiority to femininity, represent the dominant value system embedded in popular culture.

Consequently, the structural hegemonic character of popular culture in terms of processes stems from the embedded relations of production and capital ownership. The processes of organization, representation and production in which women are mostly excluded are the sites where women are hindered from possessing the capital and instruments of production, from being represented within the decision-making mechanisms of popular culture, and from having control over economic relations within its various sectors. Thus it can be seen that every process within popular culture is primarily controlled and shaped by men. As an inevitable outcome of this situation, such male-dominated economic relations at the interior sphere of popular culture also determine the discursive aspects (in other words, content in popular culture) of popular culture's structural hegemony on the exterior sphere by constructing the popular discourse on gender roles and femininity. Women in popular culture-related sectors must therefore face the prevailing gender distribution in terms of both capital ownership and managerial positions and overcome the expectations of those sectors which are based on the long-lasting popular tastes and preferences of consumers.

2.2. Content in Popular Culture

Language can be regarded as a "common social behavior" by which people disseminate their ideas about a whole range of everyday issues across the world. By means of language, institutions and people draw the boundaries of what is "natural" and what is "common sense" (Machin & Mayr, 2012: 25). According to the reconceptualization of Foucault, language is understood as a sociopolitical entity and an instrument by which specific social relations are formed. Historical, political and social conditions, which knowledge hinges on, provide the basis for determining statements as false or true. That is, discourse is the basis of power and constitutes official knowledge. On this point, Foucault did not assert the non-existence of truth. On the contrary, he agreed with postmodern theorists on the existence of truth about the same incident by underlining that particular interpretations of truth can possess privilege in terms of being official discourse (Orlowski, 2011: 39). The power of language in terms of determining the "natural," the "universal" and the "common sense" and monopolizing the construction of truth about gender roles and femininity is also valid in the field of popular culture.

Content in popular culture composed of images, discourses, auditory and visual products and tangible goods is as important as the processes of popular culture for evincing the structural hegemonic character of popular culture as it constitutes the visible discursive face of structural hegemony. The instruments embedded within society such as Hollywood films, advertisements, school education materials, art galleries, game shows and opera determine the form of women's representation and make definitions about the meaning, nature and obligations of being a woman, women's capabilities and incapabilities, their roles in society and their differences from men (Marshment, 1997: 126). As such, the truth (not reality) about femininity is constructed through instruments embedded within popular culture. What makes popular culture more important than any other types of culture is its ability to publicize and dramatically popularize a so-called truth, discourse, value, belief, taste or admiration. It therefore becomes a privileged deeper structure for the popularization of discourse about gender roles, masculinity and femininity.

The concept of "hegemonic masculinity" introduced by Connell (2005) provides guidance for understanding how masculinity, and accordingly femininity, is constructed in popular culture and diffused into society. The concept was defined by Connell (2005: 45) as "the configuration of gender practice which embodies the currently accepted answer to the problem of the legitimacy of patriarchy, which guarantees (or is taken to guarantee) the dominant position of men and the subordination of women." Accepting Gramsci's concept of hegemony as a starting point, hegemonic masculinity is the exaltation of a specific masculinity vis-à-vis other masculinities. She argued that mass culture produces an idealistic masculinity understanding which is fixed and true and based on the discourses of the "deep masculine," "real man" and "natural man" (Connell, 2005: 45).

Hegemonic masculinity is not normal in numerical terms and does not constitute a majority among different masculinities. Only a few men are able to reach such an ideal form of masculinity. However, it is definitely normative. The concept constructs idealistic standards for being an honored man and compels all men to ground on its idealistic standards while positioning themselves. By hegemonic masculinity, the worldwide subordination of female to male is ideologically legitimatized (Connell & Messerschmidt, 2005: 832). The American film industry with its violent male icons such as Sylvester Stallone, Matt Damon, Jean-Claude Van Damme, Christian Bale, Bruce Willis and Arnold Schwarzenegger is a prominent terrain for the detection of hegemonic masculinity. Similarly, the advertising sector and music video industry construct a similar discourse by reconfirming gender roles and underlining the "natural" contrasts between men and women. Symbolism in the sports industry and the military inescapably manifests itself in the full range of the media and more specifically in video games in which the muscularity is associated with "ideal masculinity" (Kareithi, 2014: 27).

Moreover, the patriarchal ideology regards men as rational and women as emotional, which is also widespread in popular culture. Hegemonic masculinity is therefore not only about the physical superiority of men, but is also about the rationality of men (Connell, 2005: 164). In this respect, popular culture's impact on the normalization of patriarchy as a universal and natural social order is actualized by the subjectivation of men vis-à-vis the objectification of women in the products of popular culture such as movies, television series, advertisements, fashion trends, music clips and so on. This situation can particularly be detected in a particular variety of television series in which men are depicted as "successful businessmen" and women are depictured as "passive figures" who are in need of men's potency. In various disaster movies, the man in the leading role becomes the rational heroic savior whereas women are dependent on the decisions of that rational man.

Advertisements form another most apparent face of popular culture by which patriarchal discourses are rapidly and easily diffused into society. They also symbolize the "fast production-fast consumption" circle of popular culture. A significant part of modern advertising is composed of visual images, in other words non-verbal symbols. Visual images in the media are very powerful means of shaping beliefs, values, behaviors and attitudes as they are quite persuasive and very sophisticated in terms of contributing the existence of meaning (Kang, 1997: 980). Advertisements are used as a tool to sell the commodified forms of both masculinity (which manifests itself in a tall and muscled body and facial hair) and of femininity (which manifests itself as a spotless and glowing skin, plump lips and long eyelashes) unintentionally and generally intentionally (Singh, 2018: 207). They therefore have the power to determine the standards for every single point of gender roles, styles and preferences. Advertisements most of the time can associate women with the home, traditional motherhood or sex/beauty-oriented roles which are not sensitive to the heterogeneity among women (Kang, 1997: 980). Being a self-sacrificing mother or a temptress at home can easily be made "popular" vis-à-vis being a successful entrepreneur woman by means of advertisements.

Courtney and Lockeretz (1971: 94–95) historically revealed particular stereotypes within famous magazine advertisements about gender roles which still have not been overcome in today's increasingly gender-friendly world. In advertisements, for instance, women belong to the home. Women are shown as incapable of making important things and important decisions. They depict women as dependent on men and as relying on male protection. Many advertisements associate women with food products, home appliances, cleaning products, beauty products, clothing and drugs. On the other hand, men are associated with cars, industrial products and companies, alcoholic beverages, entertainment media, cigarettes, banks and travel. In men's imagination, women are depicted as sex objects. Such stereotypes push women into a passive position in everyday life and especially in working life, and position men as more competent and effective than women in almost every area. The place of women is limited to the house, and all the spaces outside the home, especially those places where economic activities are carried out, are left entirely to men.

After all these detections, the structural hegemonic character of popular culture in terms of content stems from its capacity and power to determine sets of value judgments, truths, beliefs and standards which have been taken for granted by people about masculinity and femininity. Those sets constitute the discursive underlying conditions which draw limits for women's actions in everyday life. In this respect, the image of women represented in popular culture is reflexive, that is to say that the image of and discourse about women reflects the everyday lives and workplaces of women. Its impact skyrockets with the dissemination power and development speed in parallel with people's consumption speed in popular culture. Thereby, popular culture becomes a structural restrictor on women by discursively positioning them in workplace.

3. Conclusion, with a Brief Discussion of Female Entrepreneurship

It is problematic to accept popular culture as the product of a conscious and systematic agency-based endeavor, that is, popular culture is not an agency side of the gender struggle, but it constitutes a vast structure which determines the rules of the game, in other words determines the underlying conditions of and puts limits on women's actions and reproduces the male-dominant historical social order in everyday life and particularly in work life.

Such a vast structure of popular culture has been investigated by dividing it into two spheres: processes of popular culture composed of organization, production and representation constitute the inner sphere. The limits of women's action in this sphere are drawn by preventing women from controlling economic relations, having ownership or control over capital and instruments of production, and being represented within the decision-making mechanisms. Such an under-representation within the processes of popular culture can be regarded as the reproduction of the male-dominated social order. Another negative structural effect on women's action emerges with the diminishing opportunity for the success of counter-hegemonic projects of women which seek to construct alternative gender-friendly discourses.

The content of popular culture, on the other hand, constitutes the exterior sphere. It also forms the visible face of popular culture to the public. It is the sphere by which ordinary people are exposed to the dominant popular discourse. The most prominent feature of this situation is that it ensures women's passive position as the object in society and particularly in work life, while positioning men as the active subjects of society. By repeating stereotypes for appealing to the preferences and tastes of men who possess better economic potential than women, popular culture constitutes a structural incentive for the reproduction of male-dominated preferences and tastes.

It might be unrealistic to claim that each and every single element of popular culture is intended to reproduce patriarchy and exploit women, and it might be nonsensical to regard all men working in any sector of popular culture as misogynist. It is possible to detect gender-friendly attitudes in every economic sector. For this reason, the focal point of this study is not agencies, but rather it is the fundamental distinctive disposition embedded within the deeper structure of popular culture. Moreover, counter-hegemonic forces which seek to operate for the deconstruction and nullification of male-dominance can also be found on this terrain. However, their degree of achievement is determined by the settled structure of popular culture.

What distinguishes popular culture from any other types of deeper structures embedded within societies is popular culture's capability of diffusion. Such a capability is already what makes this culture "popular." It diffuses to every corner of everyday life, including work life, and shapes the discourse in circulation in society. It is unescapable since today's modern human beings finds no room to escape from the influence of the products of popular culture no matter whether they are written, auditory, visual or tangible. Since popular culture is based on a "rapid production – rapid consumption" circle, new ways of reproducing current "popular" gender perceptions can very easily be developed within popular culture.

When it comes to the issue of female entrepreneurship, which forms the main focus of this book, it can be argued that popular culture with its processes and content is a significant determiner of the underlying conditions for working women. More direct effects of popular culture can be seen for those women who seek to start an enterprise in one of the sectors of popular culture, such as the music, media or fashion industries. The fact that the processes have entirely been built and controlled by men creates a structural disadvantage for women when accumulating capital, possessing means of production and entering into economic relations. In other words, women have to find a place in the current male-dominated order in order to survive as a female entrepreneur. In this situation, women will be compelled to challenge both current economic relations and consumer preferences, both of which are mostly shaped by men.

More indirect but strong effects of popular culture on female entrepreneurship emerge in discursive terms. Popular culture can shape the attitudes of both ordinary people and the work environment towards women who are about to start a business. The image of the "irrational woman in need of a man's protection" might reduce confidence in women and trigger the demand for a male master. When women's place is constantly depicted as the home, for instance, such a discourse has a negative impact on the attitude of society towards working women. Consequently, women's entrepreneurship is discouraged and restrained in all other sectors of economic life. Even success stories of female entrepreneurs published in magazines and newspapers are typical examples for detecting how the successful entrepreneurship of women is presented as extraordinary and unnatural and how male entrepreneurship is perceived as the normal, ideal and expected form of entrepreneurship. In order to guarantee gender equality and nullify women's disadvantages in workplace and business life, therefore, the discourse about gender, femininity and masculinity in popular culture must completely be reconstructed.

References

Ahmed, O. (2017, March 8). A woman's work: How women can get ahead in fashion. *Business of Fashion*. https://www.businessoffashion.com/articles/news-analysis/a-womans-work-how-women-can-get-ahead-in-fashion

Beauvoir, S. de. (1953). *The Second Sex* (H. M. Parshley, Trans. & Ed.). Jonathan Cape.

Bennett, T. (2006). Popular culture and the turn to Gramsci. In Storey, J. (Ed.), *Cultural Theory and Popular Culture: A Reader* (3rd ed.) (pp. 92–99). Pearson Education.

Connell, R. (2005). *Masculinities* (2nd ed.). University of California Press.

Connell, R. W., & Messerschmidt, J. W. (2005). Hegemonic masculinity: Rethinking the concept. *Gender and Society, 19*(6), 829–859. http://www.jstor.org/stable/27640853

Courtney, A., & Lockeretz, S. (1971). A woman's place: An analysis of the roles portrayed by women in magazine advertisements. *Journal of Marketing Research*, *8*, 92–95.

Danziger, P.N. (2019, February 3). Would more women in fashion power positions mean more female customers? *Forbes*. https://www.forbes.com/sites/pamdanziger/2019/02/03/would-more-women-in-fashion-power-positions-mean-more-female-customers/?sh=1e7768da4b0b

Fortune. (2020). *Fortune 500*. https://fortune.com/fortune500/2020

Fox, E. J. (2015, February 11). These are the richest filmmakers in Hollywood. *CNN Business*. https://money.cnn.com/2015/02/11/luxury/hollywoods-richest-filmmakers/index.html

Fulton, J. (1987). Religion and politics in Gramsci: An introduction. *Sociological Analysis, 48*(3), 197–216. http://socrel.oxfordjournals.org/content/48/3/197

Gramsci, A. (1971). *Selections from the Prison Notebooks of Antonio Gramsci*. In Hoare, Q. & Smith, G. N. (Eds.) and (Trans.). Lawrence and Wishart.

Giroux, H. A. (1981). *Ideology, Culture & the Process of Schooling*. The Falmer Press.

Hay, C. (1995). Structure and agency. In Marsh, D. & Stoker, G. (Eds.), *Theory and Methods in Political Science* (pp. 189–208). Macmillan Press.

Hay, C. (2002). *Political Analyses: A Critical Introduction*. Palgrave Macmillan.

Hinchliffe, E. (2020, May 18). The number of female CEOs in the Fortune 500 hits an all-time record. *The Fortune*. https://fortune.com/2020/05/18/women-ceos-fortune-500-2020/

Joseph, J. (2000). A Realist theory of hegemony. *Journal for the Theory of Social Behaviour, 30*(2), 179–202.

Joseph, J. (2001). Hegemony in the fourth dimension. *Journal for the Theory of the Social Behaviour, 31*(3), 261–277.

Joseph, J. (2002). *Hegemony: A Realist Analysis*. Routledge.

Joseph, J. (2008). Hegemony and the structure-agency problem in International Relations: A scientific realist contribution. *Review of International Relations, 34*(1), 109–128. http://www.jstor.org/stable/41307942

Kang, M. E. (1997). The portrayal of women's images in magazine advertisements: Goffman's gender analysis revisited. *Sex Roles, 37*(11/12), 979–996.

Kareithi, P. J. (2014). Hegemonic masculinity in media contents. In Montiel, A. V. (Ed.), *Media and Gender: A Scholarly Agenda for the Global Alliance on Media and Gender* (pp. 26–29). UNESCO.

Karlberg, M. (2005). The Power of discourse and the discourse of power: Pursuing peace through discourse intervention. *International Journal of Peace Studies, 10*(1), 1–23.

Kidd, D. (2018). *Pop Culture Freaks: Identity, Mass Media, and Society*. Routledge.

Larrain, J. (1991). Base and superstructure. In Bottomore, T. (Ed.), *A Dictionary of Marxist Thought* (2nd ed.) (pp. 45–48). Blackwell.

Machin, D., & Mayr, A. (2012). *How to Do Critical Discourse Analysis*. Sage Publications.

Marshment, M. (1997). The picture is political: Representation of women in contemporary popular culture. In Robinson, V. & Richardson, D. (Eds.), *Introducing Women's Studies* (pp. 125–151). Palgrave.

Marx, K. ([1859]1904). A preface. *A Contribution to the Critique of Political Economy* (N. I. Stone, Trans. from German, 2nd ed.). Charles H. Kerr & Company.

Marx, K. ([1867]1981). *Capital (Das Kapital) Volume III* (D. Fernbach, Trans.). Penguin Books.

Marx, K. & Engels, F. ([1932]1998). *The German Ideology: Including Theses on Feuerbach and Introduction to the Critique of Political Economy*. The Prometheus Books.

McAnulla, S. (2002). Structure and agency. In Marsh, D. and Stoker, G. (Eds.), *Theory and Methods in Political Science* (2nd ed.) (pp. 271–291). Palgrave Macmillan.

Messner, M. A. (1988). Sports and male domination: The female athlete as contested ideological terrain. *Sociology of Sport Journal*, *5*, 197–211.

Mukerji, C., & Schudson, M. (1986). Popular culture. *Annual Review of Sociology*, 12, 47–66. http://www.jstor.org/stable/2083194

Nordicom. (2018). *The Media is a Male Business.* https://www.nordicom.gu.se/en/latest/news/media-male-business

Orlowski, P. (2011). *Teaching about Hegemony: Race, Class and Democracy in the 21st Century.* Springer.

Paton, E. (2018, April 5). Major fashion names among worst offenders in Britain gender pay gap. *The New York Times.* https://www.nytimes.com/2018/04/05/fashion/uk-fashion-companies-gender-pay-gap.html

Pike, H. (2016, September 9). Female fashion designers are still in the minority. *Business of Fashion.* https://www.businessoffashion.com/articles/fashion-week/less-female-fashion-designers-more-male-designers

Singh, A. (2018). Capitalism, consumerism and popular culture. *International Journal of Research – Granthaalayah*, 6(4), 205–210. https://doi.org/10.29121/granthaalayah.v6.i4.2018.1645

Storey, J. (2009). *Cultural Theory and Popular Culture: An Introduction* (5th ed.). Pearson Longman.

Strinati, D. (2004). *An Introduction to Theories of Popular Culture* (2nd ed.). Routledge.

Van Dijk, T. (1995). Discourse, power and access. In Caldas-Coulthard, C. R. & Coulthard, M. (Eds.), *Texts and Practises* (pp. 84–103). Routledge.

World Bank. (2019). Firms with female top manager (% of firms). *Enterprise Surveys.* https://data.worldbank.org/indicator/IC.FRM.FEMM.ZS

Müge YÜCE[1]

The Effect of Sociopolitical Factors on Women Entrepreneurship: An Analysis on China

The People's Republic of China (PRC)[2] attracted enormous interest on the parallel of her stable economic development which continues almost thirty years from the late 20th century to the 21st century. By initiating the policies of "reform and opening up" 改革开放 (gǎi gé kāi fang) under the government of Deng Xiaoping 邓小平 in 1978, China was no longer identified as a rigid communist one-party state. Especially after entering into the World Trade Organization in 2001, China began to focus on improving the private economy hand-in-hand with the state-controlled economy and encouraged investors and international firms to invest mainland from all over the world.

Starting in the last decade of 20th century, decentralization, marketization, and privatization increasingly became the main characteristics of Chinese economy (Chen, 2011: 1). As a concomitant of steady policies aiming the social and economic development, China became the world's second-largest economy for the first time in 2010 (McCury & Kollewe, 2011). In the same year, China surpassed the United States (US) and became the world's largest energy consumer (Swartz & Oster, 2010). To achieve a key player status in the international economic system, China had to accept main principles of the capitalist economy and to harmonize the state-controlled mechanisms with private economy.

Market-centered policies under a communist state were considered as a big contradiction and started a debate in the international system. Even though Chinese political elites identify this contradictive issue as "Socialism with Chinese Characteristics" 中国特色社会主义 (Zhōng guó tè sè shè huì zhǔ yì), the aforementioned debate regarding whether China will be a capitalist state or not gained significant momentum across the world. Accepting the free-market dynamic, openness to international economy, and integration efforts with global and regional organizations showed that China's socioeconomic development model will be based on a unique "open-door policy" in near future.

---

1 Research Assistant Dr., Ataturk University, Faculty of Economics and Administrative Sciences, Department of International Relations, muge.yuce@atauni.edu.tr, ORCID ID: 0000-0002-7593-6060

2 The People's Republic of China is going to be mentioned as China on the rest of study.

Under this unique condition, private actors, and entrepreneurship were the major components of long-standing economic development in China. Indeed, the Chinese Communist Party initiated encouragement policies to improve entrepreneurship in early 2000 and recognized entrepreneurs as an important social force (Zheng & Qian, 2017: 26). The period between 2000 and 2008 was characterized by further enhancement of private actors and entrepreneurs in China. However, Global Financial Crisis in 2008 has been a catalyst factor to motivate Chinese leaders about making the economy more open and competitive. Following the Global Financial Crisis (GFC), Chinese policymakers decided to make innovation and entrepreneurship new drivers of economic growth over the coming decades (Wu et al., 2017: 213).

The devastating effects of the Global Financial Crisis also forced Chinese leaders to improve bilateral relations not only with the advanced economies but also with the developing countries. Affected by the declining trend in global demand, Chinese political elites turned their attention to the underdeveloped countries and China's internal market. Within this context, two remarkable initiatives were launched and established a framework for the next direction of Chinese development strategy. The first one is the Belt and Road Initiative (BRI) declared in 2013 and aiming to re-build the ancient Silk Road from China to Europe through Central and West Asia. The second one is The Mass Entrepreneurship Initiative launched in 2015 and this initiative aims to remove the institutional barriers in order to mobilize and realize the entrepreneurial spirit of the Chinese people (World Bank, 2019). As a short-term consequence of these initiatives, the private sector contributed more than 60 % of China's GDP in 2017 and there were 65.79 million individually-owned businesses and 27.26 million private enterprises in China (Meng, 2018).

Because of the increasing contribution of the private sector and entrepreneurship to Chinese economy, many scholars were interested more in the theoretical and empirical studies on this issue. Studies on entrepreneurship in China focused on various research fields such as political framework, cultural factors, international dimension, and management-related context. Moreover, entrepreneurship in China is embedded in the country's unique social networks and institutional context (Lin et al., 2020: 449). Therefore, there is a substantial literature on entrepreneurship in China.

However, researches on women entrepreneurship and women's participation in the labor force in China are still in a nascent stage. Because women entrepreneurship is widely accepted as a concrete evidence of the importance of establishing new businesses for economic growth and development (Jamali, 2009: 232), Chinese case is very attractive and needs to be further studied in detail. Moreover, women entrepreneurship is also a prominent issue not only as an economic indicator but also for the social structure and transformation in a traditional relationship.

From this point of view, "women entrepreneurship in China" came to the forefront as a critical research topic in order to understand China's development and to foresee its effects on current world order in near future. The present study aims to draw a multi-disciplinary framework to analyze the interaction between women entrepreneurship and sociopolitical challenges in China. To achieve this objective, the present study will examine the current situation in Asia first and then try to reveal China's position in Asian economies. In the second part, Chinese political encouragement and social challenges will be discussed in detail.

1. Asia in World Politics and Women Entrepreneurship in Asia

21st century underwent a significant transformation in terms of power distribution among Great Powers. The initial indicators of the changing world order were observed in the economic development of Japan in 1950s and then in the growing economies of Asian Tigers (Hong Kong, South Korea, Singapore, and Taiwan) in 1970s. Even though these Far Eastern countries regularly achieved double-digit growth percentages for thirty years from 1960s to 1990s, the growing trend had come to an end due to the devastating Asian Crisis in 1997 (Economist, 2019).

Even though Japan was the leading one among the Asian Tigers in the 20th century, China took the place of Japan after the Asian Crisis and provided some fiscal and economic aids to Asian countries in order to overcome the effects of the regional crisis. China's sphere of influence expanding with the Asian Crisis across the region gained an international dimension with 2000s. The international community witnessed a decrease in the share of developed countries in total global GDP, whereas the developing Asian countries had an increasing share.

As seen in Fig. 1, developing economies contributed to the world's total GDP more than advanced economies did. Moreover, China's share in the global GDP increased from 3.6 % in 2000 to 17.8 % in 2019 (Elliott, 2020). The increasing share of the Asian region and China in the global economy led to a debate on how this rise will have implications for the current world order and Western criteria for national development.

The main focus of the aforementioned debate is whether the Chinese Model of Development will take the place of the Western-style liberal-democratic

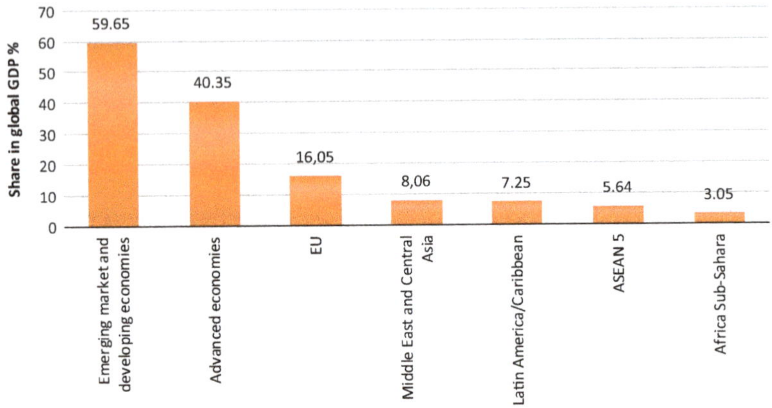

Fig. 1: Share of Global Regions in the Gross Domestic Product (Adjusted for Purchasing Power) in 2019

Source: Statista, https://www.statista.com/statistics/256340/share-of-global-regions-in-the-gross-domestic-product/

development model. Western-style development model known as "Washington Consensus" includes prudent fiscal policy, economic openness, privatization of state enterprises, and market liberalization (Williamson, 2004: 196). However, the Chinese Model of Development called "Beijing Consensus" represents a new approach to development based on China's model for economic growth and political principles of non-interference and self-determination (World Foresight Forum, 2011). Williamson (2012) listed the incremental reform, innovation and experimentation, export-led growth, state capitalism, and authoritarianism as the main development policies within the context of the Beijing Consensus.

According to Ramo (2004), who invented the term, "Beijing Consensus" is as much about social change as economic change. Therefore, struggle against poverty, equality in opportunity, educational rights, women's participation in economy, and gender equality are at the core of development policies in the Beijing Consensus. Women entrepreneurs are considered important for social development, as well as economic development. The main determinants of entrepreneurship are examined under five groups: technological development, economic factors, demographic factors, institutional factors and government intervention, and cultural factors (Verheul et al., 2006: 10). Within this context, women entrepreneurship can be examined comparatively in developed

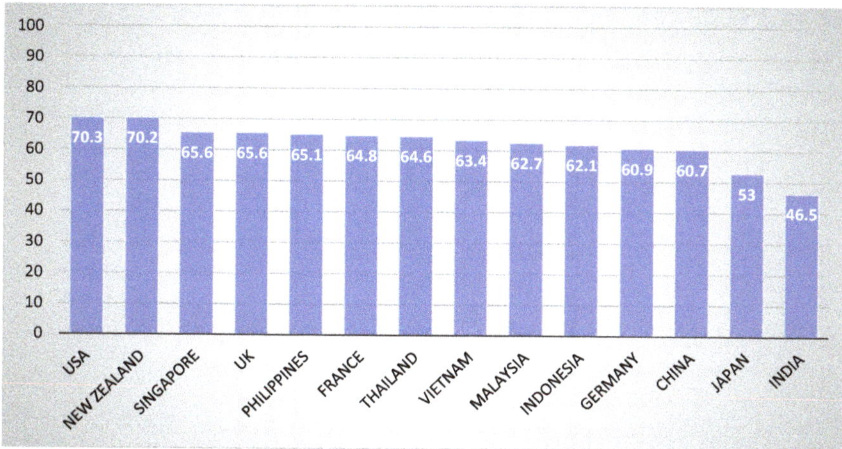

Fig. 2: MasterCard Index of Women Entrepreneurs 2019

Source: MasterCard Index of Women Entrepreneurs 2019, https://mb.cision.com/Public /18690/ 2968448/89d4464d0f5fa43e.pdf

Western countries and developing Asian countries by reflecting economic, institutional, and cultural differences.

A recent effort to compare women entrepreneurship levels of different countries is the MasterCard Index of Women Entrepreneurs (MIWE). The final report was published in 2019 and the index aims to highlight how 58 markets differ in terms of three factors: (i) Women's Advancement Outcomes, (ii) Knowledge Assets & Financial Access, and (iii) Supporting Entrepreneurial Factors (MIWE, 2019).

Mastercard index of women entrepreneurs is presented in Fig. 2. When examined comparatively, Philippines had one of the highest levels of MIWE, whereas Japan ranked at the bottom line of the list. It can also be understood in the list that Vietnam as a lower middle-income country had a higher level of MIWE than Germany, which is a high-income country. As in other parts of the world, development of women's entrepreneurship in Asian countries has also a significant potential in empowering women and transforming the society in the region (Tambunan, 2009: 28).

However, the Global Women Entrepreneur Leaders Scorecard list presented in Tab. 1 shows that the female entrepreneurs in the most influential countries of Asia (China, Japan, and India) mostly do not have suitable conditions in contrast to their Western counterparts. One explanation for the low levels of

Tab. 1: Global Women Entrepreneur Leaders Scorecard – 2015

Category 1: Business Environment			**Category 2: Gendered Access**			**Category 3: Leadership and Rights**			**Category 4: Pipeline for Entrepreneurship**			**Category 5: Potential Entrepreneur Leaders**		
Rank	Country	Score	Rank	Country	Score	Rank	Country	Score	Rank	Country	Score	Rank	Country	Score
1	USA	81	1	USA	86	1	USA	86	7	China	56	2	USA	63
3	Japan	80	8	UK	78	8	UK	78	17	USA	37	5	UK	49
4	Germany	78	14	Germany	68	14	Germany	68	22	Germany	34	6	Japan	47
5	UK	68	20	China	47	20	China	47	23	UK	33	8	Germany	39
11	China	44	23	Japan	42	23	Japan	42	30	India	7	20	China	22
18	India	34	28	India	15	28	India	15	31	Japan	1	24	India	17

Source: Dell, Global Women Entrepreneur Leaders Scorecard: Country-level five category scores, https://i.dell.com/sites/csdocuments/Corporate_secure_Documents/en/2015-GWEL-Country-Category -Scores.pdf

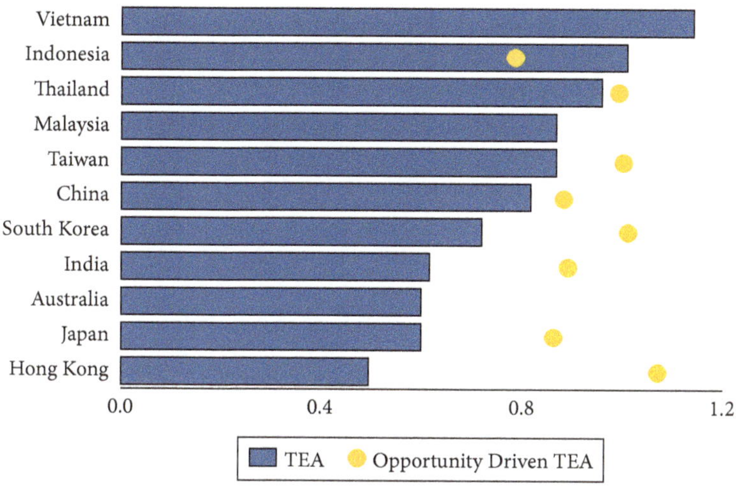

Fig. 3: Women Entrepreneurship in Asia 2016–2018

Source: Alexandra Altman, "Gender View: Women entrepreneurship in Asia," 15 March 2019, Federal Reserve Bank of San Francisco, https://www.frbsf.org/banking/asia-program/pacific-exchange-blog/gender-view-female-entrepreneurship-in-asia/

women entrepreneurship in Asia may be the sociocultural dynamics. Cho et al. (2020) explain the inferior status of Asian women with traditional culture (e.g., Confucianism), religious beliefs (e.g., Hinduism), and the lack of workplaces where cultural, religious, and organizational constraints across the region (Cho et al., 2020: 2).

Comparing the Asian countries in terms of women entrepreneurship, another instrument to be used is a report published in 2019. Women entrepreneurship in Asia between 2016–2018 is presented in Fig. 3. In comparison with their counterparts from other countries, Chinese women are more entrepreneurial. Chinese women are also as opportunity-motivated as men. However, the percentage of women starting businesses is in an alarming decline. It decreased down from the peak of 22.4 % in 2011 to 9.2 % in 2018 (Huang et al., 2020: 356).

2. Women Entrepreneurship in China: Political, Cultural and Social Challenges

The long-standing economic growth rates provide a high-level increase in education opportunities, social development, and cultural transformation in

China. Women's rights and female participation in the labor force came to the forefront as a consequence of the transformation process since 1980s. The state issued several regulations and laws to protect women in the workplace by ensuring equal opportunities including the PRC Women's Rights Protection Law, the PRC Labor Law, and the Women's Work Protection Regulations. Two decades of economic reform, ideological, legal, and experiential preparations paved the way for Chinese women entrepreneurship (Deng et al., 2011: 8).

Indeed, The Platform for Action launched in the 1995 World Conference on Women in Beijing promoted women's active participation in all spheres of public and private life through a full and equal share in economic, social, cultural, and political decision-making (Zheng & Qian, 2017: 23–24). In the late 1990s, several nationwide studies on female entrepreneurs were launched in China: Chinese Entrepreneurs Investigation System, the Association of Women Entrepreneurs in China, and the All-China Women's Federation (Deng et al., 2011: 4).

In 2001, the State Council promulgated the National Program for Women's Development in China (2001–2010). The Program major objectives, strategies, and measures were set down according to six priority areas of development, namely: women and the economy; women's participation in decision-making and management; women's education; women and health; women and the law; women and the environment (China National Program for Women's Development).

Another initiative to encourage women entrepreneurship in China is a campaign under the title of "Women's Actions for Entrepreneurship and Innovation" launched in 2015 by The All-China Women's Federation (ACWF) (ACWF, 2020). As shown in Fig. 4, the proportion of those engaged in entrepreneurial activities in China's female population reached three folds of the world average. However, this ratio showed a significant decrease in 2015 and approached the world average.

Economic restructuring, marketization, and privatization changed the world of work, management, and entrepreneurship for women in the People's Republic of China (Scot et al. 2014: 69). The Global Entrepreneurship and Development Institute (GEDI) constructed the women entrepreneurship index to measure a multidimensional aspect of female entrepreneurial development. In 2015, China's women entrepreneurship index was 38.3 out of 100, which was ranked 48 out of 77 countries (Zhu et al., 2019: 67). To understand the current status of women in China's social structure, the data about women in China should be known.

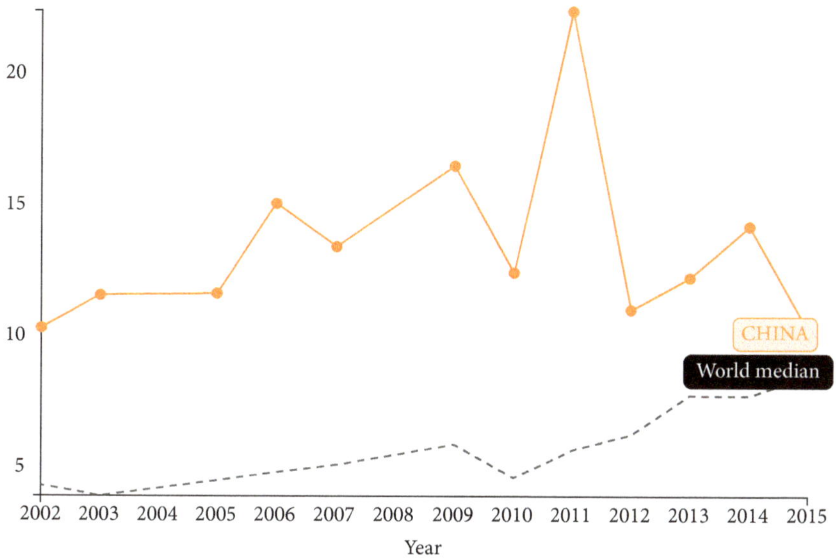

Fig. 4: Total Early-Stage Entrepreneurial Activity for Female Working Age Population, % of Female 18–64 Population

Source: World Bank, Total early-stage Entrepreneurial Activity for Female Working Age Population, https://tcdata360.worldbank.org/indicators/aps.ea.female?country=CHN&indicator=3121 &viz=line_chart&years=2001,2015

According to United Nations statistics, women constituted 48 % of China's total population as of the year 2019. The labor force participation rate of women in China in the same year was 60 % (UNDP, 2020). With this ratio, China has one of Asia-Pacific's highest labor force participation rates for women. However, women's labor force participation was declining since the 1990s from 73.2 % in 1990 to 60 % in 2019 (Catalyst, 2020).

Even though there is not the only reason to explain the recent decline in women's labor force participation, the sociocultural and political factors are accepted as one of the most important reasons. In China's case, the traditional social structure and the predetermined roles in the family groups were still a barrier to be an entrepreneur for women. Indeed, Confucian culture and Guanxi relationship pattern were examined by many scholars in order to shed light on low women entrepreneurship in China.

2.1. Confucianism and Guanxi: An Ethical Guide to Success or an Inevitable Barrier for Women

Confucianism and its teachings drew significant interest from world to understand the cultural roots of Chinese long-standing growth and development. Even though Confucianism was marginalized during the Communist restructuring of Chinese society in 1950s and 1960s, it was re-discovered after the reform and opening-up era. Being re-built as a source of growth and development by Chinese intellectuals and political elites has allowed Confucianism to expand its doctrine into each sphere of society. Within this context, Confucianism and its teaching has been researched on a wide variety of field.

In economics and business administration, Confucianism has been referred as a motivational source of hard-working, discipline, and a sense of belonging. However, it was also mentioned as a sociocultural barrier to accepting new dynamics and global trends in leadership, management, and strategic structuring.

Gender division and sexual equality of opportunities for women and men in China were also examined under Confucian doctrines. The idea that women were to serve and be subordinate to men was expressed through the belief that women should be confined to their families and homes. Commonly-heard phrases such as "man outside, woman inside" (男主外女主内) have their origin in the labor division of the traditional Chinese agricultural economy. Such "inside" versus "outside" notions reinforced the Confucian definition of women's virtue in terms of limiting their interaction with people outside the family (Chen, 2011: 4).

In this case, a relationship pattern advocated by Confucianism is called Guanxi (关系). Guanxi draws a special framework between two parties such as emperor-subject, father and son, husband and wife, elder and younger siblings, friend and friend (Nie and Lämsä, 2015: 852–854). Because Guanxi has a decisive role in Chinese society, many scholars have focused on the term from various aspects. For instance, Buckley et al. (2006) and Ramasamy et al. (2006) examined the role of Guanxi in the knowledge transfer to China, whereas Xian et al. (2019) investigated the effects of Guanxi on high-performance work systems in China. Nolan and Rowley (2020) examined the Guanxi in business and management studies, focusing on its relationship to corporate and employee performance, business ethics, entrepreneurial learning, and how Guanxi can be gendered, potentially excluding and disadvantaging women.

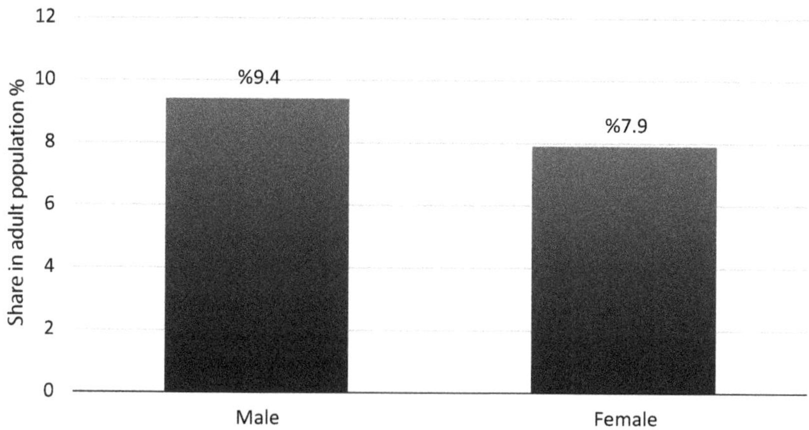

Fig. 5: Early-Stage Entrepreneur Share in China 2019 by Gender
Source: Statista, https://www.statista.com/statistics/883814/china-early-stage-entrepreneur-population-share-by-gender/

Because hierarchy and respect for superior play a central role in Guanxi, women behavior in terms of way of business and entrepreneurship can also be understood under this concept. Indeed, Leung (2000) pointed out that gender issues and Chinese cultural traditions, such as Guanxi, are the major factors influencing career development and managerial growth in China.

Early-stage entrepreneur share in China by gender is presented in Fig. 5. According to Fig. 5, the early stage entrepreneur share of women is lower than men. Nevertheless, Guanxi has not been considered as only a negative factor to gender issues and women's behavior in work-life. An important study showed that Guanxi is a way to cope with the limited resources the market can provide and the unfair treatment women could receive in their professional life (Xu and Li, 2015: 847). One of the recent studies on the Guanxi and women entrepreneurship was carried out by Zhang et al. Zhang et al. (2020) highlighted that Chinese women managers reveal the importance of Guanxi for influencing women intrapreneurship through facilitating career advancement.

Aaltio and Huang (2018) suggested that, even if working life is becoming more and more global, the local and culture-based nature of networking remains. A relatively low level of female share in earl stage entrepreneur share in China can be understood under this explanation.

3. Conclusion

China has emerged as one of the key actors of the 21st century's world order. Because China has totally integrated with international organizations, global markets, and manufacturing processes, Chinese economy is directly affected by structural crisis in the world economy. One of the most impressive cases was seen in the 2008 Global Financial Crisis and afterward. As a consequence of decreasing international demand and its devastating effects on internal markets, Chinese political elites realized the truth that economic growth should not depend on aggressive export to foreign markets and foreign direct investments. In order to overcome the destructive effects of the crisis, Chinese leaders headed towards the internal markets and put the Dual Circulation Strategy forward in early 2020.

Within the scope of the last steps focusing on internal markets, China also accepted that economic development strategy should be pursued with more comprehensive reforms on social development and welfare. Therefore, ensuring an increasing trend in the labor force participation rate of women again and removing the barriers for women's entrepreneurship emerged as the crucial targets for the near future.

As shown in the present study, although there is a large literature on entrepreneurship in China, studies on women's entrepreneurship are at a new stage of development. Although it showed significant changes over the years, women's entrepreneurship in China was an important component supporting economic development. Especially in the early years of the Communist restructuring of the state, female participation in the labor force has to be encouraged. However, there now is a decreasing trend in female participation in the labor force. Women's labor force participation was declining since the 1990s from 73.2 % in 1990 to 60 % in 2019. On the other hand, as indicated by recent researches and reports in China, women entrepreneurship rates in China are below the regional and global actors.

In the current situation, China has to reconsider women's entrepreneurship as a part of achieving its goal of becoming an influential actor in the global system. Even though the effects of Confucianism on the perceptions of women's role are perceived as a barrier to women entrepreneurship, most of the Asian countries with the same sociocultural background achieve higher levels of women entrepreneurship. Therefore, neither political conditions nor sociocultural structure of China can be seen as preventive factors for women entrepreneurship. On the contrary, the declining levels of women entrepreneurship could be seen as an obstacle to China's ambitions to become a great power.

References

Aaltio, I., & Huang, J. (2018). The guanxi ties of managers in mainland China – a critical analysis based on gender. *Gender in Management: An International Journal*, *33*(7), 577–599. https://doi.org/10.1108/gm-01-2018-0006

All China Women's Federation. (2020). *Women's action for entrepreneurship and innovation.* http://www.womenofchina.cn/womenofchina/html1/projects/20041/6088-1.htm

Buckley, P. J., Clegg, J., & Hui, T. (2006). Cultural awareness in knowledge transfer to China—The role of guanxi and mianzi. *Journal of World Business*, *41*, 275–288. https://doi.org/10.1016/j.jwb.2006.01.008

Catalyst. (2020, April 14). *Women in the workforce – China: Quick take.* https://www.catalyst.org/research/women-in-the-workforce-china/

Chen, M. (2011). *Tiger Girls: Women and enterprise in the People's Republic of China.* Taylor & Francis Group, Routledge. https://www.routledge.com/Tiger-Girls-Women-and-Enterprise-in-the-Peoples-Republic-of-China/Chen/p/book/9780415855556

Cho, Y., Li, J., & Chaudhuri, S. (2020). Women entrepreneurs in Asia: Eight country studies. *Advances in Developing Human Resources*, *22*(2), 1–9. https://doi.org/10.1177/1523422320907042

Deng, S., Wang, X., & Alon, I. (2011). Framework for female entrepreneurship in China. *International Journal of Business and Emerging Markets*, *3*(1), 3–20.

Elliott, L. (2020, December 26). *China to overtake US as world's biggest economy by 2028, report predicts.* The Guardian. https://www.theguardian.com/world/2020/dec/26/china-to-overtake-us-as-worlds-biggest-economy-by-2028-report-predicts

Huang, Q., Liu, X., & Li, J. (2020). Contextualization of Chinese entrepreneurship research: An overview and some future research directions. *Entrepreneurship & Regional Development*, *32*(5–6), 353–369. https://doi.org/10.1080/08985626.2019.1640437

Jamali, D. (2009). Constraints and opportunities facing women entrepreneurs in developing countries: A relational perspective. *Gender in Management: An International Journal*, *24*(4), 232–251. https://doi.org/10.1108/17542410910961532

Leung, A. S. M. (2000). Gender differences in guanxi-behaviors: An examination of PRC state-owned enterprises. *International Review of Women and Leadership*, *6*(10), 48–59.

Lin, Z., Cao, X., & Cottam, E. (2020). International networking and knowledge acquisition of Chinese SMEs: The role of global mind-set and international entrepreneurial orientation. *Entrepreneurship & Regional Development, 32*(5–6), 449–465. https://doi.org/10.1080/08985626.2019.1640459

McCurry, J., & Kollewe, J. (2011, February 14). *China overtakes Japan as world's second-largest economy.* The Guardian. https://www.theguardian.com/business/2011/feb/14/china-second-largest-economy

Meng, J. (2018, March 06). *China's private sector contributes greatly to economic growth: Federation leader.* Xinhua. http://www.xinhuanet.com/english/2018-03/06/c_137020127.htm#:~:text=China's%20private%20sector%20contributes%20greatly%20to%20economic%20growth%3A%20federation%20leader,-Source%3A%20Xinhua%7C%202018&text=The%20sector%20now%20contributes%20more,Federation%20of%20Industry%20and%20Commerce.

MIWE. (2019). *Mastercard index of women entrepreneurs annual report.* https://www.mastercard.com/news/media/yxfpewni/mastercard-index-of-women-entrepreneurs-2019.pdf

Nie, D., & Lämsä, A. (2015). The leader–member exchange theory in the Chinese context and the ethical challenge of guanxi. *Journal of Business Ethics, 128*(4), Special Issue on The 25th EBEN Annual Conference in Barcelona (June 2015). https://doi.org/10.1007/s10551-013-1983-9

Nolan, J., & Rowley, C. (2020). Whither guanxi and social networks in China? A review of theory and practice. *Asia Pacific Business Review, 26*(2), 113–123. https://doi.org/10.1080/13602381.2020.1737391

Ramasamy, B., Goh, K. W., & Yeung, M. C. H. (2006). Is Guanxi (relationship) a bridge to knowledge transfer?. *Journal of Business Research, 59*(1), 130–139. https://doi.org/10.1016/j.jbusres.2005.04.001

Ramo, J. C. (2004). *The Beijing Consensus.* Foreign Policy Centre. https://fpc.org.uk/publications/the-beijing-consensus/

Scott, J., Harrison, R.T., Hussain J., & Millman, C. (2014). The role of guanxi networks in the performance of women-led firms in China. *International Journal of Gender and Entrepreneurship, 6*(1), 68–82. https://doi.org/10.1108/IJGE-03-2013-0014

Swartz, S., & Oster, S. (2010, July 18). China tops U.S. in energy use. *The Wall Street Journal.* https://www.wsj.com/articles/SB10001424052748703720504575376712353150310

Tambunan, T. (2009). Women entrepreneurship in Asian developing countries: Their development and main constraints. *Journal of Development and Agricultural Economics, 1*(2), 27–40.

The Economist. (2019, December 5). *After half a century of success, the Asian tigers must reinvent themselves.* https://www.economist.com/special-report/2019/12/05/after-half-a-century-of-success-the-asian-tigers-must-reinvent-themselves

United Nations Development Programme. (2020). *Human Development Reports, China*, http://hdr.undp.org/en/countries/profiles /CHN

Verheul, I., Van Stel, A., & Thurik, R. (2006). Explaining female and male entrepreneurship at the country level. *Entrepreneurship and Regional Development, 18*(2), 151–183. https://doi.org/10.1080/08985620500532053

Williamson, J. (2004). The strange history of the Washington consensus. *Journal of Post Keynesian Economics, 27*(2), 195–206.

Williamson, J. (2012). Is the "Beijing Consensus" now dominant? *Asia Policy, 13*, 1–16.

World Bank. (2019). Innovative China. *Development Research Center of the State Council, The People's Republic of China*, https://openknowledge.worldbank.org/bitstream/handle/10986/32351/9781464813351.pdf?sequence=7

World Foresight Forum. (2011). *The Beijing Consensus: An alternative approach to development*. Issue Brief No.2. https://hcss.nl/sites/default/files/files/reports/WFF02_Issue_Brief_The_Beijing_Consensus02.pdf

Wu, Y., Guo, X., & Marinova, D. (2017). Productivity, Innovation and China's Economic Growth. In Song, L., Garnaut, R., Fang, C., & Johnston, L. (Eds.), *China's New Sources of Economic Growth,* Vol. 2, (pp.213–228). Australian National University Press. https://doi.org/10.22459/CNSEG.07.2017.09

Xian, H., Atkinson, C., & Meng-Lewis, Y. (2019). Guanxi and high performance work systems in China: Evidence from a state-owned enterprise. *The International Journal of Human Resource Management, 30*(19), 2685–2704. https://doi.org/10.1080/09585192.2017.1332670

Xu, K., & Li, Y. (2015). Exploring guanxi from a gender perspective: Urban Chinese women's practices of Guanxi. *Gender, Place & Culture, 22*(6), 833–850. https://doi.org/10.1080/0966369X.2014.917279

Zhang, C. X., Kimbu, A. N., Lin, P., & Ngoasong, M. Z. (2020). Guanxi influences on women intrapreneurship. *Tourism Management, 81*, 1–11. https://doi.org/10.1016/j.tourman.2020.104137

Zheng, J., & Qian, W. (2017). Women entrepreneurs' political participation in China. *Asian Women, 33*(2), 23–42.

Zhu, L., Kara, O., & Zhu, X. (2019). A comparative study of women entrepreneurship in transitional economies: The case of China and Vietnam. *Journal of Entrepreneurship in Emerging Economies, 11*(1), 66–80. https://doi.org/10.1108/JEEE-04-2017-0027

www.ingramcontent.com/pod-product-compliance
Ingram Content Group UK Ltd.
Pitfield, Milton Keynes, MK11 3LW, UK
UKHW020710041026
15590UKWH00002B/586

9 783631 853443